IMPROBABLE SCHOLARS

IMPROBABLE SCHOLARS

The Rebirth of a Great American School System
and a Strategy for America's Schools

DAVID L. KIRP

OXFORD
UNIVERSITY PRESS

OXFORD
UNIVERSITY PRESS

Oxford University Press is a department of the University of Oxford.
It furthers the University's objective of excellence in research,
scholarship, and education by publishing worldwide.

Oxford   New York

Auckland   Cape Town   Dar es Salaam   Hong Kong   Karachi
Kuala Lumpur   Madrid   Melbourne   Mexico City   Nairobi
New Delhi   Shanghai   Taipei   Toronto

With offices in

Argentina   Austria   Brazil   Chile   Czech Republic   France   Greece
Guatemala   Hungary   Italy   Japan   Poland   Portugal   Singapore
South Korea   Switzerland   Thailand   Turkey   Ukraine   Vietnam

Oxford is a registered trade mark of Oxford University Press
in the UK and certain other countries.

Published in the United States of America by
Oxford University Press
198 Madison Avenue, New York, NY 10016

Library of Congress Cataloging-in-Publication Data
Kirp, David L.
Improbable scholars : the rebirth of a great American school system and a strategy for America's
schools / David L. Kirp.
pages   cm
Includes index.
ISBN 978-0-19-998749-8 (hardback)
1. School improvement programs—New Jersey—Union City—Case studies.
2. Hispanic American children—Education—New Jersey—Union City—Case studies.
3. Educational equalization—New Jersey—Union City—Case studies. I. Title.
LB2822.83.N5K57   2013
371.2'070974926—dc23   2012046081

3 5 7 9 8 6 4 2

Printed in the United States of America
on acid-free paper

To
Remmert, in Love and Friendship

CONTENTS

IMPROBABLE SCHOLARS

INTRODUCTION
High Stakes

Educators have grown wearily accustomed to being slapped around in public. Still, the report of a blue-ribbon commission chaired by Joel Klein, former chancellor of New York City's public schools, and Condoleezza Rice, secretary of state in the administration of President George W. Bush, came as a shocker. *U.S. Education Reform and National Security*, published in the spring of 2012 and carrying the imprimatur of the prestigious Council on Foreign Relations, ominously concludes that the miseducation of America's students poses an imminent threat to our country's capacity to defend ourselves. "Educational failure puts the United States' future economic prosperity, global position, and physical safety"—physical safety!—"at risk."[1]

What can be done to avert this catastrophe? Klein and Rice plump for giving parents more choice about what school their children attend, arguing that charter schools and vouchers will generate needed innovation. The old-line public schools cannot merely be reformed, the report contends: if these institutions are going to do a decent job of educating our kids, a discipline-and-punish regimen of strict accountability is needed. Schools whose students aren't improving at a sufficiently rapid pace should be shuttered.

Teachers' livelihood should depend on how their students fare on high-stakes reading and math tests, with pay raises handed to some and pink slips to others. Teachers should be recruited from among the top colleges, as Teach for America does, rather than being drawn mainly from run-of-the-mill education schools.[2]

For years critics have lambasted the public schools as fossilized bureaucracies run by paper-pushers and filled with time-serving teachers preoccupied with their job security, not the lives of their students. A gaggle of influentials, among them Bill Gates, Oprah Winfrey, and David Brooks, have said as much, and it's the message of films like *Waiting for Superman* and *Don't Back Down*, which lionize charter schools as the one sure way out of the present mess.

These privately run academies have become playthings of the super-rich. The fabled Harlem Children's Zone floats on an ocean of money from investment firms such as Goldman Sachs; and when Facebook's Mark Zuckerberg wanted to make a splash, he pledged $100 million to underwrite new charter schools in the troubled Newark, New Jersey school system, announcing his largesse on *The Oprah Winfrey Show*.

Washington has been delivering similar, if less bombastic, salvos ever since the No Child Left Behind Act became law in 2002. The Obama administration's $4.35 billion Race to the Top initiative, the crown jewel of its education reform agenda, morphed into No Child Left Behind on steroids, as the Department of Education deployed the carrot of new money to prod the states into expanding charter schools and closing low-performing public schools.[3]

The administration was quick to claim that this strategy was working. In the spring of 2011, President Obama visited Central High in Miami, Florida, where a new cadre of teachers and administrators had been recruited, replacing those who weren't able to raise students' test scores. Declaring that students' "performance has skyrocketed" with this injection of new blood, the president hailed Central High as a national model.

Mission accomplished? Not so fast.

No Quick Fixes

Look dispassionately at the evidence, as I will in the last chapter, and you'll find little justification for the proposition that imposing perform-or-die accountability on teachers or expanding choice for students will cure what ails public education.

Those remade schools praised by President Obama seldom live up to their billing. At Central High, although students' math scores did improve somewhat, they remained among the worst in Florida; and the ballyhooed accomplishments of other similarly refashioned schools often vanish upon closer inspection.

No Child Left Behind, with its hyperemphasis on the three R's and its command to close or remake "failing" public schools, was supposed to end what President George W. Bush called "the soft bigotry of low expectations." But a decade later scores on the National Assessment of Educational Progress, or NAEP, the nation's report card, have improved only slightly; and poor, black, and Latino students haven't been able to close the achievement gap. What's more, despite the hosannas for charters, the bulk of the research shows that, overall, they don't do a better job than traditional public schools.[4]

In short, there are no quick fixes, no miracle cures.

Exemplary charter schools, like the national network of KIPP academies and the Green Dot schools in Los Angeles and New York City, have indeed worked wonders, giving inner-city youngsters seemingly bound for failure the skills and confidence needed to shape their own destinies. But those top-drawer academies only serve a tiny minority of students—KIPP enrolls 33,000 students, .00059% of the nation's school-age population. Nationwide 3% of students attend charters, many of them ordinary or worse.[5]

No school district can be all KIPPs and charismatic leaders and superteachers. It can't start from scratch and it can't fire all its teachers and principals when students do poorly. With more than three million K–12 teachers (3,219,458 at last count), two million of them slated to retire during this decade, there aren't nearly enough pedigreed novitiates to staff every American classroom. For better or worse, it is in nearly 100,000 ordinary public schools that most of our 55.5 million schoolchildren will be educated.

THE REAL CRISIS—THE MISEDUCATION OF POOR AND MINORITY YOUNGSTERS

The authors of *U.S. Education Reform and National Security* got one thing right—we certainly are in the midst of a crisis. It's just not the crisis they conjured.

The old saw that demography is destiny contains more than a kernel of truth. Over the past generation, fewer white students and more poor and nonwhite students have enrolled in public school. Between 1990 and 2010, the National Center for Education Statistics (NCES) reports, "the percentage of public school students who were White decreased from 67% to 54%, and the percentage of those who were Hispanic increased from 12% (5.1 million students) to 23% (12.1 million students)." Today, white youngsters no longer constitute a majority of all students. What's more, between 2007 and 2011 "the percentage of school-age children living in poor households . . . increased from 17% to 21%." Add the near-poor, those barely scraping by, and that figure doubles. For black and Hispanic youth, poverty is a double whammy. NCES notes that "higher percentages of Black (37%) and Hispanic (34%) children were living in families below the poverty threshold in 2011 than were White (12%) and Asian (14%) children."[6]

Voters and taxpayers don't carry around such statistics in their heads. But they do sense that things are changing, and many of them dislike what they see. "Why should *we* be paying for the education of *their* children?" they ask, sotto voce, and so they grow reluctant to underwrite public education with their tax dollars.

California represents the textbook example of this decline and fall.[7] The number of Latino students has mushroomed in recent decades, while the number of white youth has been rapidly declining. In 2010, the California Department of Education reports, a majority of the public school students were Latino, double the number of white students; just a decade earlier, the number of white and Latino students was almost the same. Meanwhile, public schools in the once-Golden State have been devastated by budget cuts. Once the best-funded schools in America, they now rank 47th, spending a third less than the national average. Dollars matter—you will frequently find more than thirty kids in a fifth grade classroom in California, more than forty in a senior English class. Laboring under these circumstances, how can teachers juggle their time effectively, making sure that students who need extra help don't get lost in the shuffle? Is it any wonder that California's NAEP scores are among the lowest in the country?

Nationwide, most public schools—and most charter schools, for that matter—give these kids at best a mediocre education. As a rule, says Steven Barnett, who directs the National Institute for Early Education Research, youngsters from poor families go to worse schools than middle class students.

Poor minority and immigrant youth generally wind up in factories for failure, where students flunk classes, skip school and drop out in droves: in 1,550 dead-end high schools, fewer than 60% of the students graduate.[8]

Dropping out hurts these kids—and the rest of us—in the wallet. Over the course of a lifetime the earnings difference between a dropout and someone with a high school degree can amount to more than $700,000. What's more, that dropout will cost taxpayers nearly $300,000 in lower tax revenues, additional government benefits, and incarceration costs.[9]

The "we-versus-they" crowd is blinding itself to the reality that the new immigrants aren't going away—they define our future. If we give them a bare-bones education, leaving them ill-prepared to contribute to a high-tech economy, a generation from now we'll all be paying the price.

In *The Race between Education and Technology*, Harvard economists Claudia Goldin and Lawrence Katz draw on an array of historical evidence to show that America became the world's richest nation during the first eight decades of the twentieth century mainly because of our shared commitment to education.[10] As states and communities taxed themselves to assure widespread access to decent schools and colleges, more and more students graduated from high school; and because of the GI Bill, higher education shifted from an elite to a mass system.

But in recent decades the education system hasn't kept pace. Nationwide, only seven students in ten graduate from high school. And while college enrollment continues to rise, there too graduation rates have languished— barely half of those who start college will have earned a bachelor's degree after six years. In the 1970s, the U.S. had a higher percentage of college graduates than any other nation. Now we're sixteenth and slipping.

That's the crisis in a nutshell.

The only chance we have to maintain our competitive position in the global economy is by doubling down on our investment in education and boosting the number of well-trained college graduates; and that necessarily means doing a better job of educating poor and minority youngsters. Goldin and Katz prescribe top-notch early education and rigorous K–12 instruction that gives high school graduates the intellectual tool-kit needed to make it through college.

But if superstars and clean sweeps can't deliver that, how can the typical school district, filled with ordinary teachers, most of whom grew up nearby, do it? Enter Union City.

PUBLIC SCHOOLS THAT TRANSFORM CHILDREN'S LIVES

Amid the hoopla over choice and charters, the public schools of Union City, New Jersey—a poor, densely-packed community that's mainly composed of Latino immigrants, four miles and a psychological light year removed from Times Square—point the way toward a more promising and more usable strategy.

A quarter-century ago, Union City's schools were so wretched that state officials threatened to seize control of them. But since then the situation has been totally reversed. This district now stands as a poster child for good urban education. By bringing kids, elsewhere dismissed as no-hopers, into the mainstream, it has defied the odds.

Here's the reason to stand up and take notice—*from third grade through high school, Union City students' scores on the state's achievement tests approximate the New Jersey averages. You read that right—these youngsters, despite their hard-knocks lives, compete with their suburban cousins in reading, writing, and math.*

This is no one-year wonder. Over the course of the past generation these youngsters have been doing better and better. What's more, in 2011 89.4% *of the students graduated*—that's 15% higher than the national average. Nearly 60% head to college; the top students are regularly winning state-wide science contests and receiving full rides at Ivy League universities.

Nowadays, the reputation of a school system depends heavily on its high-stakes achievement test scores. The pressure keeps intensifying as the U.S. Department of Education and its handmaidens in the state capitals expect that, year after year, more and more students must prove their proficiency in the three R's. New Jersey, like many other states, has made the outsized pledge that by 2020 every student will graduate high school prepared for college or career.[11]

Union City's schools are constantly struggling to balance this command against other priorities—sparking students' creativity, responding to the health problems and emotional baggage that many of these youngsters bring with them, generating a sense of community within the schoolhouse. Sometimes these schools succeed in maintaining that balance, always they try. What's more, those dazzling test scores don't depend on drill-and-kill instruction—the schools aim to turn kids into thinkers, not memorizers.

What makes Union City especially headline-worthy is the very fact of its ordinariness, its lack of flash and pizzazz. The district has not followed the herd by closing schools or giving the boot to hordes of allegedly malingering teachers or soliciting Teach for America recruits. And while religious schools educate a small minority of students in this city, not a single charter has opened there.

When boiled down to its essentials, what Union City is doing sounds so obvious, so tried-and-true, that it verges on platitude. Indeed, everything that is happening in Union City should be familiar to any educator with a pulse.

Here's the essence:

1. *High-quality full-day preschool for all children starts at age three.*
2. *Word-soaked classrooms give youngsters a rich feel for language.*
3. *Immigrant kids become fluent first in their native language and then in English.*
4. *The curriculum is challenging, consistent from school to school, and tied together from one grade to the next.*
5. *Close-grained analyses of students' test scores are used to diagnose and address problems.*
6. *Teachers and students get hands-on help to improve their performance.*
7. *The schools reach out to parents, enlisting them as partners in their children's education.*
8. *The school system sets high expectations for all and maintains a culture of abrazos—caring—which generates trust.*

This is a tale of evolution, not revolution, a conscientious application of what management guru W. Edwards Deming calls "total quality management." "Improve constantly and forever the system of production and service," Deming preached for half a century, and many Fortune 500 companies have profited from paying attention. So has Union City.[12]

The bottom line is simple enough—running an exemplary school system doesn't demand heroes or heroics, just hard and steady work. Stick to your knitting, as the saying goes, stay with what's been proven to make a difference and don't be tempted by every trendy idea that comes along. Of course that's much easier to say than to do—otherwise we wouldn't be talking about an achievement gap—but you don't have to be a genius to pull it off.

Success stories are to be found across the country—in communities that spend frugally on their students as well as those that are lavishly funded, in big cities as well as rural communities and in districts with black, Latino, and poor white students. In each instance, as we'll see, the school system has taken the same playbook—the same priorities, the same underlying principles, the same commitment to hard and steady work—that Union City uses, adapting it to suit its circumstances.[13]

I first heard about Union City because of its renowned prekindergarten program. After spending time in preschool classrooms so magical that I wished I were four years old again, I checked out what was happening in other grades. Was life as good for eight-year-olds and adolescents as it was for three- and four-year-olds?

When I parachuted in to a dozen or so classrooms, casually and unannounced, I sometimes saw competent teaching. More often the teaching was very good and occasionally it was world-class. Those time-serving teachers derided by the pundits were nowhere in sight.

Based on these initial impressions, Union City readily passed my "Golden Rule" test—I'd be happy if my own child went to school there. But I wanted to go beyond the superficial and find out what really made the place tick.

From the start of the school year in September 2010 to graduation day, nine months later, I dug deep into the life of this district and I returned several times the following year to pick up the threads of the story. With carte blanche to explore, I spent many days crouching in classrooms, talking with teachers and hanging out with kids, becoming "Mr. David" to a gaggle of third graders. I trailed after principals, joined top-echelon administrators' meetings when critical policy decisions about the school system's priorities were being made, and spent time crisscrossing the city with the hyperenergetic mayor who makes the schools' business his business.

THE SCHOOL SYSTEM AND THE SWISS WATCH

A Swiss watch, like a school district, is designed as an intricate system with a great many moving parts, the balance cock, the regulator, the hairspring study—those parts connect, one to the others, and if one of them breaks the mechanism will stop working.[14] But there the analogy breaks down— while skilled watchmakers know how to take a watch apart and put it back together, their counterparts in education don't possess the same grasp of the whole.

When scholars probe the schools (and they've written scads of books and articles about them) they focus on one particular aspect of the system—what makes for a good teacher, for instance, or what are the traits of an educational leader; how should reading be taught or how should achievement tests be used; does investing in technology reap benefits, and what about in-service training?

Although a watch is a complex mechanism, compared to a school system it's as simple as an Erector set, and none of the many tools in the education researchers' kitbag, from number-crunching to ethnography, can encompass the whole. The research supplied me with the high-powered lenses I've used in making sense of what I saw, extracting the patterns from the particulars. Yet it can capture only a partial truth, for when it comes to education *everything* connects, from the crucible of the classroom to the interplay among teachers, from the principal's skill as a leader to the superintendent's success in creating an intermeshed system from a host of separate schools and the politicians' role in setting the limits of a school district's autonomy. I'm brave (or foolhardy) enough to try my hand at being a watchmaker, coming at these schools from all angles.

This story begins in Room 210, a third grade class whose students start the year speaking little if any English and who, eight months later, will be taking the first high-stakes tests of their young lives. The classroom makes a logical starting point, for no matter how well-intentioned an initiative, how adroit the principal or managerially savvy the superintendent, if the teacher can't ignite fires in the students then the rest of it doesn't really matter.

All kids possess Holden Caulfield's innate talent for sniffing out the fakes and phonies. The good news is that they can be galvanized by teachers who they intuit are committed to their futures. What Barack Obama said in his 2012 State of the Union Address—"every person in this chamber can point to a teacher who changed the trajectory of their lives"—fits all of us. That's the goal of the teacher who presides in Room 210—to have an enduring impact on these kids' lives.

From the classroom to the school to the district our story opens up. The best teachers will thrive even in the educational equivalent of the Sahara desert, but most teachers will do a lot better if are part of a group effort, are given coaching, shown how to use information about their students to best advantage and encouraged to forge a "we're in this together" sense of rapport. That's where George Washington Elementary School, where Room 210 is located, enters the picture.

The narrative expands to encompass other schools, each with its own persisting challenges. Can an excellent preschool system be fabricated out of more than thirty different prekindergartens of wildly different quality, some run by the public schools and others operated as businesses? Can a visionary principal, new to the job, reform the oversized high school, which like secondary schools everywhere has become infamous for battling reformers?

Many school districts operate as loose confederacies, with each school going its own way, and only pockets of excellence amid the underwhelming, but Union City has worked hard to make the pieces fit together. For the district's administrators, maintaining a cohesive system is a never-ending grind and constantly striving for improvement is harder yet. For the system-builders in Union City the 2010–2011 school year is especially rough, for a soup-to-nuts state review is looming. School systems aren't autonomous; they operate in a world largely delineated by the politicians who oversee and fund them. In Union City, the Democratic mayor, who doubles as a state legislator, has been a godsend, and because of his clout there's a spanking new preschool and a $180 million high school. With a Republican in the governor's office, can he continue to work wonders?

Union City has done well by its children—very well indeed—but wherever you look there's unfinished business. The kids in Room 210 aren't all turning out well; not all of the teachers at Washington School are able (or willing) to improve; the quality of the preschools remains uneven; the high school isn't having an easy time going from "good enough" to good, let alone to great; and some of the ties that bind the system show signs of fraying.

It would be a mistake, however, to regard these as evidence of failure. Rather, they deliver a salutary reminder that America's public schools cannot be quickly and easily transformed—that, despite the belief of those who drafted the saber-rattling 2012 report, *U.S. Education Reform and National Security*, there's no magic bullet. In Union City, as in every school district, simple answers cannot be found and there's always work that remains undone.

1

"THE PIE"
Room 210, George Washington Elementary School

At half past seven on the morning of September 9, 2010, hordes of young-sters, many of them clasping their parents' hands, descend on George Wash-ington Elementary School in Union City, New Jersey. Although the weather is balmy, some of these kids, accustomed to the steamy climate of places like the Dominican Republic and Ecuador, come bundled in woolen overcoats.

By elementary school standards, Washington is big—its enrollment hovers near 800, preschoolers to sixth graders—but most of these kids live within easy walking distance. At almost every corner, crossing guards clad in luminescent orange jackets and wielding stop signs escort pupils across the narrow, car-jammed streets.

The first day of school comes alive with unbounded promise, the disap-pointments and frustrations of the previous year mostly erased by the months of summer. Some of the littlest children wear fearful expressions, because Washington feels cavernous and forbidding compared to the intimacy of their neighborhood preschool. But the returning students, dressed in the school's uniform—blue polo shirts emblazoned with the Union City Board of Education logo and khaki slacks or skirts—are full of chatter and high fives.

Les Hanna, the principal, is standing on the front steps. She welcomes the kids, most of whom she knows by name, with thousand-watt smiles and enveloping hugs. Vinnie Fraginals is nattily attired in a blue blazer, crisp white shirt, and tie. During the year he watches over the school from the guard's station, and his presence signals to parents that Washington is a safe haven. School superintendent Stanley M. Sanger, known to everyone as Sandy, makes an appearance, moving from parent to parent, shaking hands and introducing himself with a New Jerseyite's rendering of *buenos dias*.

Built nearly a century ago, Washington Elementary School is one of the oldest schools in Union City, and while it lacks creature comforts like air-conditioned classrooms and a cafeteria, it has retained some fine architectural details. Federalist-style columns frame the wide steps that lead to the front door and a grand stairway swoops upward from the first floor. Inside and out, the building is spotless. During the summer the school's maintenance crew has been busy painting classrooms and corridors, replacing broken desks, polishing the brass filigree in the stairwell, and buffing the floors.

As the children and parents arrive, the teachers are standing outside to greet them, class lists in hand. Les, who has been an administrator at Washington School for eleven years, has the drill down pat. The kids are swiftly matched with their teachers and by 8:15 A.M. the last of the parents have departed. The kids head to their classrooms, past the iconic Gilbert Stuart portrait of George Washington that hangs near the entrance and the school's mascot, a brightly painted Tony the Tiger lookalike. They walk in single file, goslings following their teachers to their new adventures.

Blink: initial impressions matter, and the first hour of the first day of school reveals a well-oiled machine powered by a blend of regimen and regard.

Dreaming of America

Union City ranks sixty-first nationwide in its concentrated poverty, below such famously troubled cities as Mobile, Milwaukee, and Oakland. It's also the nation's most crowded municipality. Many of the tidy, asbestos-sided houses that fill the narrow lots and hug one another have been sliced into small apartments, and three or four families are often sharing that space, all their possessions kept behind a locked bedroom door.

Over the years, this city has been the gateway to America for successive waves of immigrants. In the late nineteenth century the Germans and Dutch brought their talents as lacemakers, and the factories they set up gave the city its historic claim to fame: "The Embroidery Capital of the World Since 1872" is the boast of a faded, hand-lettered sign that still hangs over the highway leading to the heart of town.

By the 1960s, though, those émigrés, and others who had come from a score of nations, were mostly gone. Union City was being hollowed out, turned into a near ghost town, with shuttered stores and empty apartments. But a handful of Cubans, who had moved to the city a decade or two earlier, stayed on. From such roots ethnic communities grow, and when Cubans began fleeing the oppressive regime of Fidel Castro they saw Union City as a safe haven. Thousands came on Freedom Flights during the 1960s and 1970s, and the 1980 Mariel boatlifts brought thousands more. Union City became home to the second-largest number of Cubans in the United States—only Miami had more—and acquired a new sobriquet: Havana on the Hudson.[1]

There were many well-educated professionals in the Freedom Flight generation, professors and doctors, attorneys and accountants, and they quickly fashioned new lives for themselves. Most of them, like the earlier waves of immigrants, have departed for the verdant suburbs. Now the students at Washington Elementary come from across Latin America—about a third from the Dominican Republic, which everyone calls DR, a third from other Caribbean nations and Mexico, and a third from Central and South America (as well as a smattering from countries as exotic as Yemen).

These latest arrivals came for the same reasons that immigrants have always been drawn to America—the promise of earning a decent living and especially the chance to give their children a better future. But they are having a much rougher time of it than their predecessors, for most of them are poorer, less skilled, and less well educated, barely literate in their native language. While they are desperate to find work, they've come at precisely the wrong moment, amid the prolonged recession, and confront meager prospects. This unhappy concatenation of circumstances makes their children's experience at Washington especially consequential.

What will happen to these youngsters after they graduate from the Union City schools is fraught with uncertainty. Tirades against "rewarding" families that immigrated illegally have repeatedly spelled defeat for the DREAM Act, with its promise of access to college and, eventually, permanent residency for the children who, early in their lives, were brought into this country by their parents. On the floor of Congress, on December 15, 2010, Iowa GOP representative Steve King thundered: "If you support this nightmare DREAM Act, you are actually supporting an 'affirmative action amnesty act' that rewards people for breaking the law and punishes those who defend America." His California colleague Dana Rohrabacher claimed that the law would "do nothing more than bring millions of more people across our borders illegally, only now they will bring their kids, all of them."[2]

Those who would punish these youngsters for the acts of their parents miss the point—*these kids are here to stay; and, one way or another, they will help to define our future.* The real question is not whether to ship them back to countries that many of them can scarcely remember, a cruel practice that the Obama administration ended by Executive Order in 2012, but how they're going to be treated here. Give them a decent education and they'll make it in this new land—that has been the immigrant story ever since the first European settlers came to this new world. But toss them on the education scrapheap, as opponents of the DREAM Act are doing, and they'll live futureless lives.

At Washington School no one knows how many students are here illegally—*sin papeles*—and while it's estimated that 20% to 30% of them are living in this no man's land, no one is going to inquire. You can feel the perpetual undercurrent of fearfulness that families will be deported or else divided, the parents shipped home by ICE, the chillingly appropriate acronym for U.S. Immigration and Customs Enforcement. More than 90% of the students at Washington receive subsidized meals, and while this fact testifies to the prevailing poverty, the anxiety of some parents—that signing up their youngsters for this federal program will attract the malign attention of ICE—explains why even more aren't enrolled in this federal program.

Three-quarters of these kids are growing up in homes where Spanish is the language spoken at the dinner table, the language heard on the telenovelas and soccer matches that blare from the TV. Those who have lived in Union City long enough to have gone to preschool, which is free to three- and four-year-olds, have an enormous advantage: they will have received a grounding in Spanish and learned English by the time they enter kindergarten. The rest will make a step-by-step transition from Spanish to English while they're in school.

These students are as different as can be from their suburban counterparts. At Washington, more than three-quarters of them are labeled as "at risk"—less euphemistically, that means they're deemed likely candidates for failure—because they aren't fluent in English when they start school or because they are burdened by problems serious enough to require a scaffolding of supports.

Across America, immigrant children typically attend the worst public schools, but that isn't true here. The education at Washington more than satisfies what I call the Golden Rule Test—you would send a child you love to this school.[3]

The culture of *abrazos*, a nurturing culture that's evident from the very first morning, permeates the school. Les Hanna's warmth sets the tone and the teachers' personal ties to the place matter as well.

You won't find any Teach for America recruits on a mission to reinvent urban education—at Washington, as in every Union City school, almost all the teachers grew up within hailing distance of the community. Some of them, including several of the top administrators, are the children of those Freedom Flight émigrés, and for them Union City became their America. Few have ever strayed far from home. They attended local colleges like Jersey City State, Saint Peters, and Fairleigh Dickinson; Rutgers embodied the limits of their ambition. Soon after graduating they started teaching in Union City, and there they have stayed for their entire careers.

These are our kids, they say, so often and with such fervor that you're inclined to believe them. *We know them—we know where they come from and what they are going through. We're here for them.*

The Classroom Crucible

Fourteen students have been assigned to Room 210, one of five third-grade classrooms at Washington Elementary. It is no easy task to keep seven- and eight-year-olds, bundles of energy, in line, and on this first morning they run, they skip, they dawdle on their way to class. Few of them know their new teacher, but they all realize that they are launched on an adventure. Although there are lots of toothy grins, you can also see a few furrowed brows and the tiniest worry lines.

Half of the youngsters will start the year learning entirely in Spanish, and the rest have only recently begun reading and writing in English. Three of them arrived in the United States this past summer, and for them Room 210 marks their introduction to life in an American school.

For seven hours a day over the course of the next nine months, these boys and girls will be in the hands of their teacher, Alina Bossbaly. Petite and curvy, her reddish hair draping her shoulders, dressed for the occasion in an elegant turquoise blouse, black slacks, and heels, Alina looks nothing like your idea of a schoolmarm. She's always on the move, a tiger prowling among her cubs, and watching her in action you'd never guess that she's been teaching for nearly three decades.

It is hard to overestimate the impact that Alina will have on these children's lives. They will spend more of their waking hours with her than with any other adult, and during those hours they will have a nearly exclusive claim on her attention. Research by Harvard education professor Richard Elmore confirms what we all know from experience: the make-or-break factor in how much children learn is the "instructional core," the skills of the teacher, the engagement of the students, and the rigor of the curriculum.[4] Teachers' abilities vary greatly, and how much these students master will depend considerably on Alina. Does she know how to help eight-year-olds solve word problems in math? Can she turn them into confident writers? Can she help the newcomers become fluent in English? Can she prod the students into thinking critically, not just parroting what they read?

In the No Child Left Behind era of high-stakes testing, good teaching has become equated with getting students to meet state standards of proficiency in language arts (reading and writing) and math. For four days in May these youngsters, like their counterparts elsewhere, must display their skills on a high-stakes achievement test—in New Jersey, it is called the Assessment of Skills and Knowledge, the ASK for short. Twice during the year they will take locally developed tests that mimic the ASK. Because their test scores will not only show how well the students are doing in the three R's but also shape the fate of the school, the teachers at Washington will sweat to get them across the finish line.

The "no excuses" brigade of critics contends that teachers' livelihoods ought to depend mainly on their students' test scores—if students do well the teacher gets a bonus and if they do poorly the teacher gets booted. But as every good teacher understands, kids cannot be treated as machines designed for test-taking. It's folly, as the "social context" reformers point out, to ignore what's happening in the rest of their lives.[5]

Some children who grow up amid great wealth endure their share of misery—talk to a youngster whose divorced parents are warring over custody—but life is infinitely worse for many students in a place like Union City. There, some kids show up hungry because they haven't had breakfast. Some can't see the blackboard because their parents can't afford to buy them a pair of glasses; or are in constant pain because they've never seen a dentist; or have a hard time breathing because their asthma has gone untreated. Some have witnessed shootouts on their block. Some do battle against the rats that crawl over their beds at night.[6]

By inner-city standards, Union City is a peaceful place, but drugs and violence can intrude into the schoolhouse. At a statewide superintendents' meeting Sandy Sanger shocked his colleagues from suburbia when he told them that, in places like Union City, security guards were essential not just at high schools but at elementary schools as well.

These problems are emotionally draining for teachers, testing the limits of their capacity for empathy. If they erect a protective barrier between themselves and their students' lives, then academics will surely suffer; but they cannot turn themselves into social workers, a role for which they have no training. "I give a chunk of me to everyone," Alina says. "I know who these kids are. I know what I can get out of them, but I can't change their lives."

Dulce y Duro—Sweet and Hard

Every classroom evolves over the course of the year from an assemblage of individuals into a community. The shape that this community takes, whether it becomes as caring as the "Peaceable Kingdom" or as cruel as *Lord of the Flies*, is largely in the teacher's hands. "Children need to care for, respect, and love one another and the school community. Nothing can be accomplished without this," Alina tells me. The responsibility for conducting this grand symphony—weaving together the academic, the personal, and the communal—falls on her slender shoulders.

These youngsters have truly lucked out, though on the first day of class they have no reason to realize that. This is the twenty-seventh year that Alina Bossbaly has presided over Room 210, all that time helping students like these master a new tongue and settle into a new land. She appreciates what they go through because she lived through much the same experience.

On April 30, 1969, speaking not a word of English, Alina came to Miami on one of the famous *Vuelos de La Libertad*, the "Freedom Flights" that brought a quarter of a million Cubans to the United States. A few days later her family joined the steady stream of immigrants to Union City, and she enrolled as a fourth grader at Washington School.[7]

Like many Cubans, Alina's father, Jose Cardenas, had initially embraced Fidel Castro's revolution because it promised liberation from dictatorial oppression, only to grow bitterly disillusioned when the promise of equality calcified into a new form of oppression. But leaving Cuba was no simple matter, and once Jose made his intentions known the family entered a prolonged state of purgatory. He had been a pharmacist, but that life was over. After being jailed for "antirevolutionary activities"—a case of mistaken identity, as it turned out—he was banished to the sugar cane fields, permitted to see his wife and children only once a month. His wife Josefina (Josie, as she likes to be called) had always taken great pride in her looks, but now she came home every night sunburned and dirty from her state-inflicted labor in the fields.

Not even a five-year-old was safe from the long reach of the Castro government. As one of the best students in her kindergarten class, Alina looked forward to riding on a float that paraded down the arcaded main street of her hometown. But that honor was reserved for *pioneras*, she was informed, and she and her family were unworthy *gusanos*—worms.

Jose settled his family in Union City, where his relatives, six brothers and sisters, were already living. They found a three-room apartment and furnished it with castoffs. Jose went to work in an embroidery factory, later taking a job at the post office, where he worked for a quarter of a century, and Josie became a hairdresser.

Alina wasn't the only newcomer in her fourth grade class—a third of the children whose faces peer out from her class photo came from Cuba and Puerto Rico. But because Union City hadn't recruited Spanish-speaking teachers, sink-or-swim became the pedagogy by default. She was lucky with her first teacher, whom Alina remembers as "sweet, beautiful and smart," for she made the young girl feel welcome and found ways to surmount the language barrier. But when her fifth grade teacher assigned her a seat in the back of the room, he might as well have put a dunce cap on her head. And what passed for English lessons took place in the janitor's closet, taught by a woman who relied on her Italian to communicate with the Cuban kids. In math, the universal language, Alina was getting A's, as she had at school in Cuba, but she cried when she got a C in science and a D in social studies, and she didn't want to show the report card to her parents.

"That's why I went into bilingual education," says Alina, a refrain echoed by teachers with similar backgrounds. "No child should have to go through this."

In Cuba, young girls were raised strictly, chaperoned when they went on dates, expected to marry young and make their husband the center of their lives, but Josie wanted her daughter to become Americanized. Alina always had the freedom to roam, even when as a thirteen-year-old high school freshman she started dating Jesus Bossbaly, a star of the basketball team who was four years her senior. Jesus expected that they'd get married once Alina graduated from high school, but she had other ideas. She enrolled at Saint Peter's College in neighboring Jersey City; while there, she worked twenty hours a week for an accountant, partied hard, read a ton, and managed to pull down almost all A grades.

Being on her own for three years proved to be enough for Alina, and after graduating in 1981 she married Jesus. She dreamt of being a teacher, and getting married to a man who made a good living from his family's dry cleaning business meant she could afford to pursue her dream. By then, her old fourth grade teacher had become the principal at Washington School, and after subbing for a year she began to teach third grade to students who were learning English. She hasn't budged since then.

Seemingly everyone knows everyone else in the Union City schools, and those who run the school system have long since taken the measure of Alina's talents. Years ago she was Washington School's teacher of the year. She regularly represents the entire school system at statewide meetings, and every summer she is asked to help revise the elementary school curriculum. In recent years she has felt the pressure to become a supervisor, leaving the classroom to help new teachers hone their craft. Not only would she make more money, argues Silvia Abbato, the assistant superintendent responsible for academics, she would also have a bigger impact. A few years back she actually agreed, but when the time came to make the switch she wept at the prospect of leaving her classroom and ultimately backed out.

"You give to a child with *manco*," says Alina. "*Manco* literally means a person with no arms, and in Cuba that's a way of saying that you devote yourself to someone who truly needs." Those are the youngsters who, year after year, are sent her way. "Every year is different," she says, pointing to a wall plastered with photographs of her past classes, and every year there comes a time when she questions how much of a difference she can make in the arc of her students' lives, but she has always succeeded.

Other teachers at Washington School have a word for what Alina does—they say that she "Bossbaly-izes" her students. But 2010–2011 will prove to be one of the toughest years in her career.

THE MAGIC BOX AND THE GLASS JAR

At 8:30 A.M., Alina Bossbaly meets her new students for the first time. Lucia, Tomas, Mauricio, Catalina—aside from their names (which I've changed, along with some identifying details), the only thing Alina knows about them is who will be studying in Spanish and who has already begun to speak English, who is doing grade-level work and who requires extra help. Many teachers steel themselves for this moment by reading their students' files, learning what their former teachers thought of them, but Alina prefers to start with few preconceptions.

She does know one of her students, Matias, because he is repeating her class. When he came from Nicaragua the year before, the boy couldn't spell his own name or recognize numbers. He couldn't sit still, and some of the things that spewed from his mouth stunned even the teachers who thought they'd heard everything. In most school districts, says Alina, a boy like Matias would have wound up in special education, but he proved to be a quick learner. He thrived in Alina's class, making up a chunk of lost time, but he still had considerable catching up to do, and Alina persuaded his mother that he should spend another year in her class.

While the practice of leaving students back is controversial, the evidence shows that there's no cookie-cutter rule—sometimes it's a scarlet letter but sometimes it's the best thing that can happen to a kid, like pushing the "reset" button.[8] In Matias's case, repeating third grade proved the right call. He's on a roll with his schoolwork, and his behavior has changed so much that he has acquired a certain fame as the epitome of the "Bossbaly-ized" student.

Teachers usually seat their students in orderly rows, but Alina has moved the desks together to form clusters of four, so that they can work together. The kids are grouped according to their language skills and their reading ability, four separate clusters among these fifteen students. Alina's desk, blanketed with piles of books and papers, occupies one corner; rarely during the day does she have a chance to sit behind it. A bank of computers, a reading nook, and small tables for students' projects fringe the room. On the first day of school the walls are bare because Alina doesn't want to put up "canned work," and they will stay that way until the students' writing and artwork can be push-pinned onto the corkboards.[9]

Alina knows how to hush youngsters with a whisper, and with all eyes on her she explains to them what she expects. Ethics, not the familiar commands, are what's foremost on her mind. "My name is Mrs. Bossbaly, but I'm not a boss," she says, shifting from English to Spanish and back again. "Room 210 is a pie—*un pie*—and each one of us is a slice of that pie."

The pie makes a fine metaphor, a down-to-earth way of talking about a community where everyone has a place and no one gets left behind. "I like it when the art teacher, the music teacher or the ladies in the lunchroom tell me 'your class is so wonderful, *el pie es tan rico*,'" she says to the class. Judging from their expressions, some of these kids get the point immediately, but many of them don't—no matter, for the pie will regularly make its appearance throughout the year, with variations on this ideal of sharing and connectedness that reflect the circumstances of the moment.

Taking responsibility is the second theme of the morning. "The mind is powerful. Discipline comes from within," Alina tells her brood. "Right and wrong aren't just what a teacher catches you doing"—these precepts have to take up residence inside your head. This is heady stuff, Kantian autonomy for eight-year-olds, and it is hard for most of them to grasp. Whenever her students are messing around in the corridor or abandoning schoolwork for gossip, or otherwise acting like rambunctious eight-year-olds, she'll reiterate the mantra: "Discipline comes from within."

As the days go by, the class will see other sides of Alina's personality. From one minute to the next she's the actress who dramatizes the stories she reads aloud, the swivel-hipped dancer and off-key singer, the comedian, the diva, and the tease. On the first day of school, though, she's setting expectations. "I'm *dulce y duro*," Alina tells her students, neither a pushover nor a drill sergeant but sweet *and* hard. "You are part of the pie and I expect a lot from you."

Enough earnestness for the moment—the youngsters get excited, one voice piled atop another, when Alina shows off a heart-shaped metal box and a glass jar that sit on her desk and asks them to guess what's inside. This "magic box" is filled with small presents like a box of crayons, a pint-sized Superman, a mini-purse. Any student who does something especially well—gets all the answers right, improves a lot, helps out a classmate—can pick something from that box. Crayons are something special for most of these kids, and whoops of anticipation follow her announcement. And whenever the entire class accomplishes something special, Alina tells them, she puts a marble in the jar. There's a party when the jar is filled and they can choose the theme. "Pizza . . . ice cream," the kids murmur.

The magic box and the glass jar are kid-friendly ways to get across the messages of the powerful mind and the pie. Later in the day, when one of the boys complains about his seatmate and asks to be switched, Alina says no. "Accustom yourself to differences. Be positive—we are a pie." And when a girl starts to tattle about a classmate who misbehaved, Alina stops her cold. "I don't want you to tell me—take responsibility to talk with someone who's doing something wrong." Reiterate this point enough times and in enough different ways and eventually it sticks.

During these initial minutes, I'm sitting quietly in the back of the room. I'll be spending lots of time here, and Alina and I have talked about the tricky question of what the kids should call me. Children refer to their teachers as mister, missus, or miss (that's also how teachers refer to one another, out of habit, even when students aren't around), but I'm not a teacher. Nor can I just be David, which is what my students at Berkeley call me, because kids in elementary school don't refer to adults that way. We settle on "Mr. David."

My intention is to remain the invisible man, the note-taking observer, but the separation doesn't even last through that first morning, for in a class this small there's no chance of blending into the woodwork. By the end of the first day, having been lured into the classroom conversation, I'm on my way to becoming a slice of Alina's pie.

Several weeks after the beginning of school, a youngster straight off the plane from Bolivia named Clara arrives in Room 210, grasping her mother's hand. "We have a new student," Alina says, and moans envelop the room. "Don't act like that. What do we say? Hello and welcome—*hola y bienvenido*. The pie just gets bigger. You know why the new people are here—we're good!"

The reason that Clara has been assigned to Alina quickly becomes clear—she could be this year's Matias. She's bouncing all over the place, twirling when everyone else is sitting, disturbing her seatmates and then putting on a bright face of innocence. In art class, the kids are supposed to be doing a painting of a brightly colored papier-mâché globe that's hung from the ceiling. Clara thinks the globe is a piñata, and charges, wielding a stick. Her behavior is upsetting to kids who are just beginning to grasp the class routine, but Alina counsels patience. "Don't worry," she reassures them. "She's getting it." Teachable moments, these happenstances are called, and Alina relies on them to bring fifteen individuals into a collective of mutual caring and sharing—what in Latino culture is referred to as *respeto*.

Because of her reputation for succeeding with kids like Matias, she's invariably assigned a child who, like Clara, would give most teachers conniptions. "Alina can do it," goes the refrain, and in addition to the youngsters who are starting to learn English, she gets the children who are emotionally needy or hard to handle or slow off the mark—those who can benefit most from the blend of *dulce y duro* that she dispenses.

From day one, her kids are writing in their journals, sifting out the meaning of the stories they read, and solving math problems; and every weeknight they have *tarea*—homework. The Spanish-speakers are honing their skills in their native language, even as they listen to English being spoken in the class. "Exposure, exposure, exposure!" says Alina, explaining how they pick up English.

During these early weeks, though, academics aren't her highest priority. "My main mission is to get the kids to enjoy coming to school, to enjoy learning," she tells me, "and also to think of themselves as having control over their own lives, their own futures." When that happens they'll take off in the classroom.

Figuring out what's best for each child, rather than batch-processing them, is how all schools ought to be run, but that is not how things usually work. "Kids will still arrive on that first day of school full of hope and optimism, just as they do every year," observes John Merrow, education correspondent for the *PBS NewsHour* and one of the keenest observers of the American classroom. "Somehow they manage to convince themselves that 'this year will be different.'" But then comes the descent into disappointment. "The 'unnatural structure of school' sorts children into groups of 'A kids,' 'B kids' and (for most) 'C kids.' That structure works against good teaching and deep learning. For children, September, not April, is 'the cruelest month.'"[10]

This is not how life goes at Washington School—certainly not in Alina's class, where every youngster is made to feel like an "A kid."

THE RHYTHM OF THE SCHOOL DAY

For the students in Room 210, many of whom live in a world crosshatched by chaos, school becomes an anchor of stability, and a daily rhythm emerges during the course of the early weeks. At 8:00 A.M., after the youngsters have shrugged off their coats, tucked their books inside their desks, and recited the Pledge of Allegiance boomed over the PA system, they spend a solid forty minutes writing in their journals. Alina may ask them to write about what they did over the weekend, and maybe draw a picture as well, or else they'll fantasize about their dream house or explain how they can be more reliable at home.

Next come ninety minutes of math. The students carry out a math exercise called Every Day Counts, which uses the school calendar as the jumping-off point for problems that range from adding increasingly big numbers and counting coins ("which coins can you use to make 86 cents?") to reading the clock and checking the web for weather reports to graph weather patterns. Every morning one youngster, picked at random, goes to the blackboard and explains how he arrived at an answer to an Every Day Counts problem. "Is that right?" Alina asks, and if the student has made a mistake a classmate points out where he has gone wrong. Alina understands that many of her youngsters learn visually—they get better at adding big numbers by creating patterns in which different colors represent ones, tens, and hundreds—and so patterns figure prominently in her teaching. Meanwhile the students are learning an array of concepts, including three-digit multiplication, dividing with remainders, and even simple algebra.

The language lesson, which consumes the rest of the morning, varies with a student's fluency in Spanish or English. It might focus on recognizing cognates or on compound words like "cupcake" and "cowboy." Each week there are new vocabulary words to learn, like "barrels" and "spoil," or "*refunfuno*" and "*glotona*" (grumble and glutton), as well as spelling words like "acquired" and "whispered," plucked from the stories they are reading. "Don't just memorize the words," Alina tells them. "Incorporate them in your writing." After lunch she will read a story aloud, repeatedly shifting between Spanish and English, pausing to interject questions about what the tale means and how it ties into their own lives. "Last year you focused on spelling and writing," she says to the class. "This year you need to understand more."

Students don't learn "simply because their teacher gives a lecture or assigns reading," writes sociologist David Cohen. "Most need explanation, demonstration and opportunities to apply what they are learning. They need help trying out and revising their formulations, chances to try again, and opportunities to apply what they learn in new situations."[11] That's the nub of Alina's classroom philosophy.

All these kids can relate to the woes of the boy in *Alexander and the Terrible, Horrible, No Good, Very Bad Day*. "I went to sleep with gum in my mouth" begins a wonderful run-on opening sentence—the very kind of sentence that the test-makers would penalize—"and now there's gum in my hair and when I got out of bed this morning I tripped on the skateboard and by mistake I dropped my sweater in the sink while the water was running and I could tell it was going to be a terrible, horrible, no good, very bad day." Reading flows into writing, and at journal time the following day they'll write a letter to Alexander, commiserating with him and telling him how they get through their own bad days. "Your mother should give you a prize for behaving well," one of the students writes. "Don't get mad," another counsels. "Count from one to ten to calm your nerves."

For about an hour in the afternoon the class splits into groups of four or five, and over the course of the week each group switches activities, moving from the computers to the reading nook, from the CD player to a table laden with math tiles or word puzzles. All of us possess what Harvard psychologist Howard Gardner calls "multiple intelligences," and these activities (educators call them "learning centers") are designed to tap into our different ways of learning. Some kids come alive playing sophisticated math and reading games on the computer. Others need a hands-on approach, working out problems by manipulating blocks and rods, and still others can't tear themselves away from a new favorite book or an iPod or a well-recited tale. What matters is that *something* galvanizes them.[12]

"Properly implemented student-centered instruction can lead to increased motivation to learn, deeper understanding and more positive attitudes toward the subject," says Chicago physiologist Joel Michael, summarizing the research.[13] Properly implemented—that's the key. If these groups are going to run smoothly, Alina must concoct lessons that intrigue youngsters of widely varied talents and passions while also being sure to cover every topic prescribed by Union City's systemwide curriculum.

Teachers who have grown accustomed to the passive ease of prepackaged lessons would become lost in this curricular thicket. Like a juggler, Alina must keep several plates spinning, several activities going at the same time. Such a class can run smoothly only if discipline *does* come from within, as Alina preaches, but a balky computer can gum up the works and a young prankster can provoke bedlam.

During most of the day, Alina is constantly in motion, whirling like a ballerina from one small group of students to another, one youngster to another, giving hugs and tousling hair, switching languages in midsentence, English to Spanish and back again, with the occasional bit of Spanglish tossed into the linguistic pot. "*Mi corazon,*" she murmurs. "*Mi amor.*" When she reads aloud to the class, shifting between the Spanish and English translations, she acts out all the parts, her expressions as evocative as a mime's. Her English is vintage Jersey, a bit squeaky on the high notes, and her Spanish sounds like machine-gun bursts, a Cuban accent that has no time to pause for the letter "s." It's an ever-changing performance, one day to the next, one hour to the next, and for the most part these kids play their roles.

"STUDENTS WILL BE ABLE TO . . ."

Some classrooms are as muffled as a morgue, but Alina's room often echoes with the buzz and hum of kids talking to one another. "I don't mind the noise," she says, "as long as they're doing something productive. What I do insist on is that they do the work—the kids have to produce. Although my room will always be loud and full of energy, eventually these children will learn to sit still and raise their hands."

While a casual observer may think the class is impromptu, it's anything but. The daily schedule is prominently posted, so that visitors (usually the principal or assistant principal, though assistant superintendent Silvia Abbato might stop by) can see at a glance what's happening. It's also inscribed in a plan-book that divides the hours and minutes of each day almost as finely as a lawyer's calendar displays the tenths of an hour that are billed to a client. Every lesson is accompanied by what's known as SWBAT—not the Trekkies' "Star Wars Battlefront: Renegade Squadron" but "students will be able to. . . ." Walk into the classroom, ask a student what's happening, and you'll quickly find out if things are proceeding as advertised.

This is how the day is supposed to go, but whether this state of equipoise is reached depends on the chemistry of the classroom, which is potentially as combustible as phosphorous and water in a test tube. During the first week of class, Alina asked her students to draft their own constitution, which hangs on the wall. Although her class has pledged not to be noisy, to raise their hands when they want to speak, and to follow directions, here as in the outside world the constitution describes the aspiration, not necessarily the reality. The living constitution is being shaped daily by these youngsters' behavior, and this year Alina is finding it harder than usual to fabricate her pie.

These kids sometimes forget all about self-discipline and turn rambunctious, especially when they are being tutored in painting, music, and computer skills, away from Alina's watchful gaze. In the music class, John Staheli, a bulky and usually amiable man whom you'd cast as Santa in the Christmas show, works up a sweat getting the youngsters to pound in 4:4 time— "thump, thump, thump, thump," drumsticks banging on plastic buckets. Whether out of confusion or orneriness, a couple of them invariably thump to a different rhythm. But John, like the other specialist teachers, has no training in teaching kids who don't speak English, and he's having a hard time communicating with these youngsters. Frustrated by the disconnect, he loses patience, something that rarely happens when he's teaching students who speak English. "*Escuche!*" he shouts, one of the few Spanish words in his vocabulary, but the more frustrated he gets the more recalcitrant the children become.

In art class the kids normally buckle down, because Carmelina Woods knows how to tap their creativity. Their takeoffs on Van Gogh's *Starry Night* decorate the bulletin board outside the third grade classrooms and their self-portraits hang in Room 210. But one day there's an inexplicable meltdown, and in a matter of minutes the room is splashed with paint. When the youngsters return to class, hangdog expressions smeared on their faces, Alina disgustedly tosses their paintings into the trash.

Six weeks after the start of school, it has become clear that coaxing discipline from within, Alina's expectation for all her students, will be slow going. Rob Dorsett, who teaches the kids computer skills, stops by to commiserate. "You must need a glass of wine every night," he jokes. "With these students I could drink an entire bottle," Alina answers, only half-jokingly.

"These kids will get Bossbaly-ized," Principal Les Hanna predicts, "but it's going to be a hard transition."

"The Neediest Class I've Ever Had"

Time is a teacher's scarcest resource. When everyone in the class is being taught the same lesson at the same time, dividing the minutes among them doesn't pose much of a dilemma. But because these students' abilities vary greatly, as does their fluency in Spanish and English, Alina is constantly deciding where best to focus her energies. Even in a class as small as this it's always triage time, and invariably a child or two is demanding that attention be paid.

In the class photo, all the kids are wearing navy-blue polo shirts emblazoned with the seal of the Union City public schools, the uniform at Washington School. All except one, that is—Joaquin Andres Diaz stands out from the rest in his crisp white polo. This sartorial distinctiveness emblemizes the youngster who, from the first day, becomes a pivot point.

"Complex" is how Alina describes Joaquin. He's at once brilliant and erratic, focused and absent-minded, charming and infuriating, loving and jealous, bratty and mature, thoughtful and self-absorbed, impossible to ignore and ultimately impossible to resist. Read his journal and you'll find flashes of insight and inspiration as well as cavalier toss-offs, misspelled words that he's probably known since first grade, and vanished punctuation. Check his math and the usually perfect scores can be marred by sloppy mistakes.

"You're on wheels!" says Alina, in a moment of exasperation. "If the brain goes fast, the writing has to catch up."

The computer is where Joaquin does his best writing, like a clever tale about a zombie "Donut Man," and he speedily figures out the intricacies of formatting. Well before anyone else, he is turning out elegantly formatted papers that incorporate illustrations and sophisticated graphics, and he has become a wizard on the search engine. In a matter of weeks he is teaching his classmates new skills and sometimes he's instructing Alina as well.

Joaquin has shuttled back and forth between Chile, where his father lives, and Union City with his Bolivian-born mother, Pilar, and his grandparents. Born in Union City, Joaquin learned English as a child, but then forgot most of it during a year he spent with his dad when Pilar, an army sergeant, was stationed in California. Pilar tries hard to be a good mother but, overwhelmed by her day job and her night school classes, she can't always get it together. During the week, Joaquin often stays at his grandparents' apartment, where he sleeps on the living room couch, and in his journal he writes matter-of-factly about being awakened in the middle of the night. "A man in the house that I could not see was screaming 'help, help, help.' Another voice was like 'I'm going to kill you' and the police came." "The next day," he adds, as if nothing special had happened, "we went to the pool."

While other Union City youngsters are living similarly divided lives, Joaquin's absentmindedness compounds the problem. Sometimes he shows up without his backpack and has to share books with his seatmates. So frequently does he forget his new glasses that Alina starts to keep them in her desk drawer.

Most elementary school teachers expect that, by the time they're seven or eight years old, students will sit still for long stretches of the day. They would swiftly tire of Joaquin's restlessness, which leads him to wander away from his desk, perceiving his distractedness and his erratic work as proof of that overly diagnosed malady, Attention Deficit Disorder, and dispatching him to special education.[14] Here, however, he finds his place—more precisely, he contrives to make his own place. From 7 A.M., when he gets dropped off and spends the hour before school begins with Alina, until 3 P.M., when someone in the family picks him up, he makes his presence felt. The other kids acknowledge his gravitational pull. So much attention does he extract from Alina that after awhile they start to say that he's almost like her son.

Even in these early weeks of school you can learn a lot about what makes these youngsters tick by reading their journals and watching how they behave. What you'll find in Room 210 are islands of stability amid an ocean of emotional and academic insecurity. "They're the neediest class I've ever had," Alina confides.

A capable and mature boy like Emiliano—"little man," Alina fondly calls him—and bright, warm-hearted youngsters like Julieta and Lucia earn Alina's admiration. When she asks the students to describe themselves as an object, Lucia writes: "I am a sun, to help the flowers grow." (True to form, Joaquin identifies himself as a computer, "to help people work.") Youngsters like these get less than an equal share of Alina's time. She wishes that she could do more for them—she wishes that she could do more for each of them—but she figures that in a classroom overflowing with neediness they will do fine without much help. "It's the kids with issues of one kind or another, like Joaquin, who get the lion's share of attention," Alina muses. "The quiet kids fall through the cracks."

Isabella, one of Joaquin's deskmates, requires a good deal of Alina's energy. Despite her air of sweet self-confidence and her willingness to work hard, she's having a hard time. "I like writing a lot," she tells me, but she can't construct a paragraph, something she should have already learned. Veronica, who sits one seat away, stints on her homework, scribbles the barest something in her journal, and never volunteers a word in class. Alina reaches deep into her bag of tricks—she embraces, she nudges, she cajoles, she gets tough—but cannot find the elixir to cure laziness.

Matias, the boy who is repeating third grade, has become a new person, transformed over the course of a year from the wild child to the lively and responsible citizen who instinctively knows how to comfort a classmate by putting an arm around his shoulder. When asked in a journal assignment who he respects, he writes: "I respect poor people who don't have food."

Matias is a godsend to Andres, who gravitated to him from the very first day. Andres is the youngest member of the class and the smallest, a head shorter than Matias. He's bright but fretful, a perfectionist who bursts into tears if he gets a wrong answer. "No one is perfect, *nadie es perfecto*," Alina reassures him, but the words don't always register. On the day that the class is reading about Alexander's travails, he has a minor meltdown. "You're having a bad, horrible day, like Alexander," she says, "but you'll get over it." Andres plainly wants to be mothered, and Alina's ministrations don't suffice; alone among these kids, he scurries back daily to the warmth of his second grade teacher.

Samuel has bounced back and forth between Honduras and the United States, Union City and Houston. His father wants to move to Texas; his aunts, who think the world of Washington School, are anxious that he stay in Union City; and the persisting tug of war affects his ability to concentrate in ways that are entirely out of Alina's hands.

Each one of these kids is figuring out how to fit into this emerging community, and already they are helping one another. Dependable Emiliano shows Clara, the new girl, how to do Every Day Counts. Joaquin works with Isabella on her math. And when Roberto is out sick for a few days, Matias, who sits next to him, brings the homework assignment to his home.

But one of the students, Adriana, keeps herself apart. That summer, the girl had moved from Venezuela to Union City with her mother, who had come north to join her new husband. In Venezuela she lived a solidly middle class life and went to a Montessori school. Suddenly she has been plunged into the maelstrom of Union City and she hates it. There's no doubt about her intelligence; it's her attitude that's the problem. She conveys an air of disdainfulness, and the other kids respond by ignoring her and calling her "spoiled." She refuses to learn even a smattering of English, covering her ears when English is being spoken, as if through this small act of denial she can will herself back to her vanished life. Alina knows that the situation can't be sustained—the pie cannot be missing a slice—and she will go on an *abrazos* offensive.

All these kids crave affection, and the fact that I'm one of just a handful of men at Washington School makes me an affection magnet. I spend some of my time helping out the youngsters with their reading, talking with them about what they're writing, and listening to them describe their projects. Maybe an anthropologist would know how to keep his distance, but I'm drawn in by the openness of these boys and girls, their easy warmth that so starkly contrasts with the harsh realities of their lives. In a classroom where affection is so readily shown, these kids don't think twice about giving me hugs and soon enough I'm buried under an onslaught of embraces whenever I come to class.

The Halloween festivities cement this bond. Dressed in splendiferous costumes—Snow White and Cinderella, Captain America and Darth Vader, many of them home-made outfits—Washington School's students parade along nearby Bergenline Avenue, the main shopping street, as their parents dash alongside snapping photos.

Alina has cast me as Big Norman, a character in "Strega Nona," a story the kids have been reading. I'm bedecked in an oversized shirt, a mop of yellow hair, and a bumpkin's hat; Lidia, a septuagenarian teacher's aide who retains the sassiness of someone half her age, is attired as Strega Nona. Arm-in-arm we stroll down the second-floor corridor, and when word spreads every classroom wants us to visit. For them it's a cool photo op. For the youngsters in Room 210 it shows that we're part of the pie.

A Word-Drenched Class

Elementary school teachers must know a smattering of everything, from science to history, mathematics to art, but most of them have a favorite subject. Writing is Alina's first love and it's also where her students have the biggest problems.

"I put forth a love of writing," says Alina, and her students do a lot of it. The journal topic one morning is that chestnut, "What's your favorite food?" and she starts them off with a few minutes of brainstorming, sparking ideas from one another. "Pizza," the kids yell all at once. "McDonald's ... pizza ..." "What happens when you shout out?" asks Alina, and Joaquin, who was one of the quick-tongued, says, "Everyone will say the same thing." "Right," says Alina. "You're not letting others think for themselves."

Alina adores adjectives. "Don't always write 'pretty.' You can say 'attractive,' 'gorgeous,' 'beautiful,' 'stunning' ... 'atractivo,' 'precioso,' 'impresionante.' I want to see those words in your journals." And she urges them to stay focused. "Write about something important that happened on the weekend, not about everything that happened."

Week by week the "word wall" expands to include the new words the youngsters encounter in their reading. After they read a story about exchanging items—a theme that crosses the math–language divide—"merchant" and "straying" are added, and those words find their way into their writing as well.

The class is also growing more adept at brainstorming, the kids at each table checking out ideas with one another, and that too improves their writing. "What seems similar and what's different?" Alina asks, after they have read two stories, one of them about a Pilgrim's journey and the other a tale about a girl who emigrates from Russia to America. "How do they relate to your own lives? These are pioneers. When you find yourself in a new place, what problems might you encounter?"

Many of the students are making tangible progress. *"Mejor y mejor,"* Alina enthuses, "better and better," as they write longer, richer, and less rambling journal entries.

One morning when the class is being introduced to simple tools of the writer's craft—how to use "change of direction" signals like "however," "on the other hand," "but" as well as "illustrative signals" including "for example" and "in other words"—calm, collected Lucia raises her hand. She asks in Spanish whether these signals will be part of the New Jersey ASK, the achievement test that these students will be taking in the spring. "Don't worry about the exam," Alina responds, "pay attention to learning."

You might expect such a question to be posed eight months before test time in a suburb where parents, driven by the insatiable desire to give their offspring all of life's advantages, have been prepping them almost from birth.

The fact that it's being raised in a dirt-poor city by an eight-year-old who has lived in the United States for only a few years speaks volumes about how widely, and how powerfully, the pressures of testing are felt.

A month later Alina herself is regularly introducing the ASK into the classroom conversation. Those five-dollar words like "exquisite" and "stunning" are "brownie-point" words, she says. "The person who reads your essay will think, 'What a genius in Union City!'"

COMING AND GOING

It's taking considerably longer than usual for the principles that are supposed to guide the class—"the pie" and "the mind is a powerful thing"—to sink in. Compared with the first weeks, there are more good days, when all the kids are on their best behavior and a marble goes into the class-party box. But there are still those discouraging moments when Clara pouts and Andres cries, Isabella drifts off, Mauricio plays the clown, and Joaquin falls out of his seat.

"Last year, Alina's class was perfect," laments Jen Schuck, another third grade teacher whose classroom is two doors away. "It's too bad you weren't here then." Alina is more philosophical. "This is what life can be like in a third grade Union City classroom. *Es lo que es*—it is what it is."

One way to stop disruption is to alter the seating arrangement. Alina shifts the seats of some of the distraction-makers, hoping that the change will concentrate their minds, and when that doesn't do the trick she rearranges all the desks to form curved rows of four. These small groups can still work together easily, but now everyone is facing forward, making it easier for her to command their attention.

Fortunately, Alina's emphasis on helping and sharing has stuck. On a typical November day, Matias is spending time with Mauricio, who is working on *El Dia Feliz* in the reading nook. Emiliano, Alina's "little man," is lending a hand with Adriana, as they sort out the coins for Every Day Counts. Joaquin is showing Catalina how to save a document on the computer. And Andres says he will help Santiago, the newest arrival, as soon as he finishes his own project.

But Adriana continues to keep her distance from everyone, including Alina. "I touch you gently, with love," says Alina, putting her arm around Adriana's shoulder. "*Con odio*," Adriana whispers, "with hate." To a teacher like Alina, who gives her all, there can be no more hurtful word than "hate," and she sends Adriana to the corridor to reflect on what she has said. "You want to be special but here no one is special. There's *mucho amor—no odio!*" And that's not the end of it. Alina has a long conversation with Adriana's mother when she picks up her daughter after school. "Adriana needs to practice smiling in front of the mirror to see how beautiful she is when she smiles." The following day, she comes to school wearing what Alina calls a "new face"—a smile. Her transformation—from self-imposed exile to being a slice of the Room 210 pie—seems to have begun.

The other new arrivals are adjusting at a very uneven pace. Clara is doing badly, and while Alina looks for things to praise, giving the girl an *"excellente!"* when she makes a cutout of a snowflake, something she has never actually seen, those moments come rarely. Despite one-on-one lessons with Lidia, the bilingual aide, she is falling further and further behind, and when she can't complete an assignment she rips pages from her notebook. On one occasion she tips her chair back so far that she lands hard on the floor, which requires a visit to the nurse's office, and another time she surreptitiously delivers a hard kick to Matias. After a month of this, Alina wanted to send her to the second grade, where she could keep up with the class, but Les Hanna said no. "She thinks everything is a game," Alina says. "She's still a child. I'll adapt, I'll find a way that works." Perhaps Clara will become the new Matias, as Les had hoped, but the signs are inauspicious.

The newest student, a Guatemalan boy named Santiago, appears in mid-November, and he thrives. He had initially been placed in fourth grade, the level at which his transcripts said he belonged, but he couldn't master the work and was sent Alina's way. She is pleased with his quick progress. "Last week he was reading just syllables and now he can read simple stories aloud."

Still, the boy requires extra help if he's going to recover lost ground, and so Alina and Lidia spend considerable chunks of time with him. So do Matias and Andres, who are orienting him to the class regimen. Joaquin, accustomed to being the center of attention, starts to act up, much as older children do when there's a new baby in the family. He mocks Santiago, mimicking his throaty, almost guttural speech. He writes barely a sentence in his journal and is the only member of the class who doesn't finish a painting. In effect Joaquin has gone on strike, and only after a long talk with Alina does he decide that he really wants to be a part of the pie once again. When you're nine years old, attitudes can change very fast, and brattiness isn't the real

Joaquin. The day after he made fun of Santiago, Joaquin explains to him how to solve a problem on the computer.

Meanwhile, Samuel is gone, taken to Texas by his father. Together with his younger brother, he had arrived in Union City from Honduras that summer, and he was becoming close to some of his classmates. Alina had tried to persuade his father that his sons should stay, and so did Les, who knew how well the boys were adjusting. The father's decision was hastily reached, the result of a splintering among the grownups in the household whose aftershock was felt by Samuel's classmates. They cried a lot on the last day he was in school. Matias, distraught at losing his friend, clung tightly to him—a small boy, powerless in the capricious world of adults.

My own comings and goings have become the fodder for class lessons, and the fact that I'm spending Thanksgiving in Paris gets folded into the conversation. Oohs and aahs fill the room as I do a quick geography lesson. "Take me with you, take me with you!" pleads Andres. "Take me!" cries Joaquin. Tomás, who says very little in class, wears a troubled look. "*Puede volver? Tiene papeles?*" he asks me. "Can you return? Do you have papers?" That question forcibly reminds me that many of these students are living fraught and fragile lives, for Tomás's genuine concern is not just for me but most likely for himself and his family as well.

"I Am Thankful for My Mom"

La familia viene el primero, family comes first—that's essential to the idea of the pie. Most eight-year-olds cling to their families, and it will be a few years before they begin to spread their wings. For Alina's students the ties are especially close. Their parents, and perhaps an aunt or a cousin as well, are the only link between their old lives and the new lives they are making in Union City. In DR or Ecuador they played after school with other kids in their neighborhood, but in Union City many parents, fearful of the malevolent influences of the street, keep their children at home, taking them on weekends to the municipal swimming pool or the movies, the 99 Cents Only Store or Sunday Mass.

When Alina asks her class to write about their most precious possession, they don't mention the pricey store-bought item that a suburban child might brag about, an iPad or a Barbie replete with a killer wardrobe. Instead they describe a teddy bear they snuggle with every night or a cherished model of a Santo Domingo police car, mementoes from a beloved relative, an uncle or grandmother they left behind. When there's a coffee mug in the magic box, Joaquin stays on his best behavior because he wants to give it to his mom. Andres's perfect score on a vocabulary test wins him a trip to the box, and he picks out a purple plastic cup and saucer for his mother.

On the day that the journal topic is "what are you thankful for?" Joaquin writes that "I am thankful for my mom because without her I would not exist. I adore her because she is nice, pretty and intelligent. She is the most important person in my life." Matias is also thinking about his mom. "She feeds me every day, helps with my homework, washes my clothes on Saturday, takes me to the park. Weekend nights she takes me to the movies and Sundays she takes me to church. I lack nothing in my mind. It's important for me to respect and help her because she comes home tired out from work and I love her a lot."

A few parents call Alina constantly, checking up on their kids, wanting to be reassured that they're doing well. She is finding out about the lives of her students, and this knowledge shades her teaching. Emiliano, always the reliable one, the boy Alina thinks of as the "little man," comes from a solid home; Roberto, though just a middling student, has an uncle who's deeply interested in his nephew's future; and Santiago's family is involved as well. This kind of attentiveness can keep a youngster on track. But Isabella, whose family life had been relatively tranquil, has endured a series of shocks in recent months. Her father lost his job and hasn't been able to find work. Her fifteen-year-old stepbrother, raised by his grandmother in Honduras, has just landed on the family's doorstep. He has been placed in the seventh grade "port of entry" class, the way station for newcomers in middle school, where he is floundering. The landlord has jacked up the rent, forcing the family out of their apartment, and for the moment they are living with Isabella's grandparents. Saddest of all, Isabella's mother, the family's emotional ballast and breadwinner, has been diagnosed with cancer, and she is spending weeks at a stretch in the hospital. In class Isabella is as sweet as ever, and she doesn't talk about any of this, but the emotional roller-coaster surely affects her schoolwork.

Joaquin is up and down during these final weeks of autumn. When he is troubled he bites his cuticles and now, apparently fearful that his mother is again going to be sent far away by the army, he has gnawed so hard that they're bleeding. "Is something wrong?" Alina asks, on a morning when he hasn't done his homework, but he shakes his head, unwilling to talk about whatever is going on. "You're so brilliant but you get into bad habits," she says quietly, when he does something especially childish, and there's a soft sadness in her voice. "You disappoint me and yourself." But it's hard, she tells me, to stay disappointed with Joaquin. "He has a great brain and a huge heart."

LEARNING ENGLISH BY LEARNING SPANISH

Union City has pioneered in bringing immigrant youngsters, many of whom come to school unable to write a sentence in Spanish, into the education mainstream.[15] Elsewhere, these new arrivals might be handed the educational equivalent of a death sentence—inadequately taught, they never catch up, and they quit or get pushed out as soon as the law permits. But in Union City, after only a few years you can't distinguish the students whose first days in an American school are spent in a class like Alina's from those who have spent their entire lives in the United States.

In many districts you couldn't find a classroom like this one, with its continually evolving combination of Spanish and English, its mix of children still shivering in the comparatively frigid climate of northern New Jersey and those who have lived here for a few years, its child-by-child attention to differences in language fluency as well as academic skills. Instead, the new arrivals would be sent to English as a Second Language class—taught entirely in English, though specially geared for non-English-speakers—and then shifted to a regular class, where they often have a hard time making the adjustment. But Union City's educators realize that becoming fluent in English isn't an either-or proposition, with students moving in lockstep from ESL to ordinary classes, all the while being instructed only in English. Instead, these kids receive a solid grounding in Spanish before they're eased into English, lesson by lesson and student by student.

The field of bilingual education has been beset by political donnybrooks, including "English for the children" campaigns in California and Arizona that led to legislation mandating English-only instruction for newcomers, as well as ideological set-to's, fought on the battlefield of political correctness, and protracted scholarly spats. Still, the bulk of the research confirms that a solid foundation in one's home language offers the best preparation for mastery of English. And in Union City, there's no arguing with success.[16]

At the start of the year, half of Alina's youngsters were being taught in Spanish, but two months later some of them have begun to read in English. They've been prepared for that shift—from day one they have been hearing lots of English spoken in the room, and in their small groups they've been playing a game with blocks that teaches them how to construct English words. Alina won't push these kids, for she wants to make sure they've honed their Spanish before they read and write entirely in English. "There aren't many children in this country who know two languages," she reminds them. "It's a real advantage."

In mid-November, out of the blue, Julieta, one of the quietest students, writes her first sentence in English: "My most valued possession is a monster—to protect me." Then Matias decides he's going to take his math test entirely in English—"he's beginning to fly!" Alina exclaims—and Andres does half of his in English. She anticipates that Matias, Andres, and Roberto, who sit together, will start writing in English by February or March. But they floor her when, right after Thanksgiving vacation, they say they want to start writing their journals in English.

While Matias and Roberto are ready to take the plunge, Andres would benefit from a few more months of writing in Spanish; if he switches to English prematurely he might slip into Spanglish and become adept at neither language. On the other side of the equation there's the human factor—Andres would be crushed if she said no, keeping him on a leash, while Matias, his hero, speeds along. Andres is a bright kid, and over time, Alina figures, he'll make the transition to English, so she decides to let him try.

The first sentence Matias writes in his new language has to do with life in the seventeenth century, but it also speaks to his own character: "I would have a musket to hunt the animals for everybody to be safe." As Alina predicted, Andres's first paper is pure Spanglish. "You're running as fast as you can," she tells him, "but you need to slow down a bit."

MR. DAVID AND "THE PIE"

"The last six weeks of the fall are my favorite time of the year," Alina tells me. Finally this gang of needy and sometimes unruly students that she acquired in September is on its way to becoming Bossbaly-ized, conscientious and hard-working citizens of Washington School.

There are still bad days when the kids won't calm down and do their work, and on those days you're likely to hear a squeaky yell or two from an irritated Alina. But these moments have become rarer and, overall, the youngsters are doing better academically. The three seatmates who have written their first prose in English ask Alina to read their papers aloud. In turn each boy stands next to her as she recites, her arm resting on their shoulders, and the class erupts in applause.

My presence changes the classroom atmosphere, both for better and for worse. Sometimes the kids quiet down when I come, sometimes they show off. "Mr. David!" they yell, and always they want the hug or the arm around the shoulder or the quiet word. "Be my father!" Joaquin implores, holding on tightly, and I'm reminded that he hasn't seen his father for two years. "Be *my* father," cries Andres. That's harder for me to hear because Andres is in fact living with his father. Until last year, he and his mother were living in Peru. His father, who grew up in Union City and went to Peru years earlier to find a bride, returned every summer, but during the year mother and son were on their own. Then, in December 2009, they moved to Union City, and a couple of months later Andres's mom became pregnant. The boy clings to his mother and, in class, to me.

I will be leaving Washington School a few days before the Christmas holidays, and while I will be spending time there during the spring, Alina and I know that my leave-taking will stir up some feelings. We don't have a clue, though, about just how emotional things will get.

On my last day the youngsters surprise me with essays, gussied-up with clipart and crayons, about what I mean to them. One by one the kids come to the front of the room. Some of them read their papers aloud. Others, too tearful to speak, ask me to read them to the class. I'm hoping I can keep it together and so I ask Alina to do the honors. "He has been warm and caring," Adriana writes. "All the kids are excited when he comes. The class won't be the same without you."

Since her set-to with Alina there has been a marked change in Adriana's attitude, and home life is also much better. "I help my father because he is my favorite father," she writes, implicitly comparing him to the dad who remains in Venezuela. "I give him hugs and kisses to show my love." Matias says that "Mr. David is cool. He likes to hug. He is elegant. He is good to people." Joaquin knocks my socks off. "Mr. David knows how we grow, work, mature, and a lot more. I love him immensely. He is like my dad."

Alina and I have planned a surprise pizza party, the kids' favorite, and since they are such agile and excitable dancers we've left time for a Latino dance number. The idea is to make this a festive occasion, but it's hard to stop the waterworks. Joaquin and Andres won't let go of me. Neither will Adriana, who to my astonishment proves to be the most inconsolable of them all. "Go figure," says Alina.

These youngsters don't know it, but from now until May life in Room 210 will become noticeably different—sadder too, if you prize memorable teaching—as the New Jersey ASK, the achievement test that Lucia was wondering about in October, looms ever larger. It's Alina's job to keep things lively, to make sure that learning doesn't degenerate into a dull and drill-driven experience, drill and kill, while she preps these students for the high-stakes event. She works hard at it, but as the winter months tick by, that feat will become harder and harder to pull off.

2

NEW KIDS ON THE BLOCK
George Washington Elementary School

On September 20, Parents' Night at George Washington Elementary School, the rain pours down like an open spigot. Even on a picture-perfect evening most urban schools would count themselves as lucky if 10 % of the parents show up, but the gym at Washington, like other Union City public schools, is packed with parents and grandparents, aunts and uncles carrying dripping umbrellas and clammy coats.

Maria Kanik, who is responsible for connecting these families with the school, assures them that they're welcome not only on this one evening but all the time. "If you need a school uniform, I can help. If you need someone to translate when you're talking to a teacher, I can help. If you need social services, I can help." The principal, Les Hanna, offers a frothy, upbeat welcome: "It's going to be a sensational year!" she tells the families, first in Spanish and then in English. Many in the audience know Maria and Les, and the cheers they receive would gladden the heart of a rock star.

Spend an hour or two walking around any school and you'll acquire a decent understanding of how the place works. Some schools convey informality; others are more rule-bound; and some, mostly in inner cities, carry the unmistakable air of a factory or, worse, a juvenile detention center.

Washington School, with its enveloping culture of *abrazos*, seems less an institution than the simulacrum of an extended family, and its warmth feels like the public equivalent of love. It takes lots of work to make such caring an institutional virtue, and much of the credit belongs to the principal, Les Hanna.

"You Are a Star"

Not so long ago, the job of the principal was to keep the school running—ordering supplies, balancing the budget, patrolling corridors, and filling out paperwork. That scutwork hasn't gone away, though if a principal is lucky she can farm out some of it to an assistant principal, but now principals are expected to be academic leaders as well. They're supposed to know what's being taught and how to teach it effectively; how to interpret ever more sophisticated information about students' performance, using it to help teachers reach the youngsters who haven't caught on; and how to enlist parents and local talent in the shared enterprise of supporting the kids.

In short, being a principal has turned into a killer job.[1]

Les Hanna became the principal of Washington School in May 2009, a month before the end of the school year. While the appointment came at an odd time, Les was no stranger to the school, having been an assistant principal there for nine years. Her predecessor, Robert Wendelkin, had previously been a high school principal in the district, but he was overwhelmed by the demands of the job, and his transfer to Washington didn't improve his skills as an administrator. No one doubted Wendelkin's intelligence, but "his focus was entirely on his family," Les tells me. "He'd often leave early to be with his grandchildren; the school became secondary. Of course family is important, but it can't become *that* important."

Some teachers feared that they would wind up on Wendelkin's wrong side, targeted for his sharp-tongued criticism. "You never heard an appreciative word from him," recalls third grade teacher Mary Ann Rick. "It wasn't a fun place." During his six years as principal, Wendelkin was beset by health problems that surely took their toll, making it hard for him to give full attention to his job. He was on leave for several lengthy stints, and off the job for seven months when he tripped on the school stairs and broke his knee-cap. That's when Les, who had earlier filled in on an interim basis, took over. "His heart just wasn't in it anymore," she says.

Once formed, the culture of a school isn't readily changed, but from the start Les did whatever she could to alter the atmosphere. "She is thanking us constantly," Mary Ann tells me. "She makes you feel appreciated. She talks about the school as a family, and she means it."[2]

Modest gestures can make a splash. Early on, Les converted a classroom into a classy teachers lounge, replacing a small, windowless room that had previously served the purpose. Third grade teacher Marilyn Corral donated a couch, and other touches have made the place feel homey. Though the new lounge might seem like a trivial change, it mattered a lot to the teachers, for this is the only place in the building where they can take a break from the incessant demands of the job, where they can have a cup of coffee or an impromptu conversation. The old lounge had gone unused, but the new one has come alive.

Les is no pushover—as Superintendent Sandy Sanger, who has known her for many years, puts it, "she can kick ass if that's what is needed"—but her instinct is to lead by encouragement, not intimidation. On the first day of school she gave every teacher a silver star for her desk. "You are a star . . . come shine with us!" the memento says. "She's supportive and demanding," adds Mary Ann. "People are at the top of their game for her because she expects it."

What characteristics of a school predict substantial improvement in student achievement? Sociologists Anthony Bryk and Barbara Schneider posed that question in their long-term study of Chicago's public schools, and their answer can be summed up in a single word, *trust*—trust among teachers, principals, and parents; trust among the teachers; trust between the principal and the teachers.[3]

Les has worked hard to build this sense of trust. When I ask Alina Bossbaly why Washington School runs so well, she tells me to "start with Les."

TLC for the Kids

Like so many of her colleagues at Washington School, Les's life story blurs with those of her students. Her mother Olga, who was born in Puerto Rico, is the Latina daughter of a German-born entrepreneur. Because of her dark skin, he never truly accepted his daughter into the family, and at the age of nine he shipped her off to work as a maid. There must be something better than this life, Olga thought, as she slaved for wealthy families, and after getting married at age seventeen she prodded her husband, Victor, into leaving for the mainland. Miami was their first stop, but in 1958, when Victor's sister moved to Union City, he followed suit.

Union City had become world-renowned for fine embroidery, and Olga became a master at the craft. "She can make pillowcases, napkins, and dresses better than a machine," Les says proudly, but she wanted an entirely different life for her daughter. "School is your job," Olga told her. "Do your best. Get a real education and you won't have to do the dirty work. You'll become middle class."

Les became the quintessential overachiever, the president of her high school's math club and science club, a cheerleader, and an "A" student. "I was a good girl," she muses. "Too good." Yale tempted her with a scholarship, but like so many of Union City's Latino youngsters, for whom family means everything, she didn't want to leave home.

Les won a full scholarship to nearby Saint Peter's College, and after graduation she started teaching at a Union City elementary school. She fell hard for the principal, Richard Hanna, whom everyone calls Richie, an imposing figure of a man, a generation older and with children of his own, and they eventually married.

In 1983, amid a political war that roiled Union City, Richie Hanna became superintendent, but six years later he was forced out and retired soon afterward. Meanwhile Les was gradually advancing up the ranks, moving from the classroom to the guidance counselor's office, and then to the central office, where she rewrote the district's guidance standards before being assigned to Washington School.[4]

Although Les is a fulltime administrator, she hasn't lost her counselor's touch. "Les really cares about the kids," says Mary Ellen Naumann, who taught at Washington for half a century before retiring in 2009. "If she sees that a kid has a band-aid she'll ask him how he's doing."

The school used to have its own full-time social worker, but she left the previous June and her absence is sorely felt. "Children in crisis need TLC," Les says. "Our kids' lives are truly, truly horrible. We have to be there *now*, and I feel heartbroken when I'm not there." That's no exaggeration. What's astonishing is how many of these children thrive despite the jagged edges of their lives. For some of them, just making it to school represents a real accomplishment.

One morning, Marilyn Corral, who teaches third grade, was explaining the difference between a savings account and a checking account to her class when she saw puzzled looks on several faces. "My mother doesn't have that. She has to spend all her money," said one student, and other heads nodded. After a lesson on how to be smart with money, a pig-tailed girl pledged to bring her pennies to the bank so that she could buy all the books she wants. In her piggy bank there were only pennies and in her mind pennies could purchase lots of books.

"At home everything gets said in front of these kids. There are no boundaries," Marilyn tells me, thinking back to an episode when one of her students wasn't picked up after school. "My dad works till late and he can't come. My mom left with another man," the girl explained, as if this were the most normal situation in the world.

In this depressed economy, many parents can't get jobs and every month they scramble to pay the rent. A few mothers turn to what they euphemistically describe as "exotic dancing" to pay the rent and feed their kids, and maybe to pay off the *coyote* who slipped them across the Mexican border and into the country. While they surely wish it were otherwise, they have precious little time to be a mother.

Les has taken it upon herself to help fill this vacuum, to give the children at Washington the caring that they may not find elsewhere, and she's become the school's de facto social worker as well as its principal. This quality of caring can build a sense of trust between the school, the kids, and their families. At noontime it's not uncommon to see a student who threw a tantrum earlier that day sitting in Les's office, legs dangling, in the big leather wing chair that faces her desk. The kid may have attacked a classmate or smashed a chair, but unlike the typical trip to the principal—the longest voyage in a schoolchild's life, where a tongue-lashing is the best that can be expected—punishment is not the likely outcome. After lunch, with time for the youngster to cool off, they'll talk about the episode that prompted the teacher to send the student to Les's office. Usually the child will apologize, pledging that the episode won't be repeated, and most of the time this promise will be kept.

On some days the flow of misbehaving youngsters into Les's office is as constant and never-ending as the Mississippi. The girls in a fifth grade class are agog over Ramon, who recently arrived from Panama, because he's handsome, mature for a ten-year-old and a bit dashing. They're flirting madly, saying things like "I want to kiss you" and "I want to have your baby," while the boys call him a fag because he wears pink socks. "You're a fag," he shoots back, and tensions escalate. "You can't take matters in your own hands," Les tells Ramon. "That isn't how things are done here." Later in the day she lays down the law to his tormentors.

Six weeks into the school year, Les has received a spate of reports about bullying. As in Ramon's case, it's all name-calling, not physical assaults. But behavior that used to be dismissed as "kids will be kids" hijinks is now treated very seriously because of New Jersey's new antibullying legislation, the toughest in the nation. Les calls a special assembly to drive into the students' heads the point that bullying is unacceptable. She asks each one of them to pledge that they will change their ways, and then gives them rubber wrist-bands bearing the inscription "be a buddy, not a bully."[5]

Sean, a bright but sad-eyed youngster, his gaze habitually directed to the floor, poses a particularly complex challenge. He actually wants to be kicked out of school so that he can join his father, who has moved halfway across the country, and he figures that he can get booted if he messes up in class and stops doing his schoolwork. But Les, who has made it a point to look into the situation, knows that the hoped-for reunion with his dad isn't going to happen. She sits with Sean, patiently going over his unfinished assignments, searching for something to say that might make his young life feel more bearable.

Matchmaking

"The school must be inviting," Les tells me, "because it makes such a difference for the children. They spend so much of their time here—it's *their* home." Vinnie Fraginals, the security guard, personifies that message. He's the first person you see when you walk into the school, and while those who fill such positions of modest authority are often petty bureaucrats, officious and off-putting, Vinnie is about as self-important as a teddy bear. He's there for the kids, devoting hours of his time to an after-school sports program.

Because a welcoming schoolhouse ought to be spotless, Les makes sure that the building is regularly scoured. As we're walking into the building one day, back from lunch at Terry's, the local luncheonette, she catches sight of a couple of garbage bags propped against a side door. Instantly she's on her walkie-talkie, and by the time we're back in her office the trash is being carted away. During the summer, when the columns that frame the school's entry were being repainted, Les insisted on choosing the particular white—"Gardenia White"—that would be used. "No other principal gets this involved," the painters marveled.

A school's corridors also tell a tale. Many principals have a fondness for displaying rousing quotes, and they garland their building with nuggets of wisdom extracted from the classics. Les relies on the students to supply the inspiration. The walls of the corridors are covered with science projects and artwork, often accompanied by essays that elaborate on the theme. On one visit I see that the second graders have drawn cartoonish figures depicting the difference between a frog and a toad, and each child has written a paragraph of explanation. The kids in another room have been studying the environment: "Keep the Air Clean," "Help Save Water," their prettily illustrated posters read. The walls that flank the third grade classes feature a show of Paul Klee–style paintings, paired with minibiographies of the Swiss artist.

In ways big and small, Les spends a lot of time thinking about what's best for each youngster. Students in most schools normally remain with the same classmates from one year to the next, but at Washington many placements are handled individually. In making these assignments, language skills matter—once students master English, they'll be in classes where only English is spoken—and since the pace of learning varies the placements must differ accordingly. Personalities also count. Some kids thrive with a teacher who insists on order in the classroom while others respond to a lighter touch, and a student who blossoms with one kind of teacher may wilt with another. And when two youngsters have been at each other's throats all year, it's prudent to split them up.

"We have 600 kids who are going from one grade to the next. Half would do well with any teacher. The rest have hand-picked placements," Les tells me. "That keeps problems from arising and encourages good dynamics in the classroom." While this process devours many springtime hours, Les is convinced that it's worth the effort. In making these decisions, she relies heavily on the teachers' judgments. "I expect the teachers to know each student's personality. Is this kid easy-going or high-strung? Does he get along well with the other kids?" She collects scraps of information from everyone. "I talk to Olga and Nancy in the lunchroom. They give me feedback on how kids get along, and so does Vinnie [the security guard]." What's more, she has to take into account the mix of kids in a particular classroom. "It's almost like party planning," she jokes.[6]

THE WORKER BEES

"Improvements are a matter of 'will'—peoples' motivation—and of 'skill,' their capacity," asserts Ben Cohen, the former deputy minister of education in Ontario, who writes about his success in reforming the schools of that Canadian province in *How to Change 5000 Schools*. "Improvement can only occur and last where school staff are engaged and committed." In the course of molding a community at Washington School, Les has done her best to surround herself with people who share her values, the hard workers for whom the kids' needs, not the adults' egos, come first.[7]

Take Maria Kanik, who earned a prolonged round of applause at Parents' Night because of everything she has done over the years for these families. Every school in the district has a parent liaison like Maria, another indication of the value placed on keeping families close, and for Les, the social worker/principal, this connectedness is an imperative.

Maria is a glove-tight fit for the job. When parents come to her because they need medical help or are having trouble with disability benefits, can't find child care or are being evicted, she may well know by heart the phone number of the right person to call. At monthly family events she loosens things up, garbed as a pilgrim for Thanksgiving and the Mama Queen on Mother's Day. The parents understand that Maria cares about their kids' well-being—if their youngster comes to school late they'll get a 6:30 wake-up call the following morning, and if their child is absent, even for a single day, she will want to know why.

Since becoming a parent liaison in 1998, Maria had bounced from one school to the next, along the way acquiring a reputation as a troublemaker. At her first school, she tells me, a couple wanted to put their daughter, who had been assigned to special education, in a regular class. The principal said it was impossible to accommodate the request, but Maria knew the parents were legally entitled to insist on the shift. "Do I tell them the law or do what the principal tells me?" she asks me, recounting the episode. She went with the parents and was nudged out the door.

At Maria's second school, a new assistant principal proposed red and white as the school's colors. "It was a mistake because those are gang colors—the colors of the Bloods," Maria tells me. After losing the argument with her boss she went straight to Mayor Brian Stack, whose involvement in school affairs can extend to the minute particulars, and got the colors changed.

Maria was reassigned again, this time to Washington. "It's completely different here," she tells me.[8]

A steady stream of immigrant families flows into Washington School. You can spot these new arrivals, timid and perhaps fearful as they bring their children to school in America for the first time. Martha Jones—nominally a roving bilingual education specialist but in fact the assistant principal in all but the title—takes these youngsters in hand. Like Les, she has lived her own version of their stories.

Martha was born in Cuba, the daughter of an officer in Fulgencio Batista's army. After the Cuban revolution, her father, fearful of being executed by Fidel Castro's minions, escaped to the United States, where he was granted political asylum. Martha and her mother followed, traveling first to Mexico, ostensibly as tourists, then crossing the Rio Grande on a raft.

The family initially settled in New York City, but after a few years Martha's parents sought a quieter life. Without knowing where they were going, they boarded a bus bound for New Jersey, got off at the first stop, near Union City, and decided that it was a safe place. Both of Martha's octogenarian parents still live in town and both are still working. Her mother manages Casa Manito, a used furniture store; her father, a lunch monitor at Washington, has become a surrogate grandfather to many of these kids. "My parents are my heroes," she says, "they sacrificed so much for me."

"*Bienvenido*," Martha tells a new family, "welcome," as she ushers them into her office and gives the mom a reassuring hug. Each new student must be tested in reading, writing, and speaking in Spanish and, when it's appropriate, in English as well. Even though the parents may have brought school records from their home country, grade levels in the two nations don't always match.

This battery of tests consumes the better part of a day, and during breaks Martha makes it a point to learn about these youngsters' personal histories. After they're placed she keeps tabs on them. When she hears that a new third grader is craving endless attention, she connects her with a fifth grader who's living with a single mom, a girl that Martha knows wants someone to mother.[9]

But Les doesn't have free rein in picking her staff, and John Coccioli, the longtime assistant principal who likes to be called Coch, has emerged as her nemesis. On first impression, Coch comes across as a genial fellow who plays cheerful music during the morning PA announcements and promotes the never-empty coffee pot in his office. In action, though, he behaves less like an educational leader and more like a tough disciplinarian.

A meeting run by Coch, intended to help the fourth grade teachers boost their students' language arts test scores, goes off the rails when he uses the success of the third grade teachers to berate their colleagues. When he evaluated one of the school's best teachers as "proficient" but not "outstanding," the teacher, who had received the coveted "best teacher" award, sought an explanation. "There are no outstanding teachers—period!" was his response. Teachers grumble about Coch, and the most outspoken ones complain to his face. One teacher lays it on the line: "I want to knock on your door and not be intimidated. I want to talk with someone who knows about education, not just discipline."

Les and Coch are as different in temperament as chalk and cheese. To get anything done, Les knows that she must work around him, and as the year progresses she finds herself taking on more of the administrative burden. For her, the good news is that Coch keeps hinting that he'll retire in June.

Testing Times

As palpable as the culture of *abrazos* that Les Hanna fosters at Washington School is the No Child Left Behind regime in which she is enmeshed.[10] Results on the state's high-stakes tests, the New Jersey Assessment of Skills and Knowledge, usually referred to as the ASK, effectively define success for the school. In 2009, the year she became principal, only a third of Washington's students passed those exams, and she knew the school had to do better. "The test scores are weak and I need someone to turn things around," said Superintendent Sandy Sanger when he appointed her.

The New Jersey Department of Education was already hovering. In the fall of 2009, too soon in Les's tenure for her to have had much impact on how Washington was run, a team of outside experts selected by the state appraised the school. For four days the visitors scoured the records, visited classes, and met with teachers and students. Such a review is standard fare for a school like Washington that, in the language of the federal law, stands "in need of improvement" because too many of its students aren't proficient in reading or math. At the time of the review, Washington had been mired in that unhappy state for four years.

In theory, this review is a joint venture—it's called a *Collaborative* Assessment for Planning and Achievement, or CAPA—but in practice it's a one-way street. In the background lurks the recognition that, because of the students' chronically weak performance on the ASK, Washington may ultimately have to be "reconstituted." That's No Child Left Behind legalese for replacing administrators and teachers, the remedy favored by the "no excuses" critics. Union City has resisted going down this road, believing it only causes turmoil. The district is right: the evidence is that turning the school inside out "engenders the exact conditions that long lines of research have linked with persistent low performance—high turnover, instability, poor climate [and] inexperienced teachers."[11] Still, the very fact that reconstitution remains a possibility ups the pressure on Les and the staff at Washington.

The CAPA team did find some positive things to say about the school. Its report praised the smooth transition from preschool to kindergarten, noting that the kindergarten classrooms had been redesigned to make them more inviting to five-year-olds. When they visited classes, they observed instances of lively teaching and saw generally attentive students. The reviewers also acknowledged the difficulties of teaching so many youngsters who spoke little if any English and came to the U.S. essentially unschooled.

Overall, however, the report was scathing. Many teachers were emphasizing memorization and not problem-solving, said the reviewers. The school didn't target the neediest students for effective support; it didn't use the information from student assessments to improve teaching; it didn't connect the dots of the curriculum; it didn't evaluate students' portfolios; and it didn't provide useful in-service training for the teachers. Major changes had to be made—and quickly.

The school's weakest link, the CAPA team pointed out, was the sixth grade, which was falling far short of meeting the state's goals. This problem had not arisen through happenstance, nor was it unique to Washington; rather, it was an inadvertent but predictable consequence of the No Child Left Behind regime. Until 2007 sixth graders in New Jersey weren't required to take state tests, and administrators, knowing that their fortunes depended on the test results, dumped the weakest teachers there. When the state reversed course and started to test sixth graders, there was nowhere to hide those teachers. But that explanation offered Les no solace. If Washington was ever going to do better, these teachers had to raise their game, and the new principal had to figure out what could help them.

Eight months later, at the end of Les's first year as principal, the CAPA team returned. This time the reviewers came away impressed, for every one of their recommendations was being carried out. The change in leadership had made all the difference, Cathy Coyle, the former assistant superintendent in Jersey City who led the CAPA team, tells me. Cathy has a reputation for toughness—as assistant superintendent in Jersey City, she had fired a host of incompetent principals—but she has nothing but praise for Les. "When we returned, the teachers could talk about how to make good use of the test scores, identify the weaknesses and show how they were relating math and English in their instruction."

"Wendelkin was a building manager, Les is an instructional leader," says Cathy. "After our second visit I let the state know that the school is doing everything they can do. 'There's nothing more that I can recommend.'" She told Les the same thing—"with what you've done, I can't see why your scores won't improve"—and counseled patience. "It takes time to see the effects of the changes you've made." In the fall of 2010, a year and a half into Les's tenure as principal, Washington School remains a work in progress.

Mentors and Coaches

Les does her best to act as an educational leader, not a paper-pusher. She has assumed responsibility for supervising kindergarten to third grade, leaving the upper grades to Coch—"I can't do it all and he has to do something," she says. She stops by most classrooms every day, if only to stick her head in the door and say, "good morning, boys and girls," with that wide-angle smile of hers. ("Good morning, Mrs. Hanna," the kids chorus back.) Every week or so she stays longer in one or two classes, and twice a year she carries out a formal review of each teacher. But between filling out endless forms, being the impromptu social worker, and putting out fires, she can't carve out enough time to give this part of her job the attention it warrants.

Aside from observing and evaluating the teachers, Les needs to help them improve. One strategy is to break through the isolation of the classroom, encouraging teachers to work together, jointly devise projects for their students, and talk about what's working well in their classrooms and what isn't. Such collaboration, the evidence shows, can make a substantial difference in the quality of instruction.[12]

Case in point: fourth grade teacher Jennifer Mondelli. In 2009, when Jennifer graduated from Felician College, a nearby Franciscan school, the job market was tight. She took the only job she could find, a position at a tiny private academy in neighboring Hoboken. "We were paid hourly. If there was a snow day, tough luck," she tells me. "I applied everyplace." She jumped at the Union City offer.

Yet life at Washington proved to be hard going. "It was totally different," Jennifer recalls. She took over the class in February 2010, the middle of the year, after a teacher suddenly quit and a parade of substitutes had passed through the classroom. "The kids kept asking me, 'Are you our real teacher? Are you going to stick around till June?' I had to figure out what novels we should be reading, what the math sequence was, how to do a plan-book, how to teach a five-paragraph essay [that's what New Jersey ASK expects from fourth graders]. I needed to set up the classroom in the way that worked for me and I needed to learn about the kids. Before I was teaching ten third- and fourth-graders and now I had twenty students. I got to school very early and stayed very late. I was pretty stressed out."

Every new teacher in Union City is assigned a mentor. Studies have shown that a good mentor can help a novice close the gap between knowing and doing, between the theories she has imbibed in college and the ruder realities of classroom life. Although the formal pairing is Les's doing, the personalities have to click, and if the chemistry is right a mentor can become a starting-out teacher's new best friend. Les relies on experienced teachers with a reputation for being helpful and not know-it-all bossy, and they receive a modest stipend for the added work.[13]

Sue Emmerling, a fourth grade teacher who has been at Washington for more than thirty years, volunteered to be Jennifer's mentor. For Sue, the money was the least of it, and even though she wouldn't be paid until the following fall, she immediately took Jennifer under her wing. "Jennifer's a breath of fresh air," says Sue. Jennifer returns the compliment: "From day one she helped me with everything, from understanding the curriculum to little things like the procedure for lunch and dismissal." Her first full year at Washington began in September, and Sue continues to lend a hand. "If you need anything, just ask me and I'll help you," Sue says, and Jennifer often takes her up on her open-door policy.

The school used to have full-time writing and math coaches who worked with the teachers—Sue had been one of them—but two years earlier the seventh and eighth grades were carved out as a separate middle school and the coaches departed with them. When Les became principal, she asked Alina Bossbaly to serve as a part-time coach. Jennifer knew that she needed extra help with writing, and Les assigned Alina to her. "I'm a motivator," Alina says. "I want to show teachers how much fun writing can be and how the kids can really enjoy it despite all the state requirements. I want my love of writing to become contagious."

Many school systems would send a novice like Jennifer to a training session, where the glossiest new techniques are trotted out. But because these events aren't grounded in the particulars of the school and classroom, the world a teacher lives in, they're often time-wasters. Rick Stiggins, who founded the Assessment Training Institute in Portland, Oregon, has participated in scores of these sessions. "Workshops will not work," he says, echoing the research, because they "do not permit the application of and experimentation with new assessment ideas in real classrooms, and sharing that experience with other colleagues in a team effort." What Alina offers, "hands-on practice" with directly applicable teaching techniques and "personalized coaching," is a far more promising approach.[14]

"Alina has taught me how to conduct a writing class," Jennifer tells me. "I'm learning how to teach dialogue, internal thinking, break up essays into paragraphs. I didn't know how to do any of this. I could watch her—mirror her. The kids write their first draft. They volunteer to share their stories and Alina goes over the good parts and the parts they could improve on. They love her, she's so peppy and upbeat."

The previous year, Alina spent many afternoons in Mary Ann Rick's third grade classroom (while she was away, her students studied math with a substitute well versed in the subject). Mary Ann knew math cold, but writing wasn't her forte. She proved an apt and appreciative pupil. "Alina would draw on all the different words for 'smart,' like intelligent and brainy, and she knew how to encourage the students," Mary Ann recounts. "'You used sophisticated language,' she'd say. 'That's awesome.' Now if I use a big word like 'astonished' they'll give me the knitted brow and I'll define it for them." Alina also proffered helpful hints about seemingly mundane tasks, such as how to teach spelling. "You don't just hand out a list of spelling words. You have the kids write the words out and learn their meanings. It takes longer but it's worth it."

Les has called upon Alina to take another young fourth grade teacher, Veronica Pardo, under her wing. Veronica, who grew up in neighboring

Jersey City, came to Union City in 2008 fresh out of college. She'd known since she was in first grade that she wanted to become a teacher, she tells me, and she made her sisters play school, pretending to read worn-out textbooks that her father lugged home from the public library. Her students, like Alina's, were immigrants who spoke little if any English, and it's a formidable task to guide children along the path to their new language while making sure that they have a solid foundation in their mother tongue.[15]

"I knew right away that I could approach Alina with anything," Veronica says. "I didn't know how to teach these two languages. I never saw it in action. The kids were all developing at different levels and I had to learn how to differentiate the teaching."

It's gospel at Washington School, as in all of Union City's elementary schools, that for an hour or so every day students should be split into small groups, what educators call "learning centers," to expose them to varied ways of learning. In a fourth grade classroom, some kids will be navigating the web and others will be reading a book they've plucked from the classroom library or solving a word puzzle. Though the concept is appealing, it's hard going to pull it off. "At first I was confused by the idea that youngsters are on their own," Veronica remembers, and with Alina's guidance she learned on the job. What's more, because Alina had many of Veronica's students the year before, she could offer her personal insights. "'This kid has x problem,' 'that kid needs a lot of attention.'"

Veronica sometimes sat in on Alina's class during her lunch period. She admired what she saw, was amazed at the bravado, and picked up a lot. But she also knew that she had to find her own rhythm. "Alina would suggest, and I'd sometimes say no. Alina is Alina."

LEVERS OF CHANGE

Just weeks before the start of the school year, Les received the results from the previous spring's New Jersey ASK. The No Child Left Behind Act demands the impossible, that by 2014 every schoolchild in America will be proficient in reading and math, but education officials continue to behave as if this goal can be reached, setting the bar higher every year.[16]

The ASK news is mixed. As has been true for several years running, third grade is the school's bright spot. Those youngsters have consistently performed well on the state's language arts and math exams, and in the previous spring's tests they outdid themselves. However, there has been only modest improvement in the fourth and fifth grades; what's worse, the sixth graders' scores have slipped. Washington School will once again be spending the year in the "school in need of improvement" doghouse.

Detailed information about students' academic progress can potentially lead to improved outcomes, but only if it is intelligently used. Every New Jersey school system gets the same kind of data, but many of them, unsure about how to make good use of it, simply stash it away. Few mine it as thoroughly as Union City. The administration crunches the numbers, classroom by classroom, student by student, and item by item. You can tell at a glance how kids who are new to English or new to the district have done. You can see how they performed on one section of the test, such as comprehending complex passages or solving word problems in math, as well as how those results vary from grade to grade or among the teachers in a particular grade. And you can compare this year's outcomes with last year's or one teacher's scores with another's.[17]

Les reviews this information with each teacher, hoping to pinpoint and then overcome her students' shortcomings. "When you're reading to the kids, it's a good idea to deliberately make a mistake, then show them how to spot and correct it," she proposes to those whose students' reading scores are weak, borrowing one of Alina's tactics. "You can also create a cliffhanger—stop your reading and ask them to imagine what happens next." The conversations center on questions that a number of students have flubbed. "Is it because you didn't focus enough on it because the students didn't absorb it? Is it the book? Could it be the wording of the questions?" Les inquires, trying to determine why fourth grade students missed so many questions that call for analysis, evaluation, and synthesis—skills that today's educators, borrowing from a half-century-old taxonomy developed by University of Chicago psychologist Benjamin Bloom, as higher-order thinking.[18]

These teachers badly want their students to pass the ASK, for they know how much is on the line both for the youngsters and themselves, but many of them are in the dark about how to change their practice. Across the district, teachers express similar puzzlement, and so a system-wide response is called for. In midyear, assistant superintendent Silvia Abbato, who's in charge of academics, hires Standards Solution, a firm that claims a strong track record in raising schools' ASK scores. Fifth and sixth graders have done the worst, and so, starting after Christmas vacation, these outside coaches, mainly retired teachers, spend a day a week at every elementary school, sharing tips about how to teach writing. You might think of it as Alina Lite.

Perhaps the most powerful tool in Les's kitbag is transferring a teacher from one grade to another. Sometimes the teacher herself wants out. That was the case with Mary Ann Rick, who was drowning in the fifth grade, unable to control her unruly charges. She was shifted to third grade, where she has become a far more confident teacher. A fourth or fifth grade teacher whose students have fared badly on the ASK may be moved to a lower grade. Sometimes, as with longtime teacher Maria Casanovas, moving from fourth to second grade represents a return to familiar territory, and she flourishes. In other situations Les is simply moving a weak teacher and keeping her fingers crossed that the change will do her good.

In Les's world, where boosting test scores is paramount, she is making the right move, because second-grade test results don't count in the eyes of the state. But a host of studies have shown that the earlier grades have the biggest impact on how youngsters will fare in the long run, so what's good for the school, operating in the perpetual shadow of No Child Left Behind, may not be good for the children.[19]

Some problems Les simply cannot resolve. The personal lives of teachers sometimes intrude in the classroom, affecting their performance: anyone going through a messy divorce or whose father has recently been diagnosed with cancer may well suffer more than her share of bad days. Silvia is compassionate but unforgiving. "You have to leave your personal life at the doorstep," says the assistant superintendent. "You can't have bad days in the classroom." But as long as a teacher makes even a halfhearted effort, the encrusted provisions of the teachers' union contract—provisions that have come in for withering and often warranted criticism—effectively prevent disciplining, let alone firing, a teacher who's not doing her job. The best that Les can hope for is that once the teacher has sorted out what's happening outside the school she will spring back to life.

Les has been handed considerable authority, but she's hemmed in on several fronts. The imperatives of the ASK (and, one step removed, the No Child Left Behind Act), rather than the children's deeper needs, drive many of her decisions. State law prevents her from moving sixth grade teachers to a lower grade, even though they might be better off there, because they are licensed to teach only in the sixth through eighth grades. She can fire un-tenured teachers, but up-or-out decisions must be made during a teacher's third year; and once given tenure it's almost impossible to dismiss even the miscreants. (Union City hasn't fired a tenured teacher in some years.) Some pivotal determinations about what help goes to her teachers and stu-dents are also out of her hands—she has pleaded, unsuccessfully, for a part-time coach, which she thinks is the surest way to nudge the backsliders, as well as a social worker who can respond to the children's many emotional problems.[20]

Veteran Teachers at the Fountain of Youth

Within the precincts of the school, Les cannot do it alone. She needs the strongest teachers to share the responsibilities of educational leadership. When she became principal, she inherited a sizable complement of teachers who have spent decades in the classroom. A casual observer might think she's been cursed, because the conventional wisdom disparages longtime teachers as timeservers who draw big salaries and coast on what they learned long ago. The "old dog/new tricks" syndrome underscores the difficulty of retooling veterans, and studies showing that teachers' performance gets better only during their first three to five years, after which it plateaus, give ammunition to the naysayers.[21]

That's why Teach for America, which recruits smart college graduates with fine pedigrees, looks so attractive—it promises to rejuvenate the teaching profession.[22]

At Washington, however, the teachers who have been on the job the lon-gest are those who have contributed the most in making this such a fine school. With their combined experience, Alina Bossbaly, Sue Emmerling, and Maria Casanovas have taught here for nearly a century. You'd be thrilled to have them teaching your own children.[23]

These three teachers are as alive to the possibilities of teaching as they were their first day and as eager to try out promising new ideas. Year after year, their former students return to tell them how much they matter, and when one of Alina's students wins an award at his high school graduation he asks her to make the presentation. Four of Sue's students are now teaching in Union City. "They still look to me for guidance and advice," she says, "and it flatters me no end."[24]

When I spend time in their classrooms or listening in while they are helping out a colleague or huddling with a distraught student, I wonder whether the trio is imbibing at the Fountain of Youth. Many days they come to school early and stay late, leaving with piles of homework that they read at night and over the weekend. "I work until 8 P.M. sometimes," says Maria, who teaches second grade. "It's a privilege to be here. My minister says, 'I don't *gotta* preach, I *get to* preach,' and for me it's 'I don't *gotta* teach, I *get to* teach.'"

Collegiality Pays Off

Nowhere at Washington are the virtues of collegiality and collaboration more visible than in the third grade. The Dream Team—that's how other teachers at Washington School refer to Alina Bossbaly, Marilyn Corral, Jen Schuck, Marilyn Rick, and Irene Stamatopolous. Although their personalities differ greatly, they mesh as smoothly as a 400-yard relay team, and this bond helps to explain why, year after year, their students have been the school's top performers on the ASK. On the May 2010 exam, 79% passed the reading and writing test and an off-the-charts 93% were rated proficient in math—the best results in the entire district.

It's unlikely that these teachers would have been accepted by Teach for America. They all grew up within a half hour's drive from Union City and never moved away. (Two of them thought about teaching in a ghetto school in New York City, but their friends talked them out of it, and only one has ever taught elsewhere.) Only a higher education expert or someone who hails from northern New Jersey would have heard of the commuter schools—William Paterson, Jersey City, Stockton State, and the like—that they attended. Their GPAs weren't necessarily stellar, and while some of them are more naturally gifted teachers than others, they all had a hard time at the start of their teaching careers.

The best explanation for their effectiveness is what they have learned—and keep learning—from their colleagues. Experience matters, of course, but these teachers improve, the passable ones becoming solid practitioners and the good ones maturing into candidates for a demonstration video, in good measure because of the informal tutelage that the old hands give the newbies, the day-to-day collaboration, the modeling of good practice, and the swapping of ideas about what's worth trying in their classrooms. "The most productive thinking," the researchers conclude, "is continuous and simultaneous with action—that is, with teaching—as practitioners collaboratively implement, assess, and adjust instruction as it happens."[25]

The culture of *abrazos*, of love and caring, at Washington School is rooted in close relationships of long standing between Les and the teachers, among the teachers, and between the school and the families. These professionals know and trust one another, for they can draw on their history of working together, and that eases the path to collaboration. Their ties to the kids come naturally because they have an intimate understanding of their students' lives. Many of these teachers grew up and still live close by, so when they talk about the students as *our kids*, they mean it almost literally.[26]

To be sure, there are the outliers, who stand apart from this community, as well as the grumblers, who look for slights and stir the pot, for rare indeed is the organization free from outliers and grumblers. But at Washington the outliers and the grumblers are decidedly in the minority. Almost everyone at this school wants to belong to their *own* Dream Team.

You won't find any Teach for America recruits here, and with good reason—they would destabilize the school. Bright they surely are, but raw intelligence does not translate into skill in the classroom. Fresh out of college and with only the briefest of training, they are at the very beginning of the learning curve. Not only are they less effective than experienced teachers like Alina or Sue; studies show that their students actually fare worse on math achievement tests and no better on reading tests than the students of equally inexperienced credentialed teachers with bachelor's degrees from little-known colleges. Washington runs on loyalty and longevity, but 80% of Teach for America teachers quit after three years, many of them headed for careers in law or business. Presumably those who sign on with Teach for America care for children, at least in the abstract, but these cosmopolitans have been parachuted into a community about which they know nothing.[27]

Les appreciates that the third grade teachers are among her most valuable assets. When she is picking people to staff after-school classes that prep students to pass the ASK, plum jobs that pay $50 an hour, or deciding who should get new classroom computers, they usually emerge as winners. While they deserve it, Les's decisions can stir resentment, and the "Dream Team" label sometimes comes with the sour taint of jealousy. "If they're so good, why not break them up and let them inspire the other grades?" grumbled a sixth grade teacher, doubtlessly hoping to knock them off their pedestal.

"When the ASK test scores came, that teacher was only interested in how her own students did, not how sixth grade did," Alina tells me. "That's all you need to know—there's no teamwork in that grade."

"We never use the Dream Team label to put ourselves above everyone else," says Alina. Just as she perceives her colleagues' faith in her ability to "Bossbaly-ize" her students, extracting the best from them every year, as both a compliment and an incitement, she regards the "Dream Team" sobriquet as both accolade and goad. "C'mon, girls, let's keep up the good work because it's expected of us," Alina cheers on the crew. "We take a lot of pride in what we do. Just like the kids want to be praised by other teachers, we want our parents and our administration to be proud of us. There's no 'I want my bulletin board to be better,' no complaining. We do it together. The attitude is contagious. It happens—you *make* it happen."

The teacher has traditionally been treated as if she were a modern-day Queen Victoria who reigns supreme in her classroom and rarely leaves her monarchy. No one questioned what these teachers were doing, but no one came to their aid either, so they had to sort out the whats and hows of teaching on their own. Engaging in shoptalk with the teacher down the hall, pulling apart a particular lesson, or sharing ideas about how to handle a certain kind of student makes them better at their job. A wise district like Union City doesn't leave these exchanges to happenstance—it carves out time for teachers to work together.[28]

It's reality TV minus the camera crew on the second floor of Washington, where the third grade classrooms are clustered. Alina is the group's de facto leader, and from one moment to the next she may be the strategist, the influential, the calming influence, or the shoulder to cry on (occasionally she's the one doing the crying). "I see the good in every person," she says, and only rarely does she have an unkind word about anyone.

Among these teachers, only Alina has non-English-speakers in her class, though other classes include students who are in an English-only environment for the first time. In the room around the corner from Alina, Irene Stamatopolous presides in no-nonsense, meticulously organized, and perpetually unflustered mode. "Irene is the first one done with everything," marvels Marilyn Corral, whose classroom is adjacent to Alina's. "It's like she has a rocket up her butt, like she's on speed." But Irene, who came to Washington in 1990, wasn't always so sure of herself. "My first year was rough," she recalls. "The kids weren't learning and I felt like I was teaching to the walls. I put it all on me—I thought that these children should be competing at the same level as children everywhere, and that's still my goal every year."

Some kids in Irene's room came to the United States just a couple of years earlier, and this is their first experience in a class where everything is in English. Other school districts treat students like these as if they were born speaking English, tossing them in with everyone else. In Union City, these children are assigned to a teacher like Irene, who's trained to teach English as a Second Language, as they ease their way from one language to another.[29]

Marilyn Corral, whose classroom is next door to Alina's, adds spice and drama to the mix. She has Alina's vivacity, with a bit more jalapeno tossed in. Instinctively, she'll fight if she feels she's been wronged, and Alina the diplomat sometimes finds herself talking Marilyn down.

Jen Schuck, one room farther down the hall, calls to mind the girl next door grown up, everyone's best friend, and she's the shyest in the group. Mary Ann Rick, a tall, angular woman who could have sat for a Modigliani portrait, hovers slightly outside the frame. While that's partly due to the school's layout—her classroom is the farthest away—her personality doesn't lend itself to easy sociability. "I'm not really part of the social world of the other teachers," she tells me. "I'm intrapersonal—I value the quiet time."

This quintet has been together for a long time—Mary Ann, the latest addition, joined the group in 2005, a year after Marilyn. Such familiarity can breed contempt, akin to what happens in a dysfunctional family, but these teachers genuinely like and, what's more important, respect one another. Personality and teaching style are intertwined, and if you spend some time in their classrooms you can readily detect the variations. Alina will most likely be pirouetting among groups of students, Irene will be firmly in command, Marilyn passionate and boot-camp tough, Mary Ann nurturing, and Jen a gentle and soothing presence. Good teachers can't be shoehorned into a single mold. These are five distinct individuals, five distinct teaching styles—and five capable professionals.

These teachers are often in and out of one another's rooms, swapping materials and helping out, covering if one of them arrives late or has to leave for a meeting. And while some teachers safeguard the student projects that they have devised as if they were top-secret documents, everything that's generated by a member of the Dream Team is open-source. "We are all very different women who complement each other when we get together," says

Marilyn. "We plan, we share our ideas. If something works well for me or I have a cute activity I give it to my girls—I want them to look good too."

Sometimes I go to lunch with two or three of these women for *ropa vieja* and plantains at Gran Via, the Cuban hangout a few blocks away. Typically there's some girl talk, banter about who's getting married or whose kid has gotten into college. But the conversation often loops back to their work— what their students are up to, how they reacted to the latest writing prompt, what belongs in the all-important plan-book.

Walk by Room 210, Alina's classroom, most Thursdays at 9 A.M. and the din that rockets off the walls sounds like a gaggle of adolescent girls careening out of control. But the voices you hear aren't those of students—these are the third grade teachers deep into planning mode. In every Union City school, the class schedule gives teachers in each grade forty-five minutes a week for brainstorming, and the Dream Team uses this time to tackle the questions that arise in the practice of their craft.[30]

On this mid-October day I'm sitting in the back of the room, scrunched in a chair designed with an eight-year-old in mind. Alina, Marilyn, and Irene gather around a table piled high with papers, all the projects that they've devised. They are all talking at once, raising their voices so that they can be heard, while Jen is taking notes. "We get so excited," says Alina, who sounds superexcited. They are preparing their plan-books for November, a month away, and despite the racket this is serious business.

Hollywood portrays great teachers, like Robin Williams in *Dead Poets Society*, as great ad-libbers, but in this era of hyperaccountability a teacher must get the minutest and pickiest details exactly right. "We have to show what we're doing to the nth degree," Alina tells me. "Otherwise our paychecks could be withheld."

Even though the state's achievement test is more than half a year away, it is already on their minds. On the 2010 exam for second graders, a trial run for the New Jersey ASK, the seven-year-olds had a hard time understanding the passages they were asked to read, and those are the kids these teachers have inherited. "Their vocabulary is extremely small because many of them speak English only when they're at school," says Alina, by way of explanation. "When they're home, Spanish is what they hear and they're watching Spanish TV."

Words, words, and more words—if these youngsters are going to prosper academically they need to become immersed in a world of language. The more words you know the faster you acquire new words, the research shows, and so the third grade teachers spend lots of time honing the skills of comprehension. All their classrooms feature ever-expanding word walls, and each child is given a dictionary, something that most of them have never seen. "It's your tool, like the computer," Alina tells these computer-savvy youngsters. "You need to use it a lot."[31]

"The key is to make sure that from kindergarten on, every student understands the gist of what is heard or read," writes literacy expert E. D. Hirsch Jr., and that's what these teachers are aiming for. If all goes well, their students will emerge from third grade with a bigger and more evocative vocabulary. They'll be using hundred-dollar words like "gorgeous" and "exquisite," not just "pretty," and they'll know how to extract the central themes from what they read, not just regurgitate the story line. Those skills make for good writers as well as successful test-takers.[32]

Third grade math is just as demanding. By year's end these students must understand fractions; know how to convert 3/12 into its simplest form; complete the pattern, 1/3, 2/6; estimate the volume of a rectangle; and use the metric system. "Although the timetable is crushing," says Marilyn, "we like to extend certain topics even if it takes more time." They want their students to come away with an understanding of what they are doing, not simply memorizing formulas. That ability too will serve them well in later grades.

Although every teacher uses the same basic material, each of them can add to that core, and there are scores of books from which to select. Characteristically, the Dream Team agrees on the same stories, and today they're in search of a good opening question for a story their classes will soon be reading—a question that will bring the tale to life. In making this kind of decision they have character development in mind, not just on the page but among their own students. "I try to run my classroom as a community," Jen tells me. "Of course I want them to become better readers, writers, and mathematicians, but in the long run I really want them to become good people, respectful and responsible for themselves." When I ask Alina how the team chooses its stories, she responds by describing how a particular writer spins an especially engrossing tale. "Great author, great situation," she summarizes. "Those stories teach the students about character, about the importance of respect and the need to talk things through."

These teachers know intuitively that efforts designed to shape children's values can have a powerful long-term impact. They bat around several candidates for the opening gambit. "What moral lesson did you learn?" . . . "What are the moral messages behind the story?" . . . "What lessons did the author want to teach?" Eventually they agree that they'll ask how the author's moral message can be incorporated into everyday life. Each of them inserts that theme in her plan-book and each will launch a classroom dialogue with that question. But what happens next depends on their students' reactions, and in each class the ensuing discussion will bend in distinct ways. "A lot of the time inspiration comes from the kids," Jen explains. "Someone will say something that will spark an idea, and then my entire lesson will take a turn."[33]

Although this camaraderie may look effortless, it has been hard won. The two newest teachers joined the group under inauspicious circumstances. In 2005 Marilyn was reassigned from fifth grade, replacing the iconic Mary Ellen Naumann, who was shifted to second grade. "It was hard taking Mary Ellen's place," Marilyn remembers. "I liked the other teachers but I was filling very big shoes."

"Naumann was like a mother to us," says Alina, who still has lunch with her every Tuesday. "When a kid threw a desk at me, she took me to the hospital. 'We're going,' Mary Ellen shouted, as they walked down the hall. 'Get someone to fill in for us.' When we were told she was leaving third grade, Irene, Jen, and I took it hard."

Marilyn had already taught in the second, fourth, and fifth grades, and she hadn't gotten along well with the teachers in any of those grades. "During the first few months there were tensions between Marilyn and Irene," Alina recalls. "For Irene it's 'work, work, work,' for Marilyn it's 'work and enjoy life.' Each of them would come to me. One would say, 'she's ruining my kids,' and the other one would say something else. The person in the middle can't like to gossip, to set one against the other. I turned it into a joke: 'Every half day we will please one of you.'" Jen, a born peacemaker, helped to ease the situation, and so did Lourdes Garcia, a former classroom teacher at Washington who moves among the third grade rooms, tutoring youngsters in the throes of learning English.

The next year, Mary Ann followed Marilyn in the flight from fifth grade. In 2004 she had come to Union City from Harding Township, one of the twenty-five richest zip codes in the nation, where sprawling estates, some listed on the National Register of Historic Places, dot the landscape. Mary

Ann was set for life there, but she was restless and discontented. "Those children have so much," she tells me. Her thinking was profoundly influenced by her father, who for three decades taught shop in a high school located in a rough Bronx neighborhood. "His students depended on him," she says, "he mattered in their lives," and those were the kind of kids she wanted to reach.

"I was so naïve when I came here," Mary Ann says, remembering the hellish years she spent teaching fifth graders. "I had the worst of the worst. They'd say they were going to the bathroom and they were vandalizing stuff." Marilyn took her aside. "You have to get a backbone. Get tough or you'll be devoured." The move to third grade felt like a godsend. "They're two thousand times better!" she says.

To carve out a position for Mary Ann, a gifted young teacher, popular with her colleagues was assigned to another school, and that disturbed the waters. "She was understanding," Mary Ann recalls. "'There was nothing you could do,' she told me." But that didn't make things easier on the second floor. Rumors flew that Mary Ann had gotten the assignment because she was Les's favorite. "The other teachers were angry that an administrator could pluck someone out like that," Mary Ann remembers. "I tried to do whatever they were doing, so we would be cohesive, but it takes a while to work with people who are a family. It's like getting a sibling—they assume that you know certain things." In her first few years as a third grade teacher, she says, "the school gave me the worst kids. It was like reverse discrimination—I had to prove myself."

Over time, however, she has come to feel like a full-fledged member of the group. When Les asked Alina to become Mary Ann's writing coach, the bond between the two of them grew stronger. "She has so much to give," says Mary Ann, who sent Alina a gushing thank-you note that made Alina's day. Now she's on her own, and as she becomes more self-assured, her students' vocabulary expands and their papers get better.

"We are all imperfect human beings," Alina muses, in one of her philosophical moments. "We have to love each other with all our virtues and faults. We're lucky—all these girls are great human beings. You create respect because you want things to work, and now we're tight."

For her part, Mary Ann feels privileged to belong to this coterie. "They're friggin' awesome," she says. "I can't believe how dedicated they are." For "they," you can substitute "we."

OLD WAYS DIE HARD

There's no taking for granted this kind of collaboration. It depends on the personalities of the individuals and the chemistry of the group.[34]

Like the Dream Team, the teachers in the lower grades at Washington have knitted themselves together to good effect. "I always feel like I can learn something from somebody," says Maria Casanovas, who made the change from fourth to second grade several years ago. "When we sit around we make suggestions. The other teachers may decide to try it out, make it their own."

Sometimes it's the littlest tricks of the trade, such as techniques for keeping a class running smoothly, that get swapped. "Kids are always interrupting class to sharpen their pencils," Maria says. "Now I tell them that it's their responsibility to sharpen four pencils before class—it works, and the other teachers are doing the same thing."

Maria doesn't think twice about helping out other teachers. When Veronica Pardo, fresh out of college, replaced her in fourth grade, Maria bequeathed her all her files and class notes. "She said she'd help any way she could," Veronica tells me. One morning I stop by to see Maria teach a science lesson on how plants grow and come away with a lesson in the benefits of collaboration. The inspiration, Maria tells me later, was a tale about a pumpkin. As someone who relishes both science and stories, she decided to expand the topic by showing her kids how seeds evolve into pumpkins when they're planted, fertilized, and watered. That lesson shows off the creativity that administrators prize, and a teacher in a less collegial group might well decide to keep it to herself. Maria not only shared her project, she brought to school everything that the other teachers would need if they opted to use it with their own students.

However, life among the fourth grade teachers is more fraught. Three of them, veteran Sue Emmerling and her younger colleagues Veronica Pardo and Jennifer Mondelli, know how to get students excited about learning, and you can see it in the energy level in their classrooms. "It's tough," says Jennifer, "but the rewards—'*Now* I get it!'—make it worthwhile." Much like Alina, Sue has been a mentor to the two newcomers. But the other two teachers, best friends who have been teaching fourth grade the longest, stand united in their defense of the old ways. They haven't made much use of technology and haven't set up learning centers, which are supposedly de rigueur in the district. "We have to use the centers daily," Les tells them again and again. "They're not just for little kids. The centers keep these kids from being bored." She might as well be talking to a wall.

Nor do these women associate much with their colleagues. Maria Casanovas taught with them before moving to the second grade. Although she had been a teacher for decades, she was new to fourth grade and would have appreciated some guidance. She didn't get it from them. "We're much more united in second grade," Maria tells me. "There's much more camaraderie here."

Because I want to see how these teaching styles play out in the classroom, I spend some time in Sue Emmerling's class and then go straight to see Stacey Eccleston, one of the traditionalists, in action. It's a jarring fifty-foot expedition from one era to another.

Growing up in a blue-collar family in Jersey City, Sue wanted to become an actress. When she was nine or ten, she tells me, she'd write plays and put them on for the neighborhood kids, charging them a nickel. But her practical-minded father, a fire captain and the owner of a local nightclub, vetoed the idea. "You can be a nurse, a secretary or a teacher," he said. For Sue, the choice was a dead cert. "Teachers face an audience every day. Children want to be entertained and they should be, with the idea that learning is fun and necessary."

When I walk into Sue's classroom, the kids are about to write about "my favorite thing." Before picking up their pencils they start with "prewriting"—thinking aloud for a few minutes. "My favorite thing is a necklace that my mother gave to me before she left me," says Esmeralda. Max picks an object of desire, a Lamborghini, "because it's faster than a cheetah, louder than a motorcycle." Sue loves the figurative language, which they've been working on.

For their social studies project, Sue says, each of them will prepare a brochure designed to lure students to New Jersey. By going online they'll find out what's special about their state. "There's a lot we can offer," says Sue, priming the pump. "What are some examples?" "Seafood," answers one boy. "That's right—why do we have lots of seafood?" she asks, pulling down a map of the world to point out New Jersey. "It's because we're located on an ocean." Sue asks the class for directions to the ocean, a mini–geography lesson, and the kids point in the right direction.

"If you are a fisherman you can show the seashore," she continues. "If you are a hiker you can draw mountains and name them. You can go to High Point State Park and see three other states." The mention of High Point reminds Sue of the time she took a group of eighth graders there on a field trip and a couple of girls got lost. "Those girls weren't attacked by big animals," she jokes, "just by robins." The kids are enraptured by Sue's storytelling, their smiles and frowns chasing after one another.

Slipping into Stacy's classroom as she stands in front of her students, the desks lined up in tidy rows, I feel as if I've been transported back to the 1950s. The lesson completes the illusion.

On the whiteboard, Stacey has written a score of sentences in perfect script. It's the kind of labor-intensive activity that makes you appreciate the interactive board, used by almost all the teachers, which would keep this assignment stored for future use. She is calling on the students to recite by filling in the blanks in those sentences. "Recycling," "conservation," "petroleum"—this should be the stuff of a lively lesson about the environment, but Stacy's students gaze at her like zombies.

"Every day I come to school with my lunch," Stacey tells them, offering a virtuous environmentalist vignette from her own life. "I bring oatmeal in a reusable plastic container with a plastic spoon that I wash, snacks in reusable plastic bags. I make very little waste." Not a ripple of interest stirs the classroom air.

Disappointing test scores are not the only reason that Les is fretting about the fourth grade. She's also worried about the torrent of nine- and ten-year-olds that have been sent her way because of classroom fracases. "The kids are becoming little bullies," she says. "They're not getting direction." Plainly, she must do something—either convince the traditionalists that collaboration and openness to new ways of teaching are in their students' best interest, and their self-interest as well, or else break up the group by reassigning one of them. In a community like Washington it's a big decision and she has until June to make up her mind.

GOOD-BYE TO ALL THAT

The week before Christmas break, Washington School's classroom doors are decked out with fir trees and Santa Clauses (Mrs. Santas too), reindeer and candy canes, wreaths and snowflakes, all the familiar decorations, as well as one grinning tiger who's wearing a Santa hat.

Many of these doors feature pictures of the children, their hand-drawn self-portraits or photos affixed to gingerbread cookies, stockings, and Christmas tree ornaments. Alina's class has chosen a musical theme—each kid's photo is glued onto a CD, all the CDs are attached to the door, staves and notes floating in the surrounding space, and when you open the classroom door everyone bursts into song. It's not *Glee*, but it is good enough to win second prize.

Schools typically rely on an art teacher to run such a project, just as the music teacher or drama coach would normally be in charge of the performances, but at Washington the teachers, together with their students, do it all themselves. Some teachers are naturally artistic, and their doors show their skills, while others couldn't wield a paint brush to save their lives, and they solicit help from their colleagues.

Les didn't decree that all the doors be decorated. It's just a suggestion, another way to deepen the feeling of community at Washington School. A few of the doors stand out because they remain unornamented or because the embellishment is so last-minute and lackluster, like the store-bought Santa cutout slapped on with masking tape, that you wish that the teacher hadn't bothered. But almost all the teachers *have* bothered. While Santas and snowflakes are everywhere to be seen, most doors look hand-made and singular. The message comes across loud and clear: This is our classroom—"Mrs. H's Santa Land," as one door says—this is our special community.

The remarkable reputation of the Union City schools rests heavily on its success in educating the kind of students that many school systems have given up on. What's happening at Washington, and the district's other schools, delivers a useful reminder that, if they're given a solid education, they can help keep America economically competitive and politically vibrant.

The students' impressive performance on the New Jersey ASK, the high-stakes achievement test, has brought kudos to Superintendent Sandy Sanger as well as to Brian Stack, the supercharged mayor. But no one's taking success for granted—this record must be improved upon year after year. That's why, as every Union City principal knows, the top priority is to keep boosting the number of students who pass those tests. It's not exactly a prescription for joyful learning.

Between Christmas and the first week of May, when testing week rolls in, the purposeful frivolity and community-building emblemized by the decorated doors will be conspicuous by its slow, sad disappearance. For each teacher, and for Les Hanna as well, the challenge is to maintain Washington School's culture of *abrazos* amid the harsh climate of the high-stakes exams.

3

GRUNT WORK
The Endless Business of Building
a Great School System

We have heard a lot about inspirational teachers and superb schools. But excellent *school systems* are rarities. Many districts are run like a loose confederacy, with each principal calling the shots and each school free to go its own way. What sets Union City apart from the pack is that it has gone beyond this principal-as-savior approach and actually constructed an integrated school system. While there's no romance in this enterprise, nothing to titillate the media, the superintendent and his top aides are performing an indispensable role. Behind the scenes, largely invisible to the students, they buttress each school while tying all of them together, setting high expectations for the whole.[1]

Being perceived as the New York Yankees of urban school systems, expected to excel year after year, brings considerable pressure. But a generation earlier, the pressure was far more excruciating and the consequences of failure far more frightening. If the school system didn't get better, and quickly, state officials vowed to run the schools themselves.

FROM WORST TO FIRST, STEP BY STEP—THAT'S THE ESSENCE OF THE UNION CITY STORY

During the 1980s the Union City schools, which had never been particularly distinguished, degenerated into an outright embarrassment. The buildings were falling apart, with floors sagging, paint peeling, roofs leaking, and windows cracking. The teachers were demoralized. What mattered most, the students weren't learning. Three years running they flunked the state's Early Warning Test in English and math. In 1989 they bottomed out, failing forty out of fifty-two items on the state's checklist, the second-worst result in New Jersey. ("Thank God for Camden!" was the mordant response, referring to the decimated city that ranked dead last.)

The situation had grown so dire that the state threatened to inflict the ultimate sanction—seizing control. Takeover is the education equivalent of a perp walk. Had it happened, the school system would have joined the roll call of notorious urban failures like Camden and neighboring Jersey City.

Hometown pride is more than a cliché in Union City, and its leaders couldn't conceive of an occupying force of supposed experts running its schools. There were also pragmatic reasons to resist. The public schools are, far and away, the city's biggest employer. To lose control of them spelled doom for a patronage system, run by the mayor, which delivered jobs to hundreds of cleaning ladies, janitors, clerks, and bus drivers in exchange for their allegiance.

In 1989 Union City won a one-year reprieve from the guillotine. But the message from Trenton was unambiguous—if students' performance didn't improve in twelve months' time, a tall order indeed, the state would step in. To avoid that fate, someone had to set things right.

Other school districts that found themselves in a similar situation brought in outside consultants with a reputation as turnaround experts to fix things. Union City chose a different path—it looked to a midlevel bureaucrat named Fred Carrigg, who had spent almost his entire career there.

Fred was picked for the assignment because he knew a lot about the two domains, bilingual education and reading, that were indispensable to students' success. He turned out to be the right man at the right time and proved indispensable to the rescue operation.[2]

The school system opened its first bilingual classes in the late 1960s when refugees from Castro's Cuba filled the schools to overflowing. But members of the old guard refused to believe that things had changed, and for years they behaved as if the citizenry was still working-class German, Irish, and Italian. "Why don't these kids speak English?" they complained. Some principals refused to translate the messages they sent home to parents and continued to conduct "parents' night" entirely in English. The Cuban émigrés got the message. They stayed away and, if they could afford it, sent their kids to parochial schools.

As the city's population became increasingly Latino, the old-timers' reaction reflected a corrosive nostalgia. By the late 1980s nine out of ten students were Latino, three-quarters of them growing up in homes where Spanish was the only language heard at the dinner table and on TV. The educational implications should have been obvious—these youngsters had to do better if the school system was going to do better, and they needed lots of help in navigating the path to fluency in English.

By the time they are four years old, a classic study has shown, children from poor families have heard thirty million—thirty million!—fewer words than youngsters growing up in a professional household. They start school well behind and usually they never catch up.[3] This language deficit is even greater, the problem more acute, when, as in Union City, English isn't the youngsters' native language. To have a realistic chance of closing that gap, they need to inhabit a literature-filled, word-soaked world from the very first days of school.[4] In Union City a handful of teachers understood this, but no one followed their example. School district officials, untutored in the pedagogy of reading, hadn't figured out what had to be done.

"Everything starts from the fact that our kids can't read," Fred argued, and that had to change. Bringing about those changes was how he interpreted his charge. Soon enough it became his crusade.

Happenstance, not calculation, often rules our lives. It was the chance occurrence of a semester spent in Peru as a high school sophomore that got Fred Carrigg, an Irish Catholic boy growing up in Trenton, hooked on Spanish. Going to Peru wasn't a well-thought-out decision—Fred could have gone to France instead, but he would have had to spend a year there, and to a fifteen-year-old who'd never left home that sounded too long. When he returned to Trenton he kept taking Spanish classes and then majored in Spanish at Montclair State, a training ground for many of Union City's teachers and administrators. Fred had planned to pursue a Ph.D., but he took what turned out to be a life-changing detour when his college adviser told him about an opening for a bilingual teacher in Union City.

The year was 1972, the era of the Cuban Freedom Flights, and new immigrants were thick on the ground. At that time, most of Union City's immigrant youngsters were assigned to classes taught by teachers who didn't speak their language. They could only guess at their students' ability, and were quick to label as dumb anyone with whom they couldn't readily communicate. Some of these newcomers, like Alina Bossbaly and Silvia Abbato, overcame those barriers, went on to college, and returned to teach in Union City. They shudder when they think back to that time. "I cried when I got a failing grade," Alina remembers, because that had never happened in Cuba.

"The district was desperate to hire people who knew the language," Fred tells me. He interviewed for the job two days after Christmas, was hired just hours afterward, and started work a week later. During his first year, he taught English as a Second Language (ESL) for eighth graders. Although ESL teachers aren't linguists, they know a lot about the structure of language—how to address fine-grained phonetic differences, for instance, and how to identify characteristic differences in syntax and grammar—and those tools proved invaluable.

Some of Fred's students had been well educated in Cuba, but others hadn't had the same good fortune. He began using a test designed to ascertain the difference—to determine whether a youngster's academic difficulties could be attributed to skill or fluency in English. The results enabled him to figure out what combination of language instruction and academic rigor each of his students could best handle. When those kids prospered in high school, other eighth grade teachers started to adopt the same approach.

This formative experience led Fred to reach a broader conclusion, one that shapes how Latino kids are still being taught in Union City. Bilingual education is not an either-or, Spanish or English, proposition. There are many gradients of intellectual horsepower and fluency, and good teaching must take them into account.

Fred swiftly climbed the organizational ladder. Not only was he an innovator in bilingual instruction, he also proved to be an adroit grant-writer, and those grants brought in millions of federal dollars for bilingual classes. What's more, he acknowledges, the fact he was Irish, not Latino, put the old guard at ease.

In the late 1970s Fred secured an attractive offer to work in the state education department. It was appealing, because he wanted to move back to Trenton, but Union City countered with a proposition he couldn't refuse— a healthy raise, promotion to supervisor, a job for his wife, and a dirt-cheap seven-room apartment, all this at age twenty-seven.

This rapid ascent came to an abrupt halt in 1983, when political turmoil engulfed the city and infected the school system. Fred found himself on the losing side, and like everyone who backed the same city politicians, he had to fight to hold onto his job. Meanwhile, the school system drifted, as each school—each teacher—did their own thing. There were niches of excellence— an honors English class at one school, perhaps, a pioneering special ed class at another—but without an institution-builder at the top these accomplishments weren't replicated. What's more, city officials refused to raise the tax dollars necessary to maintain the schools, and the derelict state of the buildings served as a tangible symbol of the community's neglect.

Then came the state's takeover ultimatum in 1989, which upended the cutthroat political calculations. A one-year reprieve came with a condition— then-superintendent Richie Hanna had to go. Tom Highton, his predecessor, had been bounced from the job in 1983 because he, like Fred, had made the wrong political choice. But by 1989 the tide had turned and Tom was invited back. "I want the job on my terms, without all the politics," he told the school board. "I'm a realist. I know that the custodians and cleaning people are political but I need to have the sole say when it comes to hiring the education people."

The new superintendent called on Fred to shape a plan of action. His assignment was simple and seemingly unachievable—over the course of a summer he was expected to fashion a coherent curriculum out of whole cloth.

Fred Carrigg, wiry and tightly wound, is usually smarter and more knowledgeable, certainly more self-confident, than anyone else in the room. This was the chance of a professional lifetime, and no one who knew him doubted that he would seize it with both hands.

But Fred couldn't do it alone. He picked two of the ablest professionals in the district as his chief lieutenants. The math portfolio went to Silvia Abbato, the math and science supervisor for the elementary schools, whom he had nurtured since her first years in the classroom when she taught a bilingual class for gifted students. He handed Lucy Soovajian responsibility for fleshing out the reading and writing curriculum. Lucy had spent almost thirty years in the system, carrying out initiatives to improve reading and writing, and because she'd worked closely with the deposed superintendent she knew all the players. That knowledge was critical to Fred, for his circle was mainly limited to those who taught in the bilingual program.

On a humid June morning, Fred's team met for the first time in what the administration euphemistically referred to as its "conference room," a converted storeroom with boxes crowding the table where they huddled. His marching orders jolted the group.

Because many students moved frequently during the year, every school had to teach the same material in the same sequence, so that students wouldn't become lost in those transitions. In deciding what should be covered, simply picking textbooks, the practice in the past, wouldn't do. Instead, the committee had to start anew, each member boning up on her field, unearthing strategies that the research had shown to work and then matching them with materials that sharpened the skills of thinking, reasoning, and collaborating, not rote learning. "He had us reading tons of books, which was unheard of back then," recalls Diane Capizzi, a member of that committee. "We had to know the theory behind what we were talking about and the evidence to back it up."

Just as novel and as daunting, Fred insisted that the new curriculum put all students—the English-speakers, the Spanish-speakers, the gifted students, and the special ed youngsters alike—on the same academic path. While the pace of teaching might differ, the end result would be the same. The routine practice of pulling students out of their classes for remedial education would also stop because it disrupted actual learning. Instead, specialists would come into the classroom to tutor students who had learning disabilities or were learning English.

While such changes marked a revolution in Union City, they tracked the national conversation about what made for an effective education. In this insular school system, Fred was the rare bird who paid attention to that conversation. He was a magpie who picked up ideas from everywhere—as far away as California, where state standards stressed problem-solving rather than rote learning, and as close at hand as a neighboring community that taught reading and writing, math and science, in daily blocks that ran for nearly two hours, rather than the familiar bite-sized class periods.

Unless there is a raucous controversy—about the teaching of evolution, say, or sex education or the contributions of gays and lesbians—it's hard to get anyone other than educators in a lather about what ought to be taught in school and how best to teach it.[5] To many people, the recommendations made by Fred and his team sound pretty dry, but they recast the system. In the next few years, Silvia, Lucy, and Diane were promoted to senior administrative posts. They'll tell you that the time they spent sitting around the cramped conference table and hitting the books opened their eyes to new ways of educating children.

What is taught, the curriculum, was going to be revamped because of the work done by Fred's team, and so was the pedagogy, *how* students are taught. Instead of delivering a single lesson to everyone at the same time and pace, with youngsters sitting in rows of seats lined up with military precision, students would now be spending chunks of class time in "learning centers," small groups working together on a project. Teaching this way wasn't only au courant pedagogy—it matched the needs of a school district where a typical elementary school classroom might include half a dozen kids with a solid academic background, two who are functionally illiterate, three special needs students, and four non-English-speakers. There's no way, Fred argued, to reach all of them with exactly the same materials or at precisely the same speed.

Everything that happened in the classroom had to revolve around teaching students how to read—that much was clear—but how to do so was far less certain. In the late 1980s, schools of education were beset with reading wars that pitted the phonics partisans against those who saw exposure to literature, not sounding out words, as the only way to teach reading.[6]

To Fred and his colleagues, this squabble was silly. From the first day of school, the youngsters of Union City had to be drenched in literature. The team opted to begin with fables and folk tales because they convey a good-triumphs-over-evil message that resonates in both Spanish and English. The language in which parents and nursery school teachers read these books to four- and five-year-olds didn't much matter—indeed, Fred believes it does Spanish-speaking children a disservice to hear English being spoken with a broken accent. What counted the most was exposing them to evocative tales, and so Carrigg insisted that the school system provide books in both languages. But folk tales weren't enough to get these kids on track, because native Spanish-speakers were unlikely to learn how to pronounce English words without help. Consistent with the research that guided ESL practice, teachers also had to focus on consonants, like g and h, which sound different in the two languages, and to emphasize "anchor words," like light and *luz*, night and *noche*, which children can readily remember.

Because the first years of school matter so much, the group spent the summer of 1989 revising the materials for kindergarten through second grade. That fall teachers received the framework for this new curriculum, including the guts of what should be covered and a ton of resources with which to teach it. Their reception would spell success or failure for the enterprise, and no one knew how they would react.

It would be a hard sell—the teachers were wrung out by all the infighting and skeptical that the administration could excavate itself from the hole it had dug for itself. A survey revealed the depth and near-universality of their dissatisfaction. "The results," Tom Highton tells me, "showed that everything sucked." Like the rest of us, most teachers instinctively resist upending their professional lives. For one thing, they believe that they're already doing their best; and for another, change of the magnitude that Carrigg & Co. were proposing required a ton of hard work. The teachers would have to junk much of what they had been doing. Not only would they be devising new lesson plans, they would also be learning a different way of managing their classrooms, and that generated new dilemmas. To detect what's happening in several learning centers scattered around the room, they had to acquire those proverbial eyes in the back of their heads.

Wisely, Union City decided to treat the initial year as an experiment. The district's academic all-star team—Fred, Lucy, and Silvia—went from school to school, making their pitch. "No one had ever told the teachers 'these things are research-based,'" Fred remembers, and this counted for something. And for the first time bilingual teachers and special education teachers were in the same room as the general ed teachers, making it harder for the nostalgia-minded faculty to disparage "those kids."

"Most teachers aren't inherently bad or lazy," Fred tells me. "They are scared and confused. They feel left out. My experience was that if I could bring them on board before someone else characterized 'Fred' for them I could work with almost any of them."

Every school has its own culture, its own way of doing things, and reactions varied accordingly. In one building, where a member of Fred's group had already turned her first grade classroom into a model, teachers greeted the visitors enthusiastically. But the response was frosty at Robert Waters Elementary School, a K–8 factory with an enrollment of 1,400, where the principal, Sandy Sanger, exiled there because of his politics, was saddled with a coterie of naysayers. "This is crazy," those teachers fired back. "You can't expect us to figure this out for ourselves—we have to have a textbook." Even here, though, some teachers were trying the new approach behind the scenes.[7]

The most potent stimulus for reform was the calendar, with its ticking-time-bomb reminder that unless things quickly improved the state would be running the show. That fall, a watchdog from Trenton took up residence in Fred's pint-sized office. Every decision bearing on life in the classroom had to bear Fred's signature, and he was expected to show how each innovation would lead to better results. Auditors scrutinized the books, double-checking how every penny was being spent. And to assure that top jobs were awarded on the basis of merit and not politics, state monitors required the district to conduct interviews before hiring new principals, something it had never done before.

The full-court press on strengthening the first years of schooling paid off—students in the lower grades started to do better and the state extended its reprieve. In subsequent summers, Fred's team tackled the curriculum of the upper grades, and as their plan was put in place test scores continued to rise. "When most of the fifth graders are reading, that changes everything," Fred tells me. "Instead of discipline problems it's possible to deal with substance."

Gradually, Trenton loosened its hold. The monitors departed, and in 1995 the state gave the school district a clean bill of health. Rightly so—Union City had become a pioneer in what and how its students were taught, and those changes had a noteworthy impact on academic outcomes.

Parents began to take notice. In the past, families who could afford it sent their offspring to parochial schools, but between 1989 and 1995 enrollment in the public schools climbed as many of those children returned. That year the school district bought a shuttered Catholic school and converted it into a middle school.

Today you can walk into many Union City classrooms and watch kids who are growing up in a world where food isn't always on the table, books are a rarity, and ideas are rarely discussed, become engrossed by what they're studying. Put these same youngsters in the classic regimented classroom, with a teacher doing most of the talking, and it's hard to believe that they would be nearly as turned on or doing nearly as well. You can trace the way that these teachers, like many of their colleagues, approach their craft to the work started by Fred and his crew in the summer of 1989.[8]

MONEY MATTERS

New money, not just new ideas, was essential to the success of a district whose woes could be traced in part to the school board's unwillingness to raise taxes.

The state's one-year reprieve came with an edict that the city hike the tax rate, and the school budget grew by $4 million. Most of these new dollars were earmarked for long-overdue repairs, but Fred was able to squirrel away $500,000 to create minilibraries in each classroom as a way to woo children into becoming readers. This small victory won over some of the teachers. In their experience, books had been shelved in a library that children visited just once a week; and textbooks, many of them twenty years out of date, were in such short supply that students sometimes had to share them.

In subsequent years, Fred became a masterful fundraiser. His biggest coup was a 1994 grant from Bell Atlantic to wire one of the middle schools and equip it with 200 personal computers—two for each classroom, one for each teacher and another for each seventh grader. At that time computers were a rarity in public schools, and when an evaluation determined that these students were more enthusiastic about school and were doing better academically, the district attracted widespread attention. On the blustery winter morning of February 15, 1996, President Bill Clinton and Vice President Al Gore came to celebrate the technology-inflected turnaround. The president waxed poetic—"the rebirth of your city and your schools reminds us that we live in an age of great possibility"—and for the first time in ages the community could feel justifiably proud of its schools.[9]

Beginning in the early 1990s, additional help came from an unexpected source—the New Jersey Supreme Court. Over the past half-century, those justices have acquired a reputation for the boldness and controversiality of their opinions. Among the New Jersey court's landmark decisions are rulings that opened up suburbia to poor families, upheld an individual's right to die, guaranteed due process rights for students, recognized the battered woman syndrome, prohibited the Boy Scouts from expelling a gay scoutmaster, and allowed sixteen-year-olds to seek an abortion without having to notify their parents.[10]

None of the court's decrees has made a bigger splash or taken a bigger bite out of the state treasury than the epic school finance case *Abbott v. Burke*. In twenty-one decrees issued over the course of nearly three decades, the justices have read the state's constitutional guarantee of "a thorough and efficient system of education" as a charter of equality for urban youth. That 1875 provision, said the court in its historic 1990 ruling, *Abbott II*, meant that youngsters living in poor cities were entitled to an education as good as their suburban counterparts.[11]

The justices knew that they were once again entering a brave new legal world, one largely of their own making. In its 1973 *Rodriguez* decree, the U.S. Supreme Court had ruled, 5–4, that it lacked the constitutional authority to review inequities in school finance. While courts in several states had relied on their state constitutions to insert themselves in the dollars-for-scholars debate, none was so forceful as the New Jersey tribunal.[12]

In crafting its decision, the court concentrated on the state's thirty-one worst-off districts, which became known as the *Abbott* districts. "The record proves what all suspect," wrote Chief Justice Robert Wilentz. "If the children of poorer districts went to school today in richer ones, educationally they would be a lot better off.... And what everyone knows is that—as children— the only reason they do not get the advantage is that they were born in a poor district. For while we have underlined the impact of the constitutional deficiency on our state, its impact on these children is far more important. They face, through no fault of their own, a life of poverty and isolation that most of us cannot begin to understand or appreciate."

To the justices, equality didn't mean sameness—if the inner-city students were going to have a decent shot at success, they needed something extra. Urban schools were constitutionally entitled not only to "substantially equivalent" support but also to "supplemental" resources (left unspecified in the opinion) in order to confront the "unique educational disadvantages" of urban youth.[13]

Thrust and parry—beginning with its 1990 decision, the justices dueled repeatedly with lawmakers. Wealthy communities like Princeton had no interest in subsidizing poverty-ridden cities like Newark, and their representatives forcefully pressed those views in the state legislature. A pattern emerged—the court would demand "substantially similar opportunities" for cities and suburbs, and the legislature would respond with grudging half-measures that kept the inequities on the books.[14]

By 1998 the justices had become thoroughly frustrated that the lawmakers hadn't given serious thought to what extra help disadvantaged youngsters needed. They ventured deep into the educational miasma, shifting the discussion away from dollars to the particulars of meaningful reform. The court's decree ordered the state to subsidize early literacy programs (of the kind that Union City had already put into effect in its elementary schools) as well as to finance additional training for teachers and construction of new schools. Most importantly, it mandated high-quality universal preschool for three- and four-year-olds in all the *Abbott* districts.[15] And in 2000, after Republican Governor Christine Todd Whitman proposed to comply by underwriting day care, not preschool, the court became even more prescriptive, fixing the ratio of children to adults, insisting on an evidence-based curriculum, and requiring that all prekindergarten teachers have bachelor's degrees.[16]

With that opinion, the weary jurists expressed the hope that this interminable litigation had finally come to an end. "We do not run school systems," they insisted, but the case has continued to drag on as each adjustment to the school financing formula has prompted another trip to the courthouse.

Abbott opened the spigot, and money started to pour into Union City. At Washington School, Irene Stamatopolous recalls that she had been teaching as many as thirty-seven third graders and now she had only twenty students. Irene knew nothing about the litigation, but that didn't matter. "I was in heaven," she says, and across the district the story was the same. "*Abbott* left us awash in funds," former superintendent Tom Highton tells me.

Money cannot cure all the ailments of public education, and over the years some cities, such as infamous Camden and Trenton, the state capital, have wasted hundreds of millions of dollars. But the fact that New Jersey spends more than $16,000 per student, third in the nation, partly explains why a state in which nearly half the students are minorities and a disproportionate share are immigrants has the country's highest graduation rate and ranks among the top five on the National Assessment of Educational Progress, the country's report card. The additional money also helps to account for how New Jersey halved the achievement gap between black, Latino, and white students between 1999 and 2007, something no other state has come close to accomplishing.[17]

Union City knew how to make good use of its newfound riches. Every dollar went to improve instruction. Class sizes shrank, teachers received training in everything from ESL to project-driven learning, specialists were hired to work one-on-one with teachers, and all the schools were wired with a computer for every three students. (In California, the fountainhead of high-tech, the ratio is 1:5.)

Many school chiefs, seemingly unaware of the research that showed the astonishing lifelong returns from early education, disdained the preschool requirement, but Union City embraced it. It was a tall order. To succeed, the district had to change the prevailing understanding of what's best for toddlers—away from mere child-minding, toward early education that prepares children for kindergarten and beyond. And because the city's public schools didn't have space for all the three- and four-year-olds, the district also had to work with what was already in place. That meant transforming a host of private mom-and-pop day care centers, where TV watching, snack time, and naps had been the main attractions, into preschools worthy of the name, with small classes staffed by college-educated teachers who had a deep understanding of how children develop. Over the next several years, prekindergarten became a marquee program for the district, and as the preschoolers progressed through the grades its long-lasting impact has grown ever-more apparent.[18]

JOHNNY APPLESEED IN NEW JERSEY

In 2003 Fred Carrigg finally made the journey back to his home town of Trenton. He went to work at the Department of Education, where he was assigned to help floundering urban systems across the state.

The timing was propitious. After years of lip service from both sides of the aisle, a governor who championed the *Abbott* cause was finally in office. Jim McGreevey had campaigned as a vocal supporter of the judicial mandate, and as governor he matched words with deeds. The state's education department shifted gears—instead of playing the lawyers' game of emphasizing paper-clip compliance, it started to concentrate on the instructional core, especially reading and writing.

This was Fred's meat and potatoes, and when Gordon MacInnes, a jack-of-all-trades in New Jersey politics and policy, was solicited by McGreevey to convert the *Abbott* aspirations into statewide reality, he recruited Fred to be the Johnny Appleseed for this approach. The choice was obvious. "When I'd visit the schools in Union City," Gordon tells me, "I'd ask teachers 'how did this [change] happen?' The answer always came back to Fred."

At the Education Department, Gordon and Fred made a fine pair. Gordon, tall and patrician in appearance, trained at Princeton's Woodrow Wilson School of Public and International Affairs, was the policy guy, the fellow who could see the big picture. In the late 1960s and early 1970s, when he ran a major state charity, he was directly involved in an earlier school finance case, advising the litigators on how to frame the lawsuit. During his bumpy journey in and out of state elective office, he focused on education issues. He became the Democrats' point man for opposing the GOP's school aid formulas, which shortchanged the cities; and he lambasted Governor Christine Todd Whitman for proposing that the *Abbott* kids receive glorified babysitting instead of real preschool.

As the *Abbott* czar, Gordon relentlessly focused on boosting student achievement. Several times a year he met with the top administrators in each of the *Abbott* districts—"face-to-face" sessions, he called them—pressuring them to emphasize early literacy. To the superintendents who bought into this strategy, Gordon delivered the money needed to make that happen. Fred made an ideal sidekick, the guy who understood the nuts and bolts of converting policy into practice.

"Don't think about it as a miracle," Fred warned the superintendents, when speaking about what Union City had accomplished. "Miracles can't get duplicated, but the approach that we took can be used elsewhere."

That's exactly what has happened elsewhere in the state. The quality of education got better in school systems that borrowed the Union City approach—the "willing buyers," as Gordon and Fred called them—while stagnating in districts that went their own way. The tale of two cities, Elizabeth and Newark, illustrates these diverging paths.

The port city of Elizabeth, while twice as big as Union City, resembles it in important ways. Both cities are poor and both have large numbers of immigrants, though Elizabeth's population is more racially and ethnically diverse. In the mid-1990s, half of the eleventh graders in both communities were failing the state's reading and math tests. But as Union City was on the rise, Elizabeth was going nowhere. Curriculum decisions had been left to each school—each teacher, really, since the schools practiced what Pablo Munoz, a history teacher at the time, calls a "closed door approach—when the teacher's door is closed what happens in the room is up to that teacher."

In 2003, with Munoz now running the academic show, Elizabeth embraced the Union City plan. A coherent curriculum was adopted district-wide, chunks of uninterrupted time for reading and writing were blocked out, learning centers were put in place, and bilingual instruction was refined to match the students' individual skills. Fred spent a considerable amount of time in Elizabeth, continuing his work there when he left his position with the state in 2007. By 2012, with Munoz the superintendent of schools, the payoff, measured in the students' reading and math skills, was obvious. The Elizabeth public schools had measurably improved over the course of a decade.

Those students were also doing considerably better than youngsters in cities that rejected Fred and Gordon's message. Consider Trenton. The city is economically better-off than Union City, with far fewer English-language novices, and the school system has pocketed considerably more state dollars for after-school programs, summer school, and the like. It stands to reason that its students would do better academically, but they have actually done much worse.

Trenton embraced the Great Leader theory, opting to rely on superstar principals to run the show. Unlike Union City, which adopted a system-wide model of reform, in Trenton each principal was given carte blanche. In his 2009 look-back at his experience with the *Abbott* districts, *In Plain Sight: Simple, Difficult Lessons from New Jersey's Expensive Effort to Close the Achievement Gap*, Gordon makes a strong case against the Trenton approach, and he has continued hammering at that argument. As he points out in a 2011 *Newark Star-Ledger* opinion piece, Trenton lacks both a curriculum and evidence of how its students are faring. "There is no coherence, no clarity, no follow-up to obvious instructional problems." The results have been dismal—between 1999 and 2008, for example, the percentage of students who passed the eighth-grade math test barely rose, from 18.2% to 21.9%, yet "no steps were taken to try to improve instruction district-wide in the middle grades." During the same period, Union City eighth graders who passed those tests rose from 42% to 71%, close to the statewide average and what you'd expect from a middle-class suburb.[19]

Perhaps the most instructive tale, and certainly the saddest, comes from the city of Orange. After Fred left Union City for Trenton, several of his old colleagues decamped to that nearly all-black community, bringing with them the approach that was working so well in Union City. During the next few years, as the literacy pipeline was put in place, third graders' test scores in reading rose dramatically, almost reaching Union City levels. And as the reforms took effect further up the grade ladder, middle school students started to do better.

Then, in a drearily familiar scenario, the school board was ousted. The new board fired the Union City team and abandoned its approach. Old political grudges, not arguments over teaching and learning, drove this decision to change course, as the games of adults trumped the needs of children. The consequences were predictable—within a few years, the gains that had been made by the children of Orange were wiped out.[20]

Charisma Isn't a Job Requirement

"The real story of Union City is that it *didn't* fall back. It stabilized and has continued to improve," Fred Carrigg tells me, and he deserves much of the credit. Margaret Honey, who evaluated the computers-in-the-classrooms project in the mid-1990s, learned a lot about the school system during the time she spent there. "Fred's the real deal," she says. "He's smart, deeply committed and understands the politics. He had a plan and he cultivated a new generation of leaders who could help carry it out."

Well before his departure, Fred's approach to problem-solving was cemented into the school system. It is an organization—a system, not a cult of personality—that Union City has constructed, and this commitment to continuous improvement is essential to its success.

A century ago, Max Weber, an architect of modern social science, wrote about the "routinization of charisma," and while Weber had religious leaders in mind, his analysis characterizes any enterprise that hopes to endure when an inspirational leader departs. Flashy companies have forgotten this lesson to their detriment. "The organizations that are most successful are the ones where the system is the star," writes Malcolm Gladwell, contrasting the enduring success of dishwater-dull Procter & Gamble with the multibillion-dollar debacle at Enron. "The talent myth assumes that people make organizations smart. More often than not, it's the other way around." This understanding of how the world works captures Union City's approach—people come and go but the organization endures.[21]

Fred Carrigg tosses off ideas like the New England Patriots' Tom Brady throws touchdown passes. Those who followed him have built on his work, turning those ideas into common practice. They have also added new ideas based on promising practices to an ever-evolving mix. This is how good organizations typically thrive, through continuous improvement.[22]

Except for a handful of school chiefs who style themselves as crusaders, superintendents don't sweep anyone off their feet. There's no glamour to what they do, no dash and swagger either. It's just the daily grind. In "To Be of Use," poet Marge Piercy honors the work of such people. "I want to be with people who submerge in the task, who are not parlor generals and field deserters," she writes. "The work of the world is common as mud. . . . But the thing worth doing well done has a shape that satisfies, clean and evident."

Sandy Sanger, Union City's superintendent since 2003, typifies the breed. His Irish German family, who moved to Union City when he was a young boy, was perpetually poor—"a bit dysfunctional," he says, skipping the details. He earned his bachelor's degree at nearby William Paterson College, and for his entire career he has been on the Union City school payroll, as a history teacher, basketball coach, and administrator.

That's a familiar career path for a conventional guy—you might even call him a "square"—and in Union City being conventional counts as an asset. Sandy knows how to use bluntness—his motto is "GOYA," legendary pro football coach Lou Holtz's admonition to "get off your butt"—and when to deploy gentle suasion as well. Square-jawed and often stern-visaged, his gray hair receding, he has put on considerable weight since his college basketball–playing days, and the six-packs of Diet Coke in his office refrigerator vouch for his never-ending attempts to shed pounds. He spends his summer vacations on the Jersey Shore, devouring thrillers by Lawrence Sanders, not boning up at Harvard on the latest theories of leadership with high-flying colleagues. On the school district's website he identifies his hero as Jesus Christ, and he tells me that after he retires he plans to spend his time "giving back to the Lord through local missions and outreaches."

"I'm no genius," says Sandy, "but I do have a talent for choosing good people," and selecting Silvia Abbato to be the assistant superintendent in charge of academics illustrates this talent. Silvia arrived in Union City in 1969 in the first wave of migration from Cuba and, despite having to learn English on her own, she did well at school. As an undergrad at Jersey City College she thought hard about becoming a doctor, but teaching was in the family's bloodstream. Both her parents had Ph.D.s from the University of Havana, but when they came to the United States they had to start over. Her father drove a truck and her mother did embroidery to support their family while they learned English. They persevered, receiving their teaching certificates, and they eventually made it into the classroom. Those life stories conveyed a potent message—that teaching is not just a career but the secular equivalent of a religious vocation.

When she became assistant superintendent in 2003, her first big assignment was to convince the high school math teachers that they needed to rewrite the curriculum. At that time fewer than 40% of the high school students were passing the math section of the state's graduation exam, but the teachers didn't want to hear from her. "When I arrived at the high school, the teachers were angry," she remembers. "They sat with their arms crossed. The message was plain: 'What is this kid going to show me?'" "I know you are working hard," she reassured them, "and we are going to show you how to get better." By the end of that workshop "the arms were uncrossed and teachers were volunteering to write new material, and as the math scores improved they wanted to do more."

No one would describe Sandy or Silvia as a charismatic personality, but charisma is not a job requirement in Union City. "We're worker bees," says Silvia.

Ask Sandy Sanger what accomplishments he's proudest of and he'll tell you about two things—the school system's blueprint, which lays out what it takes to run an effective school, and its homegrown assessments of student performance. There's nothing in this recital that will earn headlines or bring a president to town, but it's the sort of incrementalism that can keep a successful enterprise humming.

The "Blueprint for Sustained Academic Achievement" emerged in typical Union City fashion, as a practical way to solve a problem. In 2005, the district's reading and math test scores slipped, and while the dip was slight it prompted serious soul-searching. Sandy's message was unequivocal: "This can't happen again."

One plausible explanation for the drop-off was the uneven quality of stewardship at the schools—too many managers and too few educational leaders—and that realization prompted the drafting of the blueprint. Silvia, its principal author, looked to see what the principals in the highest-achieving schools were doing and catalogued those effective practices. She describes the seventy-three-item checklist as a how-to book—"Leadership 101"—that spells out what had worked best in the school district.

"I tell the principals, 'if you follow this blueprint you will be successful,'" Sandy says. "No one else is doing this," he adds. "We should copyright it and sell it to other districts."

The precepts sound obvious, even platitudinous, but before the blueprint was drafted some principals weren't following them. Take the first item on the checklist: "Analyze testing results for targeted students [those on the verge of passing] to maximize student potential." A history of counterproductive behavior underlies that dictate.

In recent years, Union City has invested considerable time and money to construct its own reading and math tests. These assessments—the second item on Sandy's checklist of major accomplishments—mimic the New Jersey ASK, and students' scores have proven to be good predictors of how they will do on the state tests. The results are supposed to focus teachers' energies on skills the students haven't picked up, such as solving word problems in math or making sense of complex prose passages.

The data also pinpoint which students, as well as which teachers, most need help. They specify how the youngsters in, say, Sue Emmerling's fourth grade class at Washington School are doing overall; how this year's results compare with last year's as well as how they compare with the scores of other fourth grade teachers; which kinds of questions are causing trouble for her students; and which students—those who take the test in Spanish, those with special needs, those who are new to the school district—are having the toughest time, and which are on the verge of passing.

The "no excuses" camp of education reformers—those who are pushing for greater "accountability" and who believe that teachers should be judged on the basis of how much they raise students' test scores—would salivate at the opportunity these tools offer to reward and punish teachers, but this isn't how the information gets used in Union City.[23] There, the emphasis is on helping teachers do a better job. Armed with this information, a principal knows where to send a coach or an experienced teacher to model what works in the classroom—an Alina Bossbaly at Washington School, for instance, helping out Mary Ann Rick.

In every school, these test results are intended to launch one-on-one conversations between the principal and the teachers, and out of those meetings a strategy for improvement is meant to emerge. But Silvia discovered during her school visits that some principals, perhaps fearful about potential confrontations or unaware of what intervention might work, were stashing the scores in a desk drawer. Hence the first precept of the blueprint: use them.

Other checklist items sound similarly commonsensical: "conduct professional development with staff," "assist the administration in the development of the school's budget," "review teachers' plan-books for instructional strategies to support best teaching practices," "deploy data-driven decision-making," "emphasize learning experiences that require all students to use higher-order thinking skills, develop in-depth knowledge about concepts, and be able to apply what they learn to real life situations." Each one of them responds to a failure of leadership that Silvia encountered in the field.

Principals who have been on the job for years may not want—or may not be able—to do things differently. "Change comes hard," says Sandy. But in recent years several principals have retired, and this has created an opening for improvement. "We can build leadership capacity," Silvia tells me. "Mentors have been working with teachers but not administrators. We are beginning to change that."

To Gordon MacInnes, who saw every troubled urban school system up close and personal during his years in the state education department, the lesson is plain—"good management matters."

Supervision and "Snooper-vision"

Twice each year, in October and February, Sandy, Silvia, and the rest of the senior staff spend an hour or two at each of Union City's fourteen schools, conferring with the principals and their top assistants. "Face-to-face," these sessions are called—it's an idea that Sandy borrowed from Gordon, who organized similar meetings with each superintendent when he ran the *Abbott* program. They afford the administration a chance to learn what is happening on the ground.

Sandy and his colleagues joke that they always gain a few pounds during face-to-face week, and they're probably right. At most schools the food is piled high in welcome—there might be jelly donuts, bagels, and cream cheese for the morning meetings and meat lasagna, baked ziti, and Kung Pao chicken at midday sessions—as hospitality is pinned to the hope that the calories will dull the senses or soften the criticism.

Each school produces a binder that lays out what initiatives are in the works—everything from launching an artist-in-residence program and tutoring students at breakfast-time to finding attention-grabbing activities for parents—and runs through the big-ticket items at the meeting. But Union City's sterling reputation rests on its test scores, and those results drive the conversations. The district's blueprint, with its benchmarks for demonstrating effective leadership, hovers in the shadow.

After showcasing their wares, a school's leaders are peppered with questions by Sandy, who often focuses on the big picture, and Silvia, who dives into the teaching and testing. (Others at the table comment on the bilingual program, the use of technology, the budget, and the like.) Sandy conveys seriousness of purpose. Silvia comes across as more genial but no less focused—like Alina Bossbaly, her style can be characterized as *dulce y duro*, sweet and hard. Both of them are on the lookout for innovations like an electronic plan-book developed by one school to replace the handwritten tomes that drive teachers around the bend. "When we find a good idea, we bring it to the other schools," says Sandy.

Near the end of the discussion, the principals are invited to lay out their wish lists. Sandy and Silvia sometimes say "yes" on the spot, but more often they're studiously noncommittal, and if the wish list grows overlong Sandy will intervene. "Easy with the disease of 'more.'" A few days later, the school receives a summary of the discussion that highlights what is working well and what needs improving.

Principals are encouraged to flag their problems, and occasionally they do, but the understandable urge to spin the story, to put the school in the best possible light, is evident everywhere. "We're probably getting 20% that's exaggerated."

Sometimes the administration follows up with what's called a "SWAT Team" visit, an infelicitous term in a district that emphasizes collegiality. It's "supervision, not 'snooper-vision,'" Sandy emphasizes, but nonetheless the prospect of such a visit makes the principals apprehensive. A team led by Silvia comes to a school, unannounced, to spend time in the classrooms, talk with teachers and students, and peruse students' portfolios. Then they head to the principal's office to share what they've learned. Sometimes they have changes to propose. "This is how I really learn what's going on," Silvia says.

No two schools are entirely alike, and during the face-to-face meeting the variations in their culture and styles of leadership emerge.

At the Hostos Early Education Center, the flagship prekindergarten, Adriana Birne presents a bevy of detailed assessments of the prekindergartens by a team of outside experts. You'd never know that just a few minutes before she had been in crisis mode because a four-year-old had heaved a ball straight at the face of her classmate, knocking out her two front teeth. Sandy and Silvia both possess an intimate knowledge of this program—Sandy ran it, with backup from Adriana, before becoming superintendent; and Adriana and Silvia are sisters. ("I have to be tough on her," Silvia tells me. "Otherwise people will say I'm playing favorites.") The quality of the evidence she produces and the progress she has made in strengthening the privately run preschools earn Adriana unqualified praise. "You're a model for the district," Sandy effuses.

The praise also flows at Union Hill Middle School, which opened a year earlier. Principal Vicki Dickson, previously an assistant principal at Washington School, has moved the needle on reading and math scores—the main measure of success—while working hard to build a community of what she calls "upstanders." Her PowerPoint presentation and several-hundred-page binder detail an impressive array of innovations for the special ed students and high-flyers alike. "If I were a student attending an urban middle school," says Sandy, "this is the place I'd love to be."

But the situation isn't nearly so rosy at Jose Marti, the ninth grade academy, also beginning its second year. The problems start with the presentation, a hokey slide show as well as a PowerPoint summary of accomplishments that contains enough spelling mistakes to make Silvia wince. Principal Joe Polinik describes the first year of the school as a "dress rehearsal," seemingly forgetting that for nearly 600 students it was a live performance. And when Joe portrays himself as a social worker/educator who wants to maintain an "all encompassing, nurturing environment," Silvia, usually the epitome of calmness, jumps in. "Last fall lots of students received grades in language arts so low that they could never pass. What signal does that send?" she asks acidly. In her tone you can hear the echoes of the girl who came to Union City from Cuba and received bad grades because she didn't speak the language.

At Washington School Les Hanna does all the talking. The school's binder is flawless, because she has gone to great pains in making it so. "Two years earlier, a state review roughed up the school, but Washington has come a long way," says Sandy, after Les makes her presentation. In a city where most children grow up poor the youngsters at Washington are among the worst off—fewer than a quarter of them can be described as mainstream students—and they bring their emotional baggage to school. There have been more than eighty meltdowns in the first six weeks, "kids kicking, punching and throwing desks. We've been putting out fires." Les isn't a complainer—"what's the point?" she shrugs—and she doesn't add that she is largely shouldering this burden herself. "Whatever these children's backgrounds, the bottom line is that they all have to master it," says Les. "We're up for the challenge."

By the time of the second face-to-face meeting of the year, which takes place in February, things are looking up at the school. More students passed the district's reading and math test, which they had taken two months earlier, than were rated proficient on the ASK the previous spring. Fingers crossed—the latest results could be a harbinger of improvement on the achievement test these children will take in a couple of months.

"The teachers are making better use of the technology," Les reports, as computerized whiteboards, which enable teachers to manipulate lots of material at the same time, are replacing the old blackboards. And teachers like Alina Bossbaly, who know how to communicate their devotion to writing, are helping their less experienced colleagues.

Silvia is impressed. "Compared to the state's review two years earlier, when nothing was going on, you can feel the change." It's no miracle, but it embodies the kind of slow and steady improvement Union City has built its strategy upon.

THE CHAIN OF COMMAND

If you credit the educator's rule of thumb, most Union City students should be regarded as "at risk," a jargony way of saying they are likely candidates to drop out or flunk out. But these kids are thumbing their noses at such predictions. From elementary school through high school graduation, they do about as well as the typical New Jersey student, and that performance catapults them into the mainstream.

This glowing record, unheard of among the state's urban districts, has prompted educators from across New Jersey to trek to Union City, pilgrims to this Lourdes of public education who hope to bottle the elixir. State schools chief Chris Cerf, appointed by the acerbic governor, Chris Christie, to clean house, comes bearing compliments. "Can you teach other districts how to do as well?" he asks the superintendent.[24]

Nonetheless, the mandarins from Trenton are still breathing down Sandy Sanger's neck.

Local control of education was once regarded as inviolate—as sacrosanct as the "Battle Hymn of the Republic," as one superintendent put it—but the 2002 No Child Left Behind Act rewrote the rule book, and on many policy matters the state now has the final say.[25]

Whether the measure is the NAEP test, the nationwide metric, or the percentage of students who graduate, New Jersey ranks near the top. This accomplishment matters, especially in a state trying to shed its massive inferiority complex, its status as the butt of New York's jokes, and naturally it is hell-bent on remaining among the best. The baleful gaze of state education officials focuses on its weakest links, *Abbott* school districts such as Trenton, which graduates fewer than half of its students despite having received buckets of money.[26]

The state acts as a middleman, obliged to bring its districts in line with federal dictates. Since the passage of the No Child Left Behind Act, the rule has been that every child must be proficient in math and reading by 2014, and every year each school district is supposed to be progressing toward that goal. The command remains on the books, but as it became blindingly obvious that no state could meet it, in 2012 the U.S. Department of Education effectively nullified the law by allowing many states, including New Jersey, to set their own benchmarks. With these waivers came new marching orders—the states had to guarantee that, by 2020, every student would graduate from high school prepared for college or career. Never mind that this new aspiration is as unachievable as the old one—Washington still passes the buck to the states, which in turn send it along to the school systems and on down the line.

"Do better or face the consequences" is the unvarying message. That's where the nation's 13,500 districts, Union City among them, enter the picture.

The Perpetual Grind

Reports by the carload flow from Sandy Sanger's office to the masters in Trenton. The most onerous state intrusion is the audit conducted every few years—the Quality Single Accountability Continuum or, less tongue-trippingly, QSAC, jargon that camouflages a world of pain.

Asking a school system to look in the mirror, as QSAC does in requiring a detailed self-evaluation, sounds like a good idea. Trust but verify: inviting knowledgeable outsiders to look over the administration's shoulder also makes intuitive sense. "QSAC keeps you on your toes," Sandy says philosophically. But when bureaucrats are given free rein, good ideas can spin out of control and what's worth doing disappears under an Everest of paper.

Preparing for QSAC devours thousands of hours and can turn into a travesty of bureaucratic overreaching. A few years earlier, the district lost points in the state's arcane grading system because its Asian American students—all two of them—had "only" scored in the 98th percentile on the state's English and math tests. Even though those scores nearly topped the charts, they didn't demonstrate the "adequate yearly progress" that the federal law requires for each racial and ethnic minority, as well as for English-language learners and special needs students.

This audit not only covers the big ticket items, like the overall academic record and the safety of the schools. It also extends to the minuscule, such as the text of every pamphlet that's sent home to parents and the minute-by-minute details of teachers' plan-books. For every meeting that involves the administration and a school principal or a parents' group, the agenda, attendance lists, and minutes must be gathered—thousands of discrete items that fill binders fat enough to fell a small forest. This process is repeated every three years—more frequently if the schools come up short, which is typically the case with the *Abbott* districts.

For Union City, the QSAC reviewers will come calling in the spring of 2011. Sandy, who has been through this ordeal twice before, knows what must be done to satisfy the overlords in Trenton. He sets the wheels in motion during the preceding summer, marshalling his troops with the precision of a military operation.

As the year starts, the mega-audit is hardly the superintendent's only worry. He's also got a budget crisis on his hands. Although New Jersey has been generous in channeling money to the *Abbott* districts, Republican Governor Chris Christie, elected in 2009, has been making a nationwide name for himself by beating up on educators. (In the midst of a donnybrook with the teachers union, he derided teachers as drug dealers who used their students as "drug mules" to carry a prounion message.) In the spring of 2010 Christie pushed through substantial cuts in the state's education budget, costing Union City $10 million, about 5% of its budget. What's more, he clawed back $29 million that the district had socked away for the proverbial rainy day, a penalty for prudence.

"There's no way we can save that kind of money by eliminating cleaning lady and custodian jobs," Sandy tells me, reviewing his options. Serious cuts must be made.

"We will be fiscally responsible but we won't do anything to disrupt education"—this is the message the superintendent delivers to the school board, teachers, and parents, as he considers what's essential and what can be dispensed with. While other communities in the same boat are firing art and music teachers, in Union City not a single teacher is let go. Peripheral activities like transportation and information technology are outsourced. More money is saved by not filling some of the positions left empty by the retirements of administrators with six-figure salaries.

There are also savings to be had in special education. For years, Union City has sent youngsters diagnosed as autistic to private schools that cost upward of $60,000. Sandy thinks that the school system can do a better job of educating these kids in-house, and for a fraction of the money, and his opinion is shared by Jeanette Pena, a school psychologist who chairs the school board. Here's a chance to do well financially by doing good, and while some parents are understandably skeptical, they're reassured when they are shown what Union City is planning for their kids. On the first day of school seven new classes for autistic children, four or five students in a class, each with a teacher and an aide, are up and running.

Meanwhile, the results have arrived for last spring's New Jersey ASK, the three R's test for which George Washington Elementary School, like every elementary and middle school in the district, has spent months prepping its students. The weeks of waiting for the results are always nail-biting time for Sandy and Silvia. They know that better test scores will bring praise, while disappointing results will generate unwelcome questions from state officials as well as from Mayor Brian Stack, who takes an intimate interest in school affairs.

Although the results generally show improvement, there is one glaring exception—fourth grade reading scores have plummeted. "I almost had a heart attack," Sandy tells me. When he calms down long enough to contact school chiefs in neighboring towns, he learns that they're in the same boat, and when he reaches out to superintendents in the verdant suburbs he hears similarly woeful tales. What's going on? the superintendents demand of the state, and the answer isn't one they want to hear. Trenton has gotten tougher about the meaning of "proficiency" for fourth graders, and so fewer students have passed statewide.

Proficiency—the word conveys authority. But while it sounds like a clear and reliable gauge of students' performance, based on an expert consensus about what students should know, in fact it's arbitrary. What counts as proficient differs from state to state—what's acceptable in Arkansas may not suffice in Massachusetts—and, as in this instance, it may change in a particular state from one year to the next.

Whatever the explanation, perturbations arise in the political arena when more students start to fail, for no official likes to be told that students aren't getting smarter and smarter. Sandy and his fellow school chiefs fight the revised proficiency standard for fourth graders and the state retreats to its old formula. Peace, if not educational progress, is restored.

Each month on the school calendar arrives with its own time-consuming and energy-draining demands—conducting the face-to-face sessions; participating in the CAPA school reviews; revising the blueprint for principals; negotiating employment contracts; designing a two-day retreat for all the teachers; documenting what's being done to combat violence, sexual harassment, and bullying; and prepping for the monthly drumbeat of school board meetings. Some things, the *crises du jour*, you simply can't prepare for.

The pace picks up in the spring. A new budget must be prepared and, lacking certainty about the size of the state's contribution, the superintendent must assume the worst. For untenured teachers, a worst-case budget means layoff notices, and while everyone hopes it won't be necessary to follow through, teachers without tenure turn to Tylenol PM to combat their sleepless nights. In addition to the QSAC dissection two federal audits are on the calendar, one to examine how the No Child Left Behind funds are being spent and the other to review student assessment practices.

The outsiders' ceaseless demands, with one review following on the heels of another and multiple reviews occurring at the same time, take their toll. Silvia responds to the mounting tension by eating junk food, while Sandy, too nervous to eat, loses weight.

By the following summer Union City will learn whether it has survived the QSAC inquisition. But whatever the outcome there won't be time or laurels on which to rest. Sandy, Silvia, and their colleagues will be scrutinizing a new batch of state test results, picking principals, revising the curriculum, addressing budgetary concerns, and the like. Theirs is a story without an ending.

Over the long term, demography poses the most profound challenge to Union City's public schools. As more poor and uneducated youngsters from across Latin America throng the community, students whose profile differs markedly from those who came from Cuba years earlier, the schools' task becomes harder and harder. The administration is too smart to leap at the facile answer, too self-aware to believe in a magic bullet. It will stick with its strategy of continuous improvement—*plan, do, review.*

4

THE MAGIC KINGDOM
Preschool for All

Loosely coupled systems—that's how Karl Weick, a renowned student of organizations, describes school districts. There's really no "system" at all, Weick adds, just "largely self-functioning sub-systems" in which each school goes its own way—in other words, a herd of cats.[1] But if Union City is to continue working wonders, Superintendent Sandy Sanger must keep those cats on a leash. As we've seen, that's a Herculean job—and nowhere is the difficulty of the task as palpable as in the district's early education program.

In the poverty-plagued metropolises of New Jersey, every three- and four-year-old is entitled to attend free, full-day, high-quality preschool for six hours a day, 245 days of the year, a commitment that no other state has come close to making. While Latino families have generally been chary of early education, preferring to keep their toddlers at home with mom, in Union City they have absorbed the message that preschool is the best place for their youngsters. More than nine families in ten avail themselves of this option, choosing among thirty-three different prekindergartens.[2]

These preschools don't much resemble one another. Some are run by the school system but most are operated by the city or a nonprofit or else maintained as businesses. A few enroll as many as several hundred children, while others, set up in the homes of the proprietors, take care of a dozen toddlers.

Out of this agglomeration, Adriana Birne, the effervescent, apple-cheeked head of the early education program, is trying to mold a system of uniformly high quality—in effect, it's the Union City public schools in miniature. If she gets it right, a few years from now you could find yourself in a prekindergarten classroom in Union City and, because all the classes are equally good, you won't be able to tell whether the sign outside reads "Hostos Center for Early Childhood Education," the district's showpiece, or "Tiny Seed of the Big Future," a one-room operation. What's more, these children will have a leg up when they begin school, because the prekindergarten experience can potentially remake their futures.

THE BEST INVESTMENT

During his 2009 campaign for governor of New Jersey, Chris Christie derided preschool as "babysitting" and mocked his Democratic opponent for supporting it. Nothing could be further from the truth.[3]

The prevailing belief used to be that intelligence was largely inherited, that your destiny was determined at birth. But a host of research—in neuroscience, genetics, and child development—has revolutionized our understanding of how the mind and the emotions take form. Those findings put early education at center stage.

Consider the brain as if it were an unfinished work of art. Just as the form that a sculpture eventually takes is most influenced by the artist's initial creative choices, so too, scientists tell us, the brain is profoundly affected by what happens in the first years of life. Instead of thinking of nature *versus* nurture, as used to be the case, the new paradigm focuses on nature *through* nurture. "The real question," as the authors of *From Neurons to Neighborhoods*, the landmark multidisciplinary work in the field, point out, "is not which matters more, early or later experience, but how later experience is influenced by early experience." What's learned in childhood makes the biggest difference, not because it provides an unalterable blueprint for adult well-being but because it embeds "a set of capabilities, orientations to the world, and expectations about how things and people will behave that affect how new experiences are selected and processed."[4]

The scientists' conclusions have been backed up by iconic field studies— most famously, the Perry Preschool Study—that have proved beyond peradventure the powerful long-term impact of preschool. In the Perry experiment, poor children who attended a well-conceived prekindergarten in the 1960s were significantly more likely than an otherwise identical group that lacked the same opportunity to have graduated from high school and gone to college. A stream of subsequent reports has shown that, forty years later, they are also more likely to own their own home, own a car, and have a savings account; and they are less likely to have used drugs or had serious health problems, been in prison, or gone on welfare. They are also earning 25% more, enough to lift them out of poverty.[5]

Recent evaluations of state-funded prekindergartens with small classes and well-trained teachers confirm the Perry findings. A five-state assessment of such initiatives concludes that the preschoolers gained an additional three months' worth of vocabulary, compared to youngsters who lacked the same experience—a vital difference, since the vocabulary test does a good job of predicting a child's reading skills—and recorded equally impressive gains in early math skills. A similar evaluation carried out in Tulsa reported even bigger differences.[6]

"Skill begets skill"—that's how Nobel Prize–winning economist James Heckman pithily sums up these findings. Economists have put a dollar sign on the value of a good preschool experience, estimating a return on investment that runs as high as seventeen-to-one. When Clive Belfield, coauthor of the latest Perry Preschool study, found that public schools would realize big savings by offering high-quality preschools, he received calls from a dozen states that sought his expertise.[7] New Jersey is ahead of the game, because it has underwritten good preschools for over a decade, and Union City is widely regarded as maintaining the best preschools in the state. That's a principal reason why it has done so well.[8]

A Cornucopia of Teachable Moments

To really understand just why preschool matters so much, you have to visit a well-taught class, for it's here that knock-your-socks-off teaching happens. Becoming immersed in the lives of three- and four-year-olds is a nonstop activity—just spending a morning watching a class unfold can wear you out—and the best prekindergarten teachers are so good that they should be conducting tutorials in pedagogy for their K–12 counterparts.

You can find memorable preschool teachers at academic hothouses like the University of Chicago's Lab School, where MacArthur genius grant recipient

Vivian Paley taught for years and parents register their children even before they're born, or the 92nd Street Y in Manhattan, which is harder to get into than Harvard. Once in a while you'll come upon treasure troves in unlikely places such as Chicago Commons, a prekindergarten where young artists bloom, located in a neighborhood so dicey that the playground is surrounded by barbed wire. In Union City, Eugenio Maria de Hostos Center for Early Childhood Education (Hostos for short) belongs in this rarified company.[9]

When evaluators appear, they invariably award this preschool top marks for what's on hand, everything from working kitchens to banks of computers, and wax lyrical in their praise for the staff. Most of the teachers have master's degrees in child development, and they know that "age-appropriate" isn't just jargon. They've been handpicked by Adriana for their classroom wizardry as well as their rapport with kids whose families, as often as not, are barely making it.[10]

As soon as I enter Room 111, Suzy Rojas's class at Hostos, I'm sucked into the hum and buzz of activity. Some of these three- and four-year-olds are designing paper clothing and others are painting. They've given their pictures titles in a mix of English and Spanish—*Make a Man Out of Spagetty, Girafo Como El Tail*. One group has built a pink cardboard chair—*A Chair for My Mother*.

Toddlers are in some ways "smarter, more imaginative, more caring and even more conscious than adults are," Berkeley psychology professor Alison Gopnik writes in *The Philosophical Baby*.[11] French psychologist Jean Piaget, whose ideas held sway half a century ago, regarded little children as if they were heathens, irrational and immoral. But if you think of them as Gopnik does, as little explorers with open-ended and seemingly unlimited intellectual curiosity, then it's a breathtaking experience to drop into a classroom like Suzy's, which invites these explorations.

Art plasters the walls, plants hang from the ceiling, and in every niche there's something to seize a child's imagination. Angel, Victor, and Rodrigo are peering at insects through a microscope, and they're happy to explain to me what they're seeing. "Remember when we went to the museum and the butterfly landed on my arm?" Angel asks his friends. "Are these *all* insects?" Suzy wonders aloud. "How do you know?" "That one has eight legs," Victor responds, "and that means it's not an insect." Then Suzy brings over a prism. "What do you see when you look through it?" she asks, and Rodrigo looks up to say that he can't tell them apart, that they look like leaves. "Why do you think so?" she inquires. The boys have already learned about lenses, and she tells them that the prism is a special kind of lens.

There's still more to be gleaned from these creatures. "How about an insect salad—would you want to eat it?" Suzy inquires. When the boys answer in chorus, "Ugh," she bounces it back to them: "How come?" They stare once more at the insects. "How many parts does an insect body have? Do you remember what they're called?" Angel knows the answer: "Three parts—the antenna, abdomen, and legs." Then Suzy walks over to a group of kids who are solving a puzzle on a computer, but she returns when she sees Victor and Rodrigo fighting over who gets the next look at the insects. "Use your words," she says—familiar teacher-talk—but then she adds a twist. "What can we do?" *We,* not "you"; the boys think about it. "How about adding another container for insects—that way you can all take turns."

Cognitive and noncognitive, thinking and feeling, Descartes's mind-body dualism—in a preschool classroom this line vanishes. The good teacher is always on the lookout for both kinds of lessons, always aiming to reach both head and heart.

"My goal is to bring these kids all the wonderful experiences their parents can't expose them to—to do for them what I do with my own children," Suzy tells me. "It's all about exposure to concepts—wide, narrow, long, short. 'I have three brothers, three sisters and an uncle—let's graph that.' I bring in breads from different countries. 'Let's do a pie chart showing which one you liked the best.' I don't ask them to memorize 1, 2, 3 or A, B, C—I could teach a monkey to count."

Most of these toddlers come from homes where Spanish is the only language that's spoken, but by the time they're kindergarteners they'll have grown comfortable learning entirely in English. Getting them from here to there is Suzy's job. One fall day she is teaching the kids about the parts of the body. "My hands on my head, what does this mean?" She croons the familiar ditty in Spanish and English, gesturing as she sings. All the youngsters, those who already know English and those who don't, sing along. "They're getting different experiences and that's okay," says Suzy. "For Victoria, this activity has to be repeated, but Sophie can take it to the next level, writing the words or cutting out the letters." By June, Suzy tells me, Victoria will have caught up.

These kids are also coming to understand why you should wait your turn, how to share, how to control your feelings—the emotional skills that report cards once summarized as "works and plays well with others." At the outset they put their heads together to decide what will make their classroom safe and fun. Suzy puts a positive spin on their suggestions. "Use your walking feet," reads the agreement posted on the wall, rather than "do not run." Learning that they shouldn't shout out a response takes a while to master. "I would have liked it if you raised your hand," Suzy tells Joey when he blurts out an answer, but she's speaking gently. "I will let them say it because they're small kids," she confides, "but by the end of the year they'll raise their hands."

On a mid-December morning the topic is latkes, the potato pancakes that are a Chanukah staple. That's not exactly what you might anticipate in a room filled with Latino children, few if any of whom have ever met a Jew in their lives, and all the more engaging for that reason. These kids have been listening to *The Chanukah Guest*, the beguiling tale of ninety-seven-year-old, nearly blind Bubba Brayna, the best latke-maker in her village, who cooks a batch of them for the rabbi and inadvertently feeds them to a grumpy old bear. Now they are going to prepare latkes from scratch.

Everything that transpires during the next ninety minutes could be called a "teachable moment"—describing the smell of an onion ("Strong or light? Strong—*duro*. Will it smell differently when we cook it? We'll have to find out."); pronouncing the "p" in pepper and *pimiento*; getting the hang of a food processor ("When I put all the ingredients in, what will happen? All of us helped to get to the idea that the chopper chops food."). The children serve the potato pancakes with the traditional sour cream and apple sauce, as well as salsa. I try one—it's delicious.

"I think of Hostos as the Magic Kingdom," Adriana tells me. "Whatever is happening in the rest of these children's lives, this is a wonderful place to be." By keeping her door open to anyone who wants to talk with her, hiring talented and committed teachers and creating opportunities for them to work with one another, reaching out to parents, and giving youngsters a safe haven where they can stretch their minds and explore their feelings, Adriana has created a community of caring. She has accomplished exactly what Les Hanna is working toward at Washington School.

What "Preschool for All" Really Means

As director of early education, Adriana's responsibilities extend well beyond Hostos, encompassing all the prekindergartens in the city. Hostos can take only 10% of the nearly 2,000 preschoolers, and prekindergarten classes in five elementary schools enroll just 20% more. The rest of these kids attend Angel's Learning Center or Junior Prep, Happy Times or St. Francis, Tata's or ABC or Tiny Seed of the Big Future—thirty-three preschools in all, mostly run by mom-and-pop business operations, churches, or nonprofits like the National Association of Cuban-American Women.

In the first phases of the *Abbott v. Burke* litigation, the New Jersey Supreme Court focused exclusively on K–12. Later on, however, the justices were persuaded by mountains of evidence that good preschool was essential if children living in the state's poorest communities, who started kindergarten well behind their better-off peers, were going to have a truly equal chance of success. Thanks to the Court's 1998 ruling, every three- and four-year-old who lives in an *"Abbott* district" is entitled to attend a high-quality prekindergarten.[12]

Quality is the key, for without it those remarkable long-term benefits attributed to prekindergarten disappear. "Preschool without quality is just high-cost day care," Gordon MacInnes, the strong-willed state official whose job was to give teeth to the court order, points out. "It is not a simple matter of buying colorful alphabetic rugs, supplying age-appropriate toys, and finding two adults to supervise play." In New Jersey, the sizable infusion of money, an average of $12,000 for each child, was coupled with stiff new standards. Every prekindergarten teacher had to have a bachelor's degree, there could be no more than fifteen children in a class, and only a curriculum with demonstrated efficacy could be used.

Until the *Abbott* ruling, the only option available to most poor families in Union City was private day care, babysitting establishments presided over by women from the neighborhood who spoke little English and regarded themselves as mother hens, not educators. There, moms could park their toddlers while they earned a living. But the best you could say about such places is that they were safe, and sometimes even that wasn't the case. "What some of those providers did was sinful," Adriana tells me. "There was no stimulation, kids were left in cribs or parked in front of the TV all day."

With *Abbott* on the books, Sandy Sanger, at the time an elementary school principal, was handed the assignment of organizing a full-blown prekindergarten system in Union City. He chose Adriana as his deputy, and that proved to be a wise move.

When Adriana Correa arrived in Union City in 1966, a nine-year-old who had spent her early years amid the splashiness of Havana and lived in glitzy

Miami during her first few weeks in the United States, she was horrified. "I thought it was the ugliest town I had ever seen," she tells me. "Those homes were so close together, old and dark. I wondered why on earth we had to live here." She and her twin sister, Silvia—the same Silvia who is now the assistant superintendent in charge of academics—had to learn English by the sink-or-swim method. But, like Alina Bossbaly, the Correa girls soon blossomed into star pupils. Adriana graduated from Jersey City State College, summa cum laude, in 1979, and a few months later she was teaching second graders in Union City. She was just nineteen, so young-looking that an eighth grader, thinking that she was a new classmate, asked her for her phone number.

Adriana rose quickly through the ranks, moving to the central administration at thirty-one. The "Parents College" that she launched caught the attention of the White House, and in 1997 the program was spotlighted in Vice President Al Gore's "Family Reunion." A year later, Adriana and Sandy set out to give the city's three- and four-year-olds something of value; and when Sandy became superintendent in 2004, Adriana took over the post.

Because the overcrowded public schools couldn't possibly meet the parents' demand for good preschools, the district was forced to refashion the existing day care centers. State dollars paid for major renovations and covered the cost of tuition for staff members who pursued bachelor's degrees. Sandy and Adriana deployed standout master teachers as mentors to the newly minted graduates. "Twenty straight days teachers from our preschools would work with them," Sandy recalls. "We had to change the paradigm. Instead of the centers being just places for play, they would become centers for learning." As you might expect, bringing about this transformation has proven a long and arduous process.

On a crisp autumn morning, Adriana and I head off to visit the private prekindergartens that send their children to Washington School.

Our first stop is the NACAW Child Care Center, run by the National Association of Cuban-American Women. The living room of this creakily comfortable home has been turned into a prekindergarten for fifteen children. It's small and cramped, nothing like Suzy Rojas's classroom, but it's packed with temptations—a minipond where a plastic shark swims lazily and a sandbox where bucket brigades are constructing and demolishing castles, cushions piled next to shelves full of books, a make-believe store and a doctor's office, a math table where kids are counting chips, an easel where a boy is painting mini-Rothkos, and more. Yet the room doesn't feel over-crowded, just full.

The teacher, Katia Garcia, is constantly in motion, as is her aide, Selma Lopez, a grandmother who came from Cuba half a century ago. When I walk in, Katia, who is on her knees so that she's at eye level with the small circle of children, is reading *Beauty and the Beast*. It's a good sign that the kids are so engrossed that they barely look up.

The preschool's director, Xiomara Sanchez, was among the hundreds of professional women who fled from Castro's Cuba and wound up in Union City. "I had to help my people," she tells me, "and I decided on just one class-room for the kids in one very poor neighborhood." With donations and bake sales, Xiomara raised the money to buy the house in 1999. "I subbed in one of the elementary schools," Katia tells me, taking a quick break, "but I love this—it's amazing how quickly they are learning, so exciting when they get it."

If every privately run preschool in Union City were as good as NACAW, Adriana's work would be done, but what I see at our next stop, Tiny Seed of the Big Future, is eyebrow-raising. I wanted to visit this particular prekin-dergarten because of a comment that Les Hanna, the principal at George Washington Elementary School, had made. "When I have trouble with kids," Les told me, "they always seem to come from Tiny Seed." It's not hard to see why.

Adriana and I walk across the skimpily equipped, hard-surface playground, where skinned knees must be commonplace, and into a converted living room divided into two small spaces. Noise bursts through the paper-thin par-tition. While some kids are reading with a teacher and others are construct-ing houses out of blocks, several are aimlessly milling around.

The more socially adept parents in Union City have become knowledge-able about what makes a good preschool, and they've enrolled their children in other centers. As a result, many of the kids at Tiny Seed have no one to champion them. They arrive knowing no English and many of them have only a bare-bones command of Spanish. Some of their parents have been deemed neglectful or abusive, and these children have become enmeshed in the social services bureaucracy. Some of the youngsters have passed through a succession of foster care families, while others live with their families in a padlocked bedroom, sharing an apartment with other, similarly walled-off adults and children.

Adriana has no intention of glossing over the persisting problems. "Building rapport here is a challenge," she tells me. The proprietor, an Ecuadorian immigrant, is a businesswoman and not an educator. "I walked in once and she had candles burning everywhere," Adriana recalls, shaking her head in disbelief. Until recently, the teachers knew little English and less about child development. "The owner didn't understand what goes into the well-tested measures of quality that we use. 'There's no money,' she'd say, whenever we pointed out areas that needed improvement."

Patience is Adriana's strong suit—it has to be, when you're working with businesspeople who are focused on the bottom line—and at Tiny Seed her constancy has begun to pay off. "We're there all the time and we're making small strides," she says. While the building will always be cramped and loud, a coat of paint and a new floor have made it less shabby. The noise level has come down because the daily schedule has been rearranged.

What matters most, the newer teachers are considerably better-educated and more fluent in English than their predecessors. "The owner now understands the dual language goal," says Adriana. "The youngsters should leave here speaking English." The novices get tons of help from several master teachers—"more eyes," says Adriana. The vocabulary that the kids are exposed to, in both Spanish and English, is growing more sophisticated, not "thing" but "watering can" or "knife," and the teachers are acquiring the pedagogical tools that are used throughout the district. Instead of spending the entire day telling the children what to do, they're asking the kids to explain what they're doing—why they're designing a car from LEGO building bricks or what they anticipate discovering when they pour out cupfuls of sand. Watch one, do one—the experts deliver a lesson and then the rookies try it out for themselves.

You'll see the same kind of teaching with similar materials in preschools across Union City. Everywhere there's a rhythm to the day: "plan, do, review." First thing in the morning the youngsters decide what they want to pursue; then they set about making it happen, talking with their teacher when they get stumped; and at day's end they come together to reflect on what they've learned. When this technique, adapted from the Perry Preschool model, works well, kids make remarkably rapid progress. It's easy to flub, though, and so advice from a practiced hand proves invaluable. At Tiny Seed, Adriana pins her hopes on the fact that the proprietor's daughter, a recent college grad and a fireball of energy, is one of the new teachers. She's acquiring the craft while gradually taking over the business.

Reaching the Hostos preschool level of excellence may be out of reach for Tiny Seed, but a high-quality enterprise isn't unattainable. Two years from now, Adriana anticipates that Tiny Seed will be just as good as NACAW. The metamorphosis of NACAW from problem to model in just two years persuades me she's not a cockeyed optimist.

In 2008, Adriana tells me, NACAW was floundering. Katia, who had come straight from a business career, was in her first year, and while she had taken a handful of child development courses she felt overwhelmed. Though Veronica was nominally the aide, she had been at NACAW since it opened and regarded herself as captain of the ship. She treated Katia like a youngster, bossing her around. But with lots of coaching, Katia got better, gaining confidence as she did so; and with counseling from a master teacher, Katia and Veronica have found a way to work together.

The "no child left behind" emphasis on reading and math scoops up even three-year-olds in its net. It coincides with the culture of achievement that Adriana is bringing to the network, and every year ten preschool teachers, some from Hostos and others from the private providers, are randomly selected for evaluation by a team of outside experts.

This year the teachers earned a near-perfect score for organizing activities that promote language development, such as reading aloud, encouraging hands-on problem-solving, and staying flexible to kids' interests—all the things I saw in Suzy Rojas's room. While they weren't as successful at devising math activities, there was a healthy 20% improvement over the previous year's score.

"We keep working on this," says Adriana, sounding a lot like her K–12 counterparts. "No other school district has as comprehensive a system for linking test results with professional support. When teachers in the private prekindergartens are having trouble with, say, higher-order thinking, they spend a day or two at Hostos." That's why, from time to time, you'll see a teacher sitting in Suzy Rojas's class, diligently taking notes.

"At this point I'm comfortable with 75% of these providers," says Adriana. "Other districts give up after awhile, but if I had to sum up what I do in a single word it would be 'persistence.'" That sentiment sounds like the byword of the school system—*stay focused and keep doing the work.*

What Preschool Can Teach K–12

The benefits of prekindergarten, the great academic and social leap forward, can vanish when children wind up in uninspiring elementary schools—the dread "fadeout effect," as it's called. If preschool is followed by a solid K–12 education the gains, including higher incomes and better health, persist well into adulthood—but if K–12 is uninspiring, those benefits can disappear.[13]

The research shows that good preschool pedagogy works just as well for older youngsters. But it's not easy to persuade elementary and secondary school teachers, many of whom think of prekindergarten as just preparation for school, not the real thing. Adriana's second big challenge is to combat the threat of fadeout by purveying a vision of teaching that reaches from her preschool domain through third grade and beyond, with each year's experience expanding on what has gone before.

The master teachers who are overhauling day care centers like Tiny Seed have also fanned out to kindergarten classrooms across the district. There, they are helping teachers to reimagine the education of five-year-olds.

Barbara Tellechea's kindergarten at Washington School looks a lot like Suzy Rojas's room at Hostos. "In my community you'll find helpers of most any kind," reads a poster, and kids have picked their favorites, the boys saying they want to be policemen or firemen, the girls interested in pursuing careers as doctors. They're learning in much the same way as well, sometimes sitting in a circle and listening to Barbara's dramatic recitations, more often in small groups, hunting and pecking at the "Centro de Escritorio" computer program or designing a costume for the pooch in *Clifford the Big Red Dog*.

At a moment of ever-stiffening academic expectations, when kindergarten has tacitly been transformed into the new first grade, many of these teachers have come to regard their job as prepping five-year-olds for the make-or-break reading, writing, and math tests that lie several years down the road. They expect preschool to have taught children how to comport themselves in a standard elementary school classroom, sitting together and passively absorbing the lesson.[14]

But if you are a five-year-old who has spent two years with a teacher like Suzy Rojas you've formulated an entirely different notion of learning. You see yourself moving around the classroom, not sitting still; deciding what you'd like to do, rather than constantly being told what comes next; and working mainly in small groups or on your own, not with twenty classmates.

For such a youngster, the expectation of passivity doesn't go down well—after all, you can't learn how to make latkes simply by listening to a recital. In Union City, mini rebellions have broken out in kindergarten classrooms, as bored children vent their frustration or drift off. They're misbehaving, the traditional kindergarten teachers insist, and they blame prekindergarten for not getting children ready for the rigors of a "real" school. As you'd expect, Adriana stands with the kids—becoming the educational equivalent of a couch potato isn't the best way to learn.

In most school districts, the kindergarten teachers wouldn't give a damn about the views of someone in Adriana's position. A wall typically separates these two bailiwicks, but in Union City things don't work this way—the line separating prekindergarten and elementary school has been effaced, and the master teachers who've been helping the preschools are also revamping kindergarten.

"Kindergarten teachers typically lack a solid background in child development," says Marlene Lupo, who works closely with them. "They don't understand the 'why.' That's why some kids lose it when they get to the first grade—there hasn't been active learning in kindergarten." Marlene should know, since she taught kindergarten before being recruited by Adriana as a coach.

When Marlene ventures into a classroom, she demonstrates to teachers how they can move away from the one-way-communication/child-as-empty-vessel approach. Some of them, game to change their ways, welcome the chance to spend a few days at Hostos, watching one of the star teachers there. But when this preschool-to-kindergarten policy was introduced a few years back, some old timers didn't want to do things differently. They became so irate that they filed a grievance with the union, contending that the master teachers should stick to the toddlers, but with Adriana and Sandy arguing on the other side their grievance went nowhere.

"In some ways, kindergarten is harder to teach than preschool," Marlene tells me. "The classes are bigger, so the teachers have to captivate a larger audience, and the school is much bigger. What really counts is getting the kids to love school, to want to learn how to read. It's the transition year—it should be the golden year."

Barbara Tellechea's own learning curve shows how much someone like Marlene can contribute. Barbara had taught second grade for fourteen years, and when she switched to kindergarten she started out by treating her five-year-olds as if they were simply pint-sized seven-year-olds. "I needed all the children around me all the time so I could keep control," she says. "The master teacher would come in and I'd still be on the rug with all the boys and girls. I wanted them to learn a hundred words fast." But when the class started to spin out of control, Barbara was ready to try something new, and Marlene had a kit bag of suggestions that have worked for her.

As a preschool-to-grade-three movement takes off across the country, "seamless transition" has become the watchword, and this message is slowly beginning to stick.[15] In Union City, every elementary school has been assigned its own Marlene Lupo, a master teacher from the prekindergarten world, to reinvent kindergarten in the minds of those who teach it. As the connections that extend from prekindergarten through high school are reinforced, with learning about what makes for effective teaching going up and down the age ladder, the entire school system benefits.

THE POLITICS OF PRESCHOOL

Early in the school year, when a parent couldn't find a prekindergarten that seemed right for her three-year-old, she called the mayor, Brian Stack. Elsewhere the top city official wouldn't get involved in such a personal matter—it's what a principal normally deals with—but in Union City the impress of politics is felt everywhere. Adriana reports to the superintendent, but she's also beholden to the mayor, and when he reached out to her she responded with alacrity. With excellent reason—not only is the mayor the dominant figure in local affairs, he also doubles as state senator, and from that perch he has been an indispensable ally to early education.

Thanks to Brian's political pull in Trenton, the $13 million tab for the 38,000-square-foot, cutting-edge Hostos early education center, which opened in 2007, was entirely picked up by the state. And when Governor Christie, no fan of early education, floated a proposal to cut state-supported preschool to half a day, Brian came to the rescue. "We need your help," Adriana told him. "We've come so far—it would be a shame to go back ten steps." Brian, who emphasizes the value of early education whenever he's speaking with young parents, reassures her. "I'm always bringing the message of the importance of prekindergarten."

Brian's prowess as a state lawmaker stems from his talent at forging alliances across the aisle. He invites several of his fellow senators, among them a GOP colleague, Tom Kean Jr., the son of a much-admired former governor, to visit Union City and see for themselves what an exceptional preschool looks like. The visit turns Kean and his compatriots into advocates for prekindergarten. Christie moves on to other issues and the threatened cutback never materializes.

Helping to rescue the *Abbott* preschool program is just one of myriad ways in which Brian has insinuated himself in decisions about how the schools are run. His voice can be heard on matters big and small, from securing $180 million for a new high school to hiring a crossing guard. And when he speaks, the district rushes to respond.

5

MOTHER TERESA MEETS
MAYOR DALEY
Good Schools = Smart Politics

In many cities the school district stands on its own, with an elected board, separate from city government, that's empowered to hire and fire, tax and spend. The mayor, while free to offer advice, is powerless to make anything happen. Not so in Union City. Here, school policy and city politics are tightly intertwined in the person of Mayor Brian Stack, known to everyone as Brian.[1]

Since 2000 Brian has been the city's unquestioned leader, winning reelection by margins that would please Vladimir Putin. The mayor, who's in his mid-forties, vows that he'll remain on the job as long as the voters will have him. Two years after being elected, he won the power to appoint the school board, and its members act in the long shadow he casts. They rubber-stamped his decision to name Sandy Sanger, a political comrade-in-arms, as superintendent in 2003. Wearing a second hat as state senator, he has secured hundreds of millions from the state's coffers to build new schools, including the megalithic $180 million high school.

There's considerable disagreement, both among academics and educators, about whether mayoral control of the schools is a good thing. In some locales, putting the mayor in charge and making him accountable for the results works well, while in others it has been noisily controversial. In Union City mayoral control has been a blessing, at least to date, because it has secured the stability essential to an effective school system.[2]

Still, a public official, even one as powerful and as committed to the welfare of his hometown as Brian, can only accomplish so much. His options are constricted by the changing demography of Union City—on one side increasing poverty and joblessness and, on the other, a growing number of young professionals drawn to the city by its relatively cheap prices and proximity to Manhattan who aren't interested in the city's welfare. Over time, these gathering forces will have a marked, if as yet undefined, impact on the school system. And Brian won't be in office forever—who knows what role the next mayor will decide to play? That's why it's worth detouring into the land of politics.

"Brian Is 24–7"

Union City Superintendent Sandy Sanger eases his burly frame into a red leather banquette at the Coach House Diner. It's the first day of school, and now, at the end of a grueling twelve-hour day, Sandy finally has a chance to unwind. As he tucks into his steak, his cell phone rings. The mayor is on the line. "Hey, Brian," Sandy says, steadying himself for whatever is to come.

Sitting across the table, I can hear Brian's booming, angry voice. "The buses that are supposed to pick up the special needs kids blew it. All day long I've been getting calls from hysterical parents. Some of their kids were never picked up and some of them didn't make it home when they were supposed to."

This barrage comes as news to Sandy, though he quickly figures out what has gone wrong. The drivers working for the company that the school district, in a budget-trimming move, had hired to ferry disabled children to school don't have their routes down pat. They are getting lost on Union City's narrow streets.

Brian wants to fire the company immediately, but Sandy talks him down. "Let's give it a few days," he says, and by the end of the week the drivers have gotten their routes down pat.

Anywhere else, parents whose children go missing would call the principal's office, or maybe the school superintendent or the police, to find out what's happened. They wouldn't think of phoning the mayor, and even if the idea did cross their minds they'd be shuttled from one aide to another. But Brian is the first stop for anyone in Union City with a beef, whether it's about a city agency or a landlord or an employer. Even complaints about rude service at the post office come his way, though it's not within his purview. Everyone who has met the mayor knows his cell phone number, 201-376-1942, because it's handwritten on each of his business cards, and he receives about 200 calls a day.

"I am available seven days a week. I am only a call away," says a flyer distributed by his office. People know that all those calls will be answered promptly—the mayor checks his messages hourly—and that he'll do whatever he can for them. "Brian is 24–7," says Tom Highton, the former school superintendent. "There's no one like him—literally."

But the course of Union City politics hasn't always run so smoothly. Over the course of a generation, a take-no-prisoners fight raged, and the fallout profoundly affected the schools.

Take-No-Prisoners Politics

In Hudson County, home to Union City, politics has long been a blood sport, kickboxing in suit and tie. Next door in Jersey City, the legendary Frank Hague ran one of the country's most commanding and corrupt machines for over three decades.

"I am the law," Boss Hague said, and he meant it. His influence reached to Trenton, where his puppets were elected governor, and Washington, where his get-out-the-vote support for Franklin Roosevelt was rewarded with federal funds for a huge medical center complex (the maternity wing is named for Hague's mother). As mayor, Hague never earned more than $8,500 a year, but by the time he died in 1956, ensconced in a Park Avenue penthouse, fearful that if he crossed the Hudson River he'd be indicted, he had amassed a fortune estimated at $10 million.

While Hague has been dead for nearly sixty years, the legacy of corruption lives on. So many elected officials in the Garden State have been sent to prison that the phrase "crooked Jersey politician" has come to be used almost as a single word, and when two veteran observers wrote about New Jersey politics, they titled their book *The Soprano State*.[3]

Although Bill Musto, Union City's dynamic mayor during much of the 1960s and 1970s, never had as much clout as Hague did, no one doubted that he ran the show. "Anything in Union City gotta go by Bill Musto first," says Anthony Olszewski, recounting how his father went to the mayor to get an assault charge dropped.[4]

But Musto was no hack. Astutely, he reached out to the city's fast-growing Cuban American constituency, finding jobs for the newcomers and becoming an early advocate of bilingual education. Bob Menendez, an ambitious young politician who as a twenty-year-old won election to the school board, became his protégé and heir apparent.

In 1982 the four-term mayor was hauled into federal court and charged with taking millions of dollars in kickbacks. The court case divided the city. On one side stood the pro-Musto faction, convinced that the charges were trumped up, while a reform faction, led by Menendez, thought otherwise. The protégé testified against his boss, who was convicted of racketeering.

The saga didn't end there. Despite his conviction, Musto was reelected, defeating Menendez, and when he went to prison his wife succeeded him as mayor. The ensuing battle intruded into every domain, dividing the merchants on Bergenline Avenue, Union City's main shopping street, generating splits in the churches and union halls and even within families.

Inside the school system, the war also raged. Political loyalty had always played a part in who got the top jobs, but now loyalty became the sole criterion. From teacher's aides to superintendents, careers were made or wrecked because of which side you were on.

Sandy Sanger, a principal at the time, stood with the Musto forces, and when the Menendez faction came into office he was punished accordingly. Although Sanger couldn't be fired because he had tenure as a principal, he was put through the bureaucratic equivalent of hell, forced to manage a school with 1,400 students and notoriously inept teachers without a single administrative staffer to help him. "They really went after me," Sandy recalls. "They hung me out to dry."

Bob Menendez—"a man always in a hurry," as Kay Licausi, a political consultant and his former aide, describes him—became a congressman in 1993. But although he was heading to Washington, he had no intention of absenting himself from local affairs. He anointed his successor, longtime ally Bruce Walters; and four years later, when Walters died in office, Menendez tapped

Rudy Garcia, a thirty-four-year-old Cuban American lawyer with a Colum-bia University pedigree, for the job.[5]

Dynasties inevitably weaken over time, though, and after Walters's death, Brian Stack emerged as a formidable challenger to the Menendez machine. Brian was a phenom. He was working for Mayor Musto as a twelve-year-old; and two years later he started a civic association, running it out of his home, to take care of families in need. That operation became his political base. In 1998 Garcia won a costly election against Brian, but only by 400 votes, and once in office he floundered. When he inexplicably turned on Menendez, his old mentor, he found himself badly outmaneuvered. "We made his life a living hell," says Kay Licausi, who was working for Menendez at the time. Faced with the almost-certain prospect of being defeated in a recall election, Garcia resigned in 2000.

Mayor Superman

Brian Stack became the only Union City politician left standing, and Menen-dez, a political realist who later won a U.S. Senate seat, sued for peace. In 2000, with Menendez's backing, Brian was elected mayor. In the years since then, his limitless appetite for hard work and his insatiable need to bond with his constituents have made him, by all accounts, the most popular mayor in the city's history.

In 2003 Brian became what Jerseyites call a "double dipper," continuing as mayor while winning election to the state assembly, and four years later he was elected to the state senate. In the 2010 mayoral election he obliterated his opponent, garnering close to 90% of the vote.

Victories by such huge margins come rarely in American politics. What makes those outsized wins, and the clout that accompanies them, so re-markable is the fact that in an overwhelmingly Latino community, where many of the residents know no English, Brian is a third-generation Union City native of Irish ancestry whose Spanish doesn't go much beyond *buenos dias*.

Take a walk in any neighborhood of this densely packed, 1.27-square-mile city—pass by Jay's Apparel, the Argentina Bakery, Style's Barbershop, La Gran Via Restaurant, the more than three hundred *mama y papa* businesses that flank Bergenline Avenue, or else head for the numbered side streets with their three- and four-story apartments overflowing with families—and even though it's not election season, in many windows you'll see posters of Mayor Brian Stack, ruddy and bespectacled, his dark hair slicked back, wearing a dark suit and conservative tie and smiling his boyish smile. These visible displays of loyalty recall the time, half a century ago, when in windows across America you would see posters of JFK. The business cards with Brian's scribbled phone number, the calls from anguished parents with the quick follow-up—this attention to detail explains how he has claimed the affection of his city.

Sometimes the mayor sheds his Clark Kent costume and behaves as if he's Superman, on hand wherever he's most needed. He's constantly driving around the city with Mark Albiez, his chief of staff, in search of things to fix and problems to solve.

Even the seemingly trivial can catch his attention. When Brian spots a burned-out streetlight, he orders Tito Rivas, who runs the public works department, to get it replaced. "It's a crime hazard," he tells me, and a couple of days later he checks to make sure the street is lit. "We need a new sweep to identify vacant buildings," he says to police chief Charles Everett, a friend since boyhood, because those buildings can spell trouble. "Just pull up to 520 New York Avenue, you'll see that it is vacant."

At 2 A.M. on a Saturday night, once again on the prowl with Mark, he grabs his cell phone and calls the police. "Send a car," he says. "There's someone urinating at 10th Avenue and New York." A few months earlier, he'd witnessed the same behavior during a midday drive. He told Mark to stop the car, leapt out and made a citizen's arrest of the nonplussed offender. "Hi, Brian," some kids shouted while he was in action.

On Christmas morning in 2011, a Sunday, snow began to fall heavily across the Northeast, and by Monday night Union City was buried under nearly three feet of snow. Elsewhere, mayors called out the snowplows and stood by. From the first sign of wintry trouble, Brian and Mark were manning the snowplows themselves. They didn't make it home until Tuesday night.

"It's like going to Harvard"—that's how Mark, who has been immersed in the rough-and-tumble world of Jersey politics since he graduated from Rutgers a decade ago, describes his education in street politics, Brian Stack–style. One afternoon when Mark and I are driving around Union City, I spot several scorched apartment houses. You can expect fires to occur with some frequency in a place crammed with dilapidated buildings. Without having to ask, I know that the mayor will be on the scene whenever there's a fire. "Has he ever gone into a burning building to rescue someone?" I ask, reasonably confident that not even this mayor could be so hypercommitted, but I'm wrong. "Brian has had to be resuscitated several times by the paramedics," Mark tells me.[6]

The mayor's workday typically starts at 8 A.M. and stretches until late at night. On weekends he's likely to officiate at a score of weddings, one right after another, and he uses the money he receives to pay for the tickets to charity benefits that he's invited to. Most days his lunch consists of a slice of pizza wolfed down in the car, and several times a week dinner is a rubber chicken banquet. His marriage broke down a few years ago because he didn't have much time for a home life.

In the bathroom next to his office there sits a constantly replenished bottle of Extra Strength Mylanta Calci-Tabs. "Everyone here is being treated for ulcers. It's a high-stress job," says Mark, who recounts Bob Menendez's worried remark to Brian. "You can't keep this up—it's going to kill you."

Power, as the mayor knows from his own experience, can be fleeting, and so in every election he has had to prove to his potential rivals that he remains a force to be reckoned with. On June 7, 2011, primary day, the mercury topped 100 degrees. But despite this scorching heat, more than 16,000 residents— "monster numbers," headlined the *New Jersey Journal*—turned out to vote for him in the race for a state senate seat. Hundreds of people, many of whom Brian had personally helped, fanned out across the city, knocking on doors to round up voters and standing on street corners to hand out leaflets.

With this turnout, far bigger than other Hudson County politicians could manage, Brian was sending a message to anyone with the temerity to go after him—back off. "If you are using the hammer hard enough, no one will get in the way," Mark explains.[7]

Many politicians in Hudson County despise the mayor because he has refused to cozy up to the machine, instead setting up his own political organization, Union City First. This is old-style city politics, but with a twist— it's machine politics with a one-man machine. To Sal Vega, the former mayor of neighboring West New York, the sea of "Stack-for-Senate" signs brings to mind not JFK but Red Square, with Stack as Lenin running a "police state." Brian gives as good as he gets: "If [the county political organization] did more work helping people instead of negotiating in backrooms, we'd all be better off."[8]

"Union City First" aptly describes Brian's legislative priorities. Sitting in the senate chambers in Trenton, he extracts every dollar that he can for his city. He's a pragmatist who has made it a point to befriend whoever holds power at the moment. When Democrats occupied the governor's office, Brian made himself useful, and he has become especially close to Republican governor Chris Christie.

As you'd expect, Democrats have frequently done battle with the governor. After a knockdown fight over the budget, Steve Sweeney, the president of the state senate, slammed Christie as "a bully and a punk," declaring that he "wanted to punch him in the head"—and Sweeney has often been on the governor's side.[9] For his part, Brian has opted for flattery. At a town hall meeting in Union City, he made headlines by introducing Christie as "the greatest governor this state has ever had."[10] If that paean wasn't sufficiently heretical, he took on the unions by sponsoring the governor's pension reform plan that they loathe.

"Brian likes bold people—that's what it boils down to," says Mark. "Like Christie, he's not afraid to speak his mind, to go on the offensive when he needs to. And he makes his 'outsider' identity work for him. It's part of his identity." The *Star-Ledger*, the biggest-circulation paper in the state, sees things differently: "being a suck-up has its privileges."[11]

It is axiomatic that politicians reward their friends and punish their enemies, and Brian's good deeds have paid off handsomely. "No community has gotten more school construction money," says Kay Licausi, and no community has received as much money to build parks either. In October 2011 the governor delivered $13 million, one-eighth of the city's budget, in "transitional aid" targeted to municipalities hard hit by the recession. With Union City confronting a deficit because of the rising costs of firefighting and pensions, this infusion of cash made for a fine early Christmas present. It also cemented Brian's local reputation as a man of accomplishments.

17,000 Turkeys, 10,000 Toys

Every Tuesday and Thursday, the mayor spends half a day meeting with constituents. On one such December day, the line outside his office begins to form before 7:00 A.M. Outside it's below freezing, and those who are waiting, many of them recent arrivals from Latin America, are shivering, stamping their feet and rubbing their hands to get warm.

About fifty people are on hand when the doors swing open an hour later, and another hundred or so will trickle in throughout the morning. Those who have immigration issues are channeled to a specialist. The rest sit, one by one, at a fifteen-foot-long mahogany table with Brian. Piled on the table are towers of files, one pile for each city department. The telephone is in near-constant use as Brian interrupts conversations to call the responsible city official, seeking quick action. "It's the mayor of Union City," he says in his broad Jersey accent.

What unfolds over the next three hours, and what is repeated twice a week, every week, could be lifted from one of the *Godfather* movies. People lay their problems before the mayor, their presence saturated with *respeto*. I hope that you can do something for me, they say, and I would be honored to do something for you.

Rodolfo, who's first in the queue, tells Brian that he was laid off from a construction job without getting paid.[12] "My mother, who's in Ecuador, is dying," he says in Spanish, tears welling up in his eyes, "and I'm sending money home for cancer treatment. Without it she will die. I have no money for rent and I'm going to be kicked out of my room." Rodolfo has brought the contractor's business card and Brian has it xeroxed. "We track down these builders and write them a letter," he tells me. "Seventy-five percent of the time we're successful." Then he turns to his aide, Mark Albiez. "We need to get him some food too, and help with his rent."

This is where the Civic Association, which Brian still runs, enters the picture. It's an old-fashioned "chicken-in-every-pot" enterprise—a turkey in every oven, actually, since the association delivers about 17,000 turkeys for Thanksgiving. At Christmas, 10,000 families queue up for toys, perhaps a doll or a box of crayons, often the only gift these kids will receive.

Throughout the morning, the mayor scribbles detailed notes on a yellow legal pad. Chris, a longtime resident, complains that the police took forever to come after he called. "They should be there in two or three minutes. No excuses—they have to respond," the mayor says, getting the police chief on the phone. Then he turns to me. "I knocked on Chris's door thirty years ago in my first campaign, when I was fourteen."

Emilio, a landlord, has been cramming three or four families into a single apartment, illegally installing locks on his tenants' bedroom doors. When he tried to evict one of his tenants he learned that the tenant had already appealed to the mayor, and now he is making his pitch. Emilio insists that he knew nothing about the locks, but Brian isn't buying it, and when the mayor berates him for the way he is treating his tenants he stares down at the floor.

"I'm calling the Housing Department," says Brian. "We have to resolve this without going to court."

Leticia comes looking for part-time work for her son Diego, who's in high school. "We really need the money," she says. "There's a grant for summer and after school jobs," says Brian. "How's Diego doing in school? He has to keep his grades up to be eligible." Then he asks after Leticia's mother, who's in a nursing home, for he knows the family.

Sometimes the callers make an appearance simply to convey their gratitude. A delegation of immigrants from Colombia thanks the mayor for having named a new park "Colombia Park," and they are followed by a Dominican contingent that has a park named for its national hero, Juan Pablo Duarte. That organization will be marching in a Manhattan parade and the members have come by to collect a flowery official proclamation. The opening of a city park or plaza, a school or museum, affords an opportunity to pay tribute to one constituency or another—the police and the firefighters, the Colombians and the Dominicans—and because of Brian's pull in Trenton there have been many such occasions.

This is the aspect of the mayor's job—more precisely, the way Brian defines the job—that he most relishes. "Delegation" can't be found in his lexicon—if he had the time, he would handle even the tiniest details himself. When Firefighters Memorial Park was being designed, he personally selected the flowers. He has turned his obsessive-compulsive behavior, coupled with a politician's deep-seated need to be loved, into a political asset. "People don't go to city commission meetings because they can come to me," Brian tells me. "They bring their complaints about drug dealers because they say they don't trust the police. They tell me the intimate details of their lives. It's a nice feeling."

Many of the men and women who sit across from Brian at that mahogany table have the same abiding wish—to find a job. "I'll do anything," they say, and you know they mean it. This web of ties also becomes a web of obligations, and almost all of them add: "Please let me know what I can do to help out in your campaign."

Brian can sometimes tap into a grant, as in Diego's case, and sometimes he can turn to the North Hudson Community Action Corporation, a social services agency run by Chris Irizarry, a reliable vote on the city council. "Go to Olga at the community action center," he advises the supplicant, "and tell her that Brian sent you. If they have a job I'll recommend you. You have my cell number."

But much of the time the mayor has no good news to convey. In years past, city jobs were dispensed as rewards for fealty, but Brian has been forced to slash the budget. Since 2000, when he became mayor, budget cuts have halved the city's workforce, from 700 to 350, as retiring workers have not been replaced. The police department did away with the deputy chief and inspector positions, and Brian eliminated the position of city business administrator, taking on the job himself. To spread the public largesse, some full-time jobs have been split into part-time positions, but those jobs never paid much, and now the salaries barely keep families above the poverty line.

At noon, the mayor's office closes. An apologetic staffer invites those who are still waiting to come to a nearby firehouse, where a mobile city hall will be held that afternoon. Many of them show up, and so do others who live in the neighborhood, another hundred or so, for in Union City the sea of human misery seems bottomless. But the flyer that promotes these meet-Brian events contains a caveat: *"Due to current economic circumstances the mayor's office is unable to offer employment to residents."*

DISMAL ECONOMICS

Classic accounts of machine politics trace its demise to an influx of New Deal money that the bosses couldn't control as well as to the growth of a middle class uninterested in Thanksgiving turkeys and Christmas toys. But this model doesn't fit Union City. There, not a single public dollar, whatever its source, gets spent without the mayor's say-so; and because of the dolorous economy and their lack of skills, these immigrants have not followed their predecessors' path to prosperity.[13]

The economic statistics tell a grim tale. Think of those numbers as a misery index, with real lives lurking beneath the statistical surface.

During the 1990s the Brookings Institution ranked Union City among the nation's ninety-two most economically depressed municipalities, and the New Jersey Municipal Distress Index placed it at number three on its list, in worse shape than notorious Newark. The situation hasn't improved since then. Hudson County's poverty rate, 15.1% in 2010, is the state's highest, and while there's no city-by-city calculation, estimates put the Union City figure at close to 20%. Three out of every ten children are living below the poverty line, nearly 50% above the national average, and if you add in the near-poor you've accounted for a majority of youngsters in the municipality.

Immigrants have always come to Union City looking for work, the Jacob's Ladder leading out of poverty, but decent jobs are nearly impossible to come by. The unemployment rate, 13% at the end of 2013, is almost double the national average. One adult in eight cannot find a job, a figure that doesn't take into account those who have settled for part-time work or have given up searching.

Here as elsewhere, skilled workers have the best chance of finding employment, but the new generation of immigrants, which makes up more than half the city's adult population, comes with few skills. Forty-one percent, twice the statewide average, didn't graduate from high school, and just 13% have a college degree.

Warehouse jobs are among the few steady jobs paying decent wages, but warehouse workers are expected to have experience using a forklift and other heavy equipment. What's more, English is required, even to work in a warehouse. That's often a deal-breaker, since only 29% of those born abroad say they speak English "very well." These jobs aren't open to anyone lacking proof that they're in the country legally, and it's estimated that at least a quarter of the city's population is undocumented. When they do find work, they are putting themselves at the mercy of rapacious employers, forced to accept below-minimum wages, dangerous working conditions, and bosses who demand sexual favors.

The housing picture looks equally bleak. Economists consider housing to be affordable when the rent is no more than a quarter of a family's income, and by that metric two-thirds of the tenants in Union City can't afford their rent. Half of them spend at least 35% of their paycheck on rent, a burden that puts them perpetually on the verge of being evicted. Nor do those who own their own homes have it easy. The average Hudson County homeowner pays 7.5% of his income on property taxes, among the biggest hits in the nation, and in Union City, like the other communities in the county, the tax bill has been going up by an average of 3% or 4% a year.

The Power of Trust

Dismal statistics can be mustered for any down-and-out city—indeed, numbers like these are the usual measure of down-and-out—but they tell only a partial truth. In many cities, public blight accompanies individual poverty, neighborhoods descend into chaos, and the public schools degenerate into holding pens for no-hopers. But Union City remains vibrant.[14]

Civic life is thriving. Polls taken by a Republican pollster at the mayor's behest show that almost everyone who lives here believes that the city in general, and the mayor in particular, has their back. The many enclaves that comprise this community are flourishing—the multiplicity of Latino cultures, the Mexican-Americans and Ecuadorian-Americans and Colombian-Americans, each with its own hyphenated American association; the Muslims and Hasidic Jews, each with its own house of worship and its own school; and the newest arrivals from countries like India and Yemen. Despite the grim figures, Union City would surely rank high in a survey of personal happiness.[15]

The public schools both reflect and help to mold this sense of identity. In *Organizing Schools for Improvement,* a massive study of Chicago public schools, sociologist Anthony Bryk finds a straight-line connection between poor neighborhoods and failing schools—the worse-off the community, the worse the school. But there is one notable exception—poor Latino schools consistently outperform expectations. The reason boils down to a single word: *trust.*

"The trust levels, inside these schools and out to parents, are stronger," Bryk writes by way of explanation. "These schools tend to be 'nicer places'— students are calm, relations civil etc." That's a thumbnail description of Union City's schools, where the norm of *respeto* prevails. "Latino neighborhoods tend to have significantly more social capital and neighborhood organizations that create a basis for this" than other poor enclaves, Bryk adds. The personal bonds are tighter, grassroots organizations forge stronger connections, and the sense of belonging is more powerful.[16]

Those networks can powerfully change the quality of people's lives. "Community connectedness is not just about warm fuzzy tales of civic triumph," writes Harvard political scientist Robert Putnam in *Bowling Alone.* "In measurable and well-documented ways, social capital makes an enormous difference to our lives."[17] And as the eminent sociologist James Coleman has written, summing up decades of research, the fact that kids are embedded "in the enclaves of adults. . . . first the family and second, a surrounding community," shapes their futures because it helps them navigate the world.[18]

Bryk and Putnam might very well have been talking about Union City. The one and the many, identity amid diversity—the essence of community connectedness—defines the community and shapes life in the schools as well.

The Yuppie Threat

Demography is destiny, the social scientists say, and it is far from certain that this sense of connectedness—this social capital—can be maintained if the composition of the community changes.[19]

Today, the first thing that any visitor to Union City sees is a chipped, hand-painted sign that hangs over the exit from Route 495: "Embroidery Capital of the World Since 1872." Whether it was luxury fabrics in the 1920s, military insignias during World War II, or delicate designs for fancy night-gowns and confirmation dresses, the industry kept shifting gears to keep pace with the demand. Since the 1980s, however, cheaper goods from abroad have come to dominate the embroidery market and the local indus-try has shrunk to near-nothingness.[20]

That much-photographed sign with its outdated boast offers a reminder that this used to be a blue-collar city that offered good blue-collar jobs to anyone willing to work hard. But now only a quarter of the residents have manufacturing jobs, and they must commute to reach them, while the city jobs that took up some of the slack are rapidly disappearing.

Blue-collar work was Act 1 and public employment Act 2 in the life of this city, but the third act remains to be written. A few miles away, Hoboken pre-sents one possible future. Since the 1980s that city has capitalized on its waterfront location and proximity to Manhattan. A once-blighted commu-nity has reinvented itself as a destination for well-heeled young urbanites, émigrés from Wall Street and Madison Avenue, by making it financially at-tractive for developers to erect luxury condos. The downtown, which used to be mainly boarded up, has become a Saturday night hub, with bars serving craft cocktails, edgy clubs, and push-the-envelope restaurants—New Jer-sey's answer to SoHo. This is the heart of what realtors call the "Gold Coast," with housing prices to match.

Union City, next door to Hoboken, is the logical next stop for the devel-opers. Land costs less, so it's cheaper to build. And the city is only 3.7 miles from Times Square—if you build high enough there's a picture-window view of the Manhattan skyline. Previous mayors were hostile to develop-ment, Brian tells me, but he has taken a different approach. Borrowing ele-ments from Hoboken's strategy, he wooed builders by offering them handsome tax incentives and enticed buyers with five years of reduced property taxes.

By 2007, the mayor's courtships were having the desired effect. That year the city recorded $192 million in new construction and 600 certificates of occupancy, a tenfold increase in just half a decade. Anticipating a new, more upscale clientele, a few trendy restaurants, bars, and art galleries opened, and the city sponsored a municipal art gallery and a cultural center. "Hoboken Comes to Union City," forecast the *New York Times*. While that cheery prediction proved premature, as the recession forced a slowdown in development, the pressure to "Hobokenize" will resume as the economy recovers.[21]

In such a world there's no room for the people who throng the mayor's office, desperate for work—the people whose kids go to Washington School—because escalating housing prices would inevitably force them out. The residents grasp this, and they have registered their unease in the polls that the mayor, ever attentive to his constituency, regularly commissions. In his 2000 run for mayor, Brian promised to develop more taxable property without displacing the residents. "The city was stagnant and developers shied away," he told a *New York Times* reporter in 2005. "We were determined to change that"—to expand the tax base, bringing in revenues that the city badly needs—"but not forget the people living here."[22]

So far the mayor has been able to keep his promise by approving a mix of projects, some priced for families of moderate means, and rewriting the rent control law to spur landlords into fixing up their buildings. But ultimately this approach won't satisfy developers who only want to build high-rise condos with panoramic views of the Manhattan skyline. If Union City is going to maintain its identity, then the mayor will have to perform an exquisite balancing act.

In a city of modest three- and four-story buildings, the fifteen-story Thread Building, the most posh of the new condos, towers over everything, a Gulliver among the Lilliputians. It looks out of place and its residents are out of place as well. Union City serves only as a convenient address for them—"five minutes to Manhattan," as the Thread's website declares—and not a vibrant community. These commuters are unlikely to shop on Bergenline Avenue or eat at La Gran Via or come to the Cuban Day Parade.

Few of the arrivistes will even contemplate sending their children to the local public schools. And few of them will know—or care—about the quality of the school system. For the time being, such well-heeled residents remain a small minority. But if the high-rises with their fine views keep getting built there's no telling how this rootlessness will affect the character of the city and its schools.

THE SCHOOLS AND THE MAYOR

In 2002 Brian Stack added the public schools to his already bulging portfolio, convincing the voters to give him the power to appoint the school board. Depriving citizens of the vote makes for a hard sell, but the mayor pulled it off. "Hold me responsible if things aren't working out" was his pitch, and he received a 5–1 vote of confidence.

Most education reformers regard politics disdainfully, as anathema to good schools. In their influential book *Politics, Markets, and America's Schools*, political scientists John Chubb and Terry Moe fingered politicians as mainly responsible, along with unions, for the sorry state of the schools. They urged that power be taken from school boards and turned over to the unconstrained and presumably untainted market. Less ideologically driven analysts search out seemingly successful school systems, study their policies and the style of their leaders, and extract "best practices" that can be introduced elsewhere. Politics has no place in their story.

But there's really no way to take education out of politics. "Successful educational reform ultimately requires a broad and sustainable coalition of support," as Clarence Stone and his colleagues argue in *Building Civic Capacity*, "and the route to this goes directly through, and not around, politics."[23]

For education as for so much else in Union City, Brian is the go-to man. "We have heated closed-door conversations, like a family, but at the public meeting we present a united front," Jeannette Pena, the chair of Brian's hand-picked school board, tells me. Like every member of the board, her life is intertwined with the mayor's—her husband has known him since their high school days.

"Brian isn't a 'my way or the highway' guy," Jeanette adds. "He'll hear me out." But she draws a blank when I ask her to name a time when the board went against the mayor's wishes.

School politics in Union City couldn't be more straightforward—the school board echoes Brian and Brian backs Superintendent Sandy Sanger. The two men have been personally and politically close for years, and when Tom Highton, who had served since 1989, retired in 2003, Sandy's track record made him the obvious pick for the top job. He had more than paid his dues, managing a 1,400-student k-8 school without any administrative support and distinguishing himself as the first head of the district's preschool program. Although the board went through the motions of conducting a search, there was no doubt that Sandy would be selected. "I said to myself that Sanger is the right choice. He knows our strengths and weaknesses," board member Lenny Calvo told the *Hudson Reporter*.[24] For his part, the mayor is confident that with Sandy running the show the job will get done. His reaction to any school problem, like those missing schoolchildren, is always the same: "Sandy, handle it."

Across the country, school board elections sweep into office insurgents who, whether out of pedagogical differences, pique, or personal ambition, are after the superintendent's scalp. The average tenure of an urban school chief is less than three years. This churning is a recipe for drift, when what's needed is decisiveness.

In *The Color of School Reform*, a classic study of why big city school systems usually fail, political scientist Jeffrey Henig lays out how this brand of politics undermines superintendents' efforts to sustain reforms. An ever-changing cast of board members, each with his own agenda, continually forces the school system to change course. Under those fraught circumstances, teachers and principals understandably become skeptical about their new boss's big plans, for they have seen a parade of superintendents come and go.[25]

Hence the appeal of mayoral sovereignty. After conducting a rigorous statistical analysis, Kenneth Wong and his colleagues conclude, in *The Education Mayor*, that shifting from the old-style elected school board to a mayor-led school system "will lead to significant, positive gains in reading and mathematics." What is happening in Union City suggests why this might be so. Because the superintendent isn't constantly having to look over his shoulder or count votes on the board, he has the luxury of freedom to plan for the long term. That's a big reason why these schools have been able to make sure and steady progress.[26]

To be sure, the longevity of a school chief doesn't necessarily depend on there being a mayor at the helm. Some school boards know how to do their job. In several sizable districts—such as San Francisco Raleigh, North Carolina; and Montgomery County, Maryland—an elected board has given the superintendent ample time to inject major reforms into the lifeblood of the system. Almost invariably, students' test scores have risen and the achievement gap has shrunk.[27]

What's more, mayoral sovereignty shouldn't be regarded as a panacea. In some cities, such as Boston and Baltimore, this shift in authority has led to better schools; elsewhere, as in New York and Chicago, the jury is still out; while in other metropolises, like Detroit, where the state stepped in to assume control of the school system, it failed abysmally. The context matters, of course: a great deal depends on the political and social dynamics of the community, as well as the priorities of the mayor. In this respect Union City has been particularly fortunate. Brian Stack's lengthy tenure in office—thirteen years and counting—has brought revenues and stability to the district.[28]

The mayor watches the schools with a hawk's eye for detail. Every day or two he's on the phone with Sandy, talking about a parent who wants her daughter transferred to another school in the district or a cafeteria worker who complains that she's being harassed by her coworkers or a gang of teenagers whom he saw hanging out in front of the high school when he drove past an hour earlier. He wants to be sure the schools are safe—if the semiannual report on school violence shows an uptick he'll be sure to ask why. He also wants the schools to be academically strong. Partly this is a matter of the fierce hometown pride of a third-generation resident of Union City and partly it's a matter of politics. The glowing reputation of the schools burnishes his reputation in the community. It is also a calling card in Trenton, where the quality of the schools in his home town is perceived as a measure of effective leadership.

The mayor's immersion in education plainly makes for smart politics. Many voters have children in the schools, and what they think about their sons' and daughters' education rubs off on him. Nowadays, when Brian surveys the community, more than 70% of the residents report that the schools are doing a good job, a vote of confidence that few districts can match.

The stellar reputation of the school system also earns him points in Trenton. "When I'm there I talk up what Union City has done," the mayor tells me. "People get that we're doing the right thing. Christie sees districts not performing. But he's impressed by Union City. 'How do you do it?' he asks."

But more than politics is at work here—Brian's palpable, visceral bond with these youngsters motivates him as well. Before he became mayor, teachers and administrators participated in politics purely out of expediency, holding their nose as they did so, but that's no longer so. "I always played it both ways, professionally and politically," says John Bennetti, the innovator whom Sandy is counting on to turn the city's new high school into an academic powerhouse. John tells me that he and his politically connected compatriots are known, only half-jokingly, as "made men," yet he doesn't regard going door to door during election season, praising the mayor's commitment to education, as an obligation. "I know it sounds hokey, because it's not how you usually think about politicians, but Brian really cares about kids."

It's easy to be cynical about the motivations of politicians, who habitually put their reelection above everything else. But Brian, unlike the classic boss, cares about more than remaining in office. Eavesdrop on one of his many appearances at a parents' night as he implores parents to take an interest in their children's education. Dig deeper and you'll learn about the funerals for a teenager who committed suicide and a girl who died in a car crash that his civic association quietly paid for.

Part Boss Daley, part Mother Teresa: Brian Stack is passionate about wanting the kids of Union City—*his* kids—to do well in school, to anticipate a future that matches the hopes of their parents. For that to happen, secondary education had to be resuscitated.

CHARTRES ON THE HUDSON

By the time Brian Stack became mayor, the elementary and middle schools in Union City had become unrecognizably better since the threatened state takeover in 1988. But the two high schools had evaded reform. The buildings were ancient and rundown, and the education taking place there left much to be desired. The mayor and the newly appointed school chief agreed—something dramatic had to be done.

The chance to act came in 2003, when the New Jersey Department of Education selected Union City as one of six school "demonstration projects." Governor Jim McGreevey played a big role in securing the $180 million needed for a state-of-the-art high school, and Brian, an assemblyman at the time, had a lot to do with winning McGreevey's support.

To Sandy and his deputy, Silvia Abbato, this project represented the golden opportunity to transform secondary education in their city. It didn't matter to them that many experts were assailing big schools as factories for batch-processing students or that the Gates Foundation, the biggest non-profit player in the field of education, had become so convinced that small was beautiful that it was spending millions to split scores of old school-houses into diminutive academies.[29] Their rationale was partly pragmatic. They knew that Trenton wouldn't fund two regulation-sized high schools, since in choosing "demonstration projects" it was after something bold. Besides, the new high school, more than the vest-pocket parks and plazas, would stand as the mayor's legacy, his impress on the city landscape and confirmation of his political clout.

What's more, a big high school could offer so much that, because of scale, the old schools had never been able to provide—a plethora of new courses, everything from robotics and Mandarin to fashion design and modern dance, calculated to excite young minds. Once the plan was formulated, Silvia started dreaming about a school that gave its students everything they could find at a progressive suburban secondary school. She imagined a school that would aspire to being not just a good city school but a good school, period.

The new high school is to Union City what the Cathedral of Our Lady of Chartres is to Chartres or the Opera House is to Sydney—its symbol and showplace, its bid for grandeur. It sprawls across four-and-a-half acres of this cramped city, and from the athletic field, which has been scooped out of the roof, you can see the Manhattan skyline. The 360,000-square-foot building contains sixty-six classrooms, fitted out to a standard that would have made Steve Jobs smile, each outfitted with Mac computers, interactive white-boards, and Wi-Fi; science labs better equipped than you'd find on many college campuses; a 910-seat theater that would be the envy of an Off-Broadway troupe; a pediatric clinic; art, dance, and music studios that meet professional standards; a crèche for the infants of teenagers, intended to keep those parents in school; and sports facilities straight out of "Friday Night Lights."

"It was like walking through the gates of Disneyland," marveled football coach Wil Valdez, remembering the first time he laid eyes on it. To an Environmental Protection Agency staffer sent to check out the facility, it looked like "a $25,000 [tuition] private school."

At the October 3, 2009 ribbon-cutting for the new building, Jim McGreevey, the former governor, spoke movingly to the overflow crowd about his old colleague. "Brian came into my office and he told me, 'My dream is to have a school as good as any school in the State of New Jersey for the children of Union City.'" As McGreevey continued the applause swelled. "There are politicians who build monuments to themselves and then there are those who build monuments to children. Brian Stack didn't ask for politics and didn't ask for himself. He asked for the children of Union City."[30]

A scandal had driven McGreevey out of office five years earlier, but that didn't faze the mayor. In his book, the only thing that counted was the fact that the former governor had worked hard to make the high school a reality, and that's why Brian had the school's media center named after him. "No one was a bigger advocate for Union City," Brian told the gathering, "and we should never forget that."

Getting the new school built was a coup for the mayor. For the educators, though, this shiny new building was only the start. They knew that fulfilling the dream of making it an academic powerhouse—"as good as any school in the State of New Jersey," as the mayor envisioned it—would be at even harder to accomplish.

6

CAN THESE EAGLES SOAR?
Union City High School

At Union City High, the first day of the 2010–2011 school year has less to do with education than logistics. There's no ebullient Les Hanna waiting on the front steps to embrace the children, as at George Washington Elementary School, no teacher like Alina Bossbaly to create "the pie." Instead there's Dave Wilcomes, a hovering, eggshell-bald, and craggy sexagenarian principal who stands at the entrance of the school, along with a phalanx of assistant principals, and watches the students pour into the building.

These men look harried, and no wonder—2,400 adolescents must find their way to their new homerooms. The sophomores, cosseted the year before in a school just for ninth graders, are setting foot here for the first time and they look like lost puppies. They have to navigate a building so immense that security guards glide through the corridors on Segways and so intricate in its multiwing design that even teachers who have already spent a year here sometimes lose their way.

If we build it they will come—this enormous high school, which opened the year before, is Union City's field of dreams. From Brian Stack to the parishioners of St. Augustine Church across the street from Washington School and the lunchtime crowd at Terry's Coffee Shop on Bergenline

Avenue and the social workers at North Hudson Community Action—the people who send their kids to the public schools—the hope is that this spare-no-cost environment for learning will inspire students to become as impressive as the space itself. Everyone hopes that the school will be first class, and not just by the minimum-expectations standard of similarly poverty-ridden cities.

First things first—this year's goal is to shed the dread label of being a "school in need of improvement." For some years, the old high schools in Union City languished in this netherworld, and if the new high school is going to break the pattern, 10 % more students must pass the state's graduation exams in English and math. That's hyperambitious, for it is almost unheard-of for a school to jump from "level 5" purgatory, its current status, to a state-issued seal of approval in a single year. What's more, it's extremely rare for an urban high school with a comparable student profile to emerge from under the state's thumb—not only in New Jersey but anywhere in the country.

UN-PASSIVE RESISTANCE

In the 1990s, even as the rest of the Union City school system was charging ahead, the high schools remained mired in the past. Late in the decade, Fred Carrigg tried to do something about this, and he seemed like the right candidate for the job. Fred was already a local legend, renowned for having spearheaded the redesign of kindergarten through eighth grade instruction, and in the process rescuing the school system from the nightmare of state takeover. To this day, longtime teachers and administrators will tell you that his ungentle prodding made them better at their craft.[1]

When it came to reengineering the high schools, Fred's initial step was to secure foundation grants aimed at encouraging more graduates to attend top-tier universities. These initiatives were peripheral to most of the teachers and so they passed unnoticed. With the summer academics and Ivy League tours paid for by the grants, the fortunes of the top students did indeed improve. But when Fred pushed for major revisions in how the high schools were run, adapting teaching strategies that worked well for younger kids to fit the needs of adolescents, he found himself in the midst of a war zone.

In Union City as elsewhere, high schools have become notorious for warding off the efforts of those who would remake them. Most are considerably bigger than elementary or middle schools, not intimate communities where a culture of *abrazos* prevails but stony citadels with walled-off units and layers of bureaucracy. And while elementary and middle school teachers are generally a compliant bunch—as Alina Bossbaly says, "We're good girls and we do what we're told"—secondary school teachers have a very different sense of themselves. In general they take their cues about teaching from what's done in college, concentrating on what material to cover rather than ways of enlivening their lessons.[2]

"High school teachers play rough," Fred laments, thinking back to that time, and they weren't afraid to curse him out. "You have stolen my thunder, you have ruined my life!" a ninth grade English teacher screamed after being told that his beloved *Lord of the Rings* trilogy had become an eighth grade staple. When persuasion failed, Fred's style could turn abrasive, which didn't play well. "Teachers would duck into their classrooms when they saw him coming down the corridor," says a senior administrator, who recalls watching as the doors slammed shut.

While Fred did make some converts, the tried-and-dreary, the teacher talking nonstop to neatly aligned rows of zoned-out students, remained the norm; and when the foundation funding dried up, he found himself pushed aside. Soon afterward he departed for an attractive job in the state education department.

The transformation of secondary education in Union City didn't get into full swing until 2009, with the opening of the showpiece high school. But even then, the choice of Dave Wilcomes, the principal of the old Union Hill High, to run the school slowed the pace of change.

Dave had a reputation as a disciplinarian, and that kind of toughness was regarded as critical in handling 2400 hormonally charged adolescents. But what he lacked, crucially, were the skills of an educational leader, someone who could lift the high school out of the academic doldrums. After a rocky inaugural year, authority was divided—Dave would manage the building; and John Bennetti, a kinder and gentler version of Fred Carrigg, would have sole authority over instruction.

One School, Two Worlds

On my first visit to Union City High I enter via the Eagles' Nest, the fancy name for the lobby. After stopping at the security desk I walk past the stairs, labeled the "Grand Staircase," and head for Dave Wilcomes's capacious office.

The principal has prepared for this meeting by piling stacks of memorabilia on a conference table, and more boxes are resting on the floor.

Much of this material commemorates sports history at the old Union Hill High, where Dave coached football for six years before becoming principal. The pile includes stacks of programs from football games gone by; team photographs; a yellowing album of the history of the "Hillers"; and photos of the 18,000-seat Roosevelt Stadium, a New Deal project that had been home to the annual Thanksgiving Day game between Union Hill and Emerson, which was demolished to make room for the new high school.

The emotion ginned up by the Turkey Day game, which had been played since 1917 (the final tally was forty wins for each high school and nine ties), exemplified the antagonism between these schools. "That rivalry was fierce," Dave tells me. "The players, band, and majorettes took off the Monday through Wednesday before the game to practice. All the students from the winning school got a half day off on Monday. When I became the football coach it was like being president of the United States." Union Hill served the uptown neighborhood, while Emerson students came from downtown, and even though the city stretches less than two miles, uptown and downtown saw themselves as entirely separate. "When I was growing up I never went below 32nd Street," Dave remembers. "That was the dividing line."

Sherril-Marie Henriquez, a 2010 Union City High graduate who went on to Columbia, remembers Turkey Day in a way that Dave would appreciate. "There would be pep rallies for two days before the game, a homecoming king and queen and a mascot—I was the Emerson mascot, a bulldog—and the floats, which went around the stadium during the game, cost a couple of thousand dollars. People would talk about the score for months afterward."

Over the decades, the two schools had defined themselves as rivals, and that made the merger a potentially toxic venture. Police feared that that the students might carry their hostilities into the new building, with troublemakers clashing in the corridors. Sherril-Marie harbors unhappy recollections of the new school's first year. "Everyone hated the transition. There were two tiers—the top students were treated with respect but the others were spoken to like dogs."

Animosity among the adults was inevitable, since jobs were at stake. Instead of two football coaches there would be one, instead of two heads of the science departments there would be one, and even the smallest decisions were viewed through the rival-schools lens. "I know why I got my classroom," a teacher who didn't receive the space she had requested grumbled to Dave. "I come from Emerson and you're a Union Hill guy."

Although Dave strove for fairness, that teacher's portrayal hit the mark, for he was a Hiller to the core. He had gone to Union Hill, where he lettered in football, and after graduating from college he spent thirty-nine years there, as a teacher, coach, and principal. "Sometimes I wish I were still at Union Hill," he muses. "I knew what it meant to be the principal of a small high school."

Dave Wilcomes relishes the role of the genial host. When we leave his office for a tour of the building, he shows off the theater and the dance studio and lingers over the uniquely designed rooftop athletic field. In reciting his accomplishments, he takes particular pride in having maintained order on the campus and damping down the interschool tensions. He has kept the local gangs—the Uptown Zoo, Dominicans Don't Play, the Trinitarios, the Latino Kings, and the rest—off the premises. He helped pick the school's nickname, the "Soaring Eagles," to symbolize a new identity, and its colors, navy, silver, and white, to avoid colors favored by the gangs, red and black. He mentions having to handle "drugs, gangs, pregnancy, gay problems," leaving it to me to sort out how "gay" figures in this equation.

These mundane tasks rarely get discussed outside administrators' circles, but they must be done well if a school isn't going to descend into chaos. Someone has to make sure that the fire drills come off smoothly, that students can squeeze all the classes they need into their schedules, and that 600 seniors flow smoothly across the stage at graduation. "We were in and out in ninety minutes," Dave boasts, describing the school's first commencement. "No one listens to the speeches. Parents just want to see their child get handed his diploma."

Over the course of several conversations, Dave has nothing to say about what is being done to improve teaching and learning, nothing about the value of mentoring or coaching, collaboration among teachers, or the use of data. This seems a remarkable omission in an era when principals are supposed to be educational leaders, not sports boosters or disciplinarians. But it makes a certain sense, since academics are no longer Dave's responsibility. This year he is officially out of the loop, having been obliged to cede control over instruction to John Bennetti. You'd think he would be angry or at least embarrassed by the snub, but the education side of the house is plainly not his concern.[3]

One school, two worlds: When I talk with Dave, I see myself back in the mists of time, a student summoned to the principal's office, while John and I hash over current thinking about how to pique students' interest, pondering how those strategies might be adapted to fit the school. A grown-up Boy Scout in appearance and demeanor, notwithstanding his fondness for "Men in Black" outfits, buoyant, fervent about kids, an idea man and data-fiend, a mentor and system-builder, John Bennetti carries the message of innovation.

If anyone can make a difference at Union City High, it's John. But as he takes up the task, essential questions hang unanswered. Is it possible to run a high school in which responsibility for academics has been hived off from everything else? How will the school fare in the full-bore state review that's slated for March? Can John's leadership enable the school to shed its unhappy status as a "school in need of improvement"?

HOOKED ON LEADERSHIP

"I feel like I had a calling to become an educator," John tells me, borrowing the religious imagery to reflect on his career. Like so many people who work in Union City's schools, he has lived his entire life no farther than a half-hour drive away. He grew up in neighboring Jersey City, and from kindergarten through high school he attended local parochial schools.

"I never thought of being anything but a teacher," he recalls, "even though my own education wasn't that great." He carries pungent memories of his fourth grade teacher, the quintessential wicked nun. "She hit students and threw them across the room. She made us stand in the hall and sing for the school—'the pink marshmallows,' she called us." High school, though less colorful, wasn't much better educationally. His fondest memories are of teaching Bible stories to public school kids so that they could take their sacraments.

John commuted to the Newark campus of Rutgers to be near his sweetheart, whom he'd known since he was thirteen. He married her after graduating in 1992, and took his first job as a teacher in Union City. His older sister Debbie, who was teaching there, made the introductions.

Thomas Edison, the elementary school to which he was assigned, housed 1,900 students in kindergarten through eighth grade. "That school was referred to as 'Siberia,'" John says, "and going there was getting sent to the 'gulag.'" His classroom resembled a set from *Blackboard Jungle*—leaky windows, ripped shades held together with masking tape, buckling wooden floors, cracked blackboards—and his students were the toughest bunch in a school that served some of the city's poorest kids. Many of them were fourteen- and fifteen-year-olds, languishing in sixth grade.

John wasn't fazed. "I loved it," he says. "Walking in there I was like, 'this is home, this is my room.' I was over the top in getting my kids to be creative and do well academically—everything I didn't get in grade school."

Being an administrator wasn't part of John's game plan. He was thriving in the classroom; what's more, the school's leaders didn't inspire emulation. "I had to explain project-based learning to one of the senior administrators," he recalls, referring to a widely used teaching technique. When he enrolled in graduate school, though, he decided to take courses in educational leadership, thinking "they might be useful some day," and that experience changed his perspective. "I was hooked the first day of class, listening to the professor talk so profoundly about how a leader can turn a school around. It totally changed my perspective."

In 1998, when John received his administrator's certificate, the district maintained a lengthy roster of administrative hopefuls. "Too many people, regardless of their quality, were ahead of me," he recalls. Although John was no political innocent—you can't divorce yourself from politics if you want to become an administrator in Union City—unlike many on the waiting list he was an honest-to-god educator. For him, securing a top job wasn't just about having the cash to buy a summer home on the Jersey shore. It was a chance to do right by the kids.

When Sandy Sanger was tapped to be the superintendent in 2003, John's prospects for advancement measurably rose. Years earlier, when Sandy was a principal, he had dropped in unannounced on an evening adult education class that John was teaching. John remembers that moment well. "I had no idea how I was doing because I'd never taught adults before, and no one had ever seen me teach that class. I'd never spoken to Sandy, and when he called me into his office and said, 'great job,' it meant a lot."

By the time Sandy became superintendent, John was already regarded as a bright "curriculum guy." Seeing his potential, Fred Carrigg had mentored him, choosing him to run workshops around the state. "It was incredibly validating to know he had that much respect for what I could do," says John. In 2004 Sandy selected him to be an elementary school assistant principal, where he revamped the school's management. A few years later he was assigned to the central office and given the job of tutoring principals of low-performing schools across the district. In that capacity he had worked with Dave Wilcomes at Union Hill.

Watch one, do one, teach one: the training that John received from Fred early in his career and his stint as a mentor to other principals have prepared him for his new post. But it is, far and away, his most daunting assignment.

Something for Everyone

The sheer complexity of a comprehensive secondary school like Union City High—the fact that, with its large staff and many departments, it looks more like a community college than an elementary school—partly explains why meaningful change comes so hard.

The school's catalog, which runs thirty-four small-print pages, reflects the diversity of capabilities and interests. Students can take everything from Algebra 1 to Calculus, English for Today to Shakespeare, Biology to Anatomy and Physiology, World History to Constitutional Law, Spanish as a Native Language to Mandarin Chinese 3 and Honors Italian, Cisco Certification and ROTC to Hospitality Management, Band to Advanced Dance, Professional Baking to Advanced TV Production. Whether you want to attend MIT or become a chef when you graduate, this high school has something for you.

Such a school, writes Larry Cuban, a Stanford emeritus professor and former school superintendent, must juggle multiple and inconsistent goals. It is expected to be meritocratic, "creating an aristocracy of academic excellence from children of all social classes," while simultaneously being democratic, "providing access to all," as well as practical, "preparing all students for jobs, business and the professions."[4]

Under any circumstances this would be a hard trick to pull off, and in Union City the gap between the strongest and weakest students makes matters even more complicated. The top 2% or 3% take Advanced Placement chemistry and Chinese, win national science awards, and are sought out by Ivy League colleges. Students from the class of 2010 are enrolled at

Princeton, MIT, Johns Hopkins, and Brown's combined medical-BA program. One is a Gates Millennium Scholar, a highly prized and highly competitive award, given to just 100 students nationwide, which guarantees him a free ride in graduate school as well as college. At the other end of the spectrum are the students diagnosed as having "special needs," a catchall category that encompasses everything from mild learning disabilities to retardation, occasional panic attacks to persisting psychiatric problems. The multitudes in the middle expect to become programmers or health club managers, mechanics or fashion models. (These days, starring in *Jersey Shore* tops the list of students' fantasies.)

Most of these teenagers are freighted with the burdens that accompany poverty. It's not uncommon for them to be raising their brothers and sisters on their own, assuming responsibilities that no adolescent should bear but that no adult has been willing to assume. And because this is a city of immigrants, many students must confront the hazards of strangeness, the pain that can accompany adjusting not only to a new language but also to the new worlds of city and school.

THE BIG TEST

Nearly half of the students in Union City fit the official definition of an "at risk" youngster—less euphemistically, they are regarded as prime candidates to drop out or flunk out of school. Still, they must take the High School Proficiency Assessment, HSPA for short, New Jersey's test of literacy and numeracy.

A review of graduation tests in six states ranked New Jersey's as the "most challenging."[5] A sample English question requires students to "write a letter to the president of the school board stating your position on year-long school which will increase classroom time for learning. Support your position with reasons, examples, and/or other evidence." Another question obliges them to speculate on what's depicted in Joseph Wright's eighteenth-century painting *The Orrery*, which is reproduced on the test. (For those of you who, like myself, don't know the meaning of the word, an orrery is a mechanical device that represents the motions of the planets; to make matters more perplexing, nothing mechanical is depicted in Wright's painting.)

These questions are daunting for someone growing up in the inner city, who may never have been to an art museum in her life, and especially for someone who's learning English.[6] The open-ended math questions cover algebra, geometry, and trigonometry, with multipronged problems requiring graphical or formula-driven written answers. Both sections also feature multiple-choice questions, with options designed to trap the unwary.

In 2010 a quarter of Union City's high school students, twice the statewide average, failed the HSPA three times. To graduate, they had to pass a different test—the Alternate High School Assessment, or AHSA.

No one watches the clock when students are taking the AHSA, so they can take their time. There are no multiple-choice questions to trip up the unwary, only open-ended essays. The test is administered in Spanish and other native languages as well as English, giving immigrant kids who came late to the United States the chance to earn a diploma.

This two-pronged approach to testing has long been a hot-button issue among New Jersey's educators. Critics, who contend that "alternative" means "inferior" and that the exam devalues the diploma, buttress their case by pointing out that in some inner-city high schools more than half the students take this route to graduation. State officials counter that its strategy captures multiple intelligences. John is inclined to agree with the state's view, and I'm on his side. In all my years of teaching I have never given a multiple-choice test or asked students to cram their knowledge into fifty minutes, since to my way of thinking neither mode of assessment is especially informative.[7]

But even as this debate is playing out among the educators, when the state decides whether to brand a school as "in need of improvement" it takes into account only the number of students who pass the HSPA, and so these are the house rules by which John must play. It's purely a numbers game. For Union City to be out of the woods, the high school must record a 10% increase in the number of youngsters who pass the HSPA—a 10% jump for the entire student body as well as, separately, the youngsters who are learning English and the special needs students.

Last spring's HSPA scores also reflect a hidden educational deficit that must be overcome if the school is going to evolve from being a solid inner-city high school into one that can compete with the best. Many students have been passing the HSPA by the slimmest of margins—out of more than 800 test-takers in 2010, only 55 were rated as "advanced proficient" on the language test and just 34 in math. That's a problem.

The line that separates "proficient" and "barely proficient" is artificial, a matter of getting one multiple-choice question right or wrong. But students who have squeaked by, fueled by cram sessions that sharpen test-taking skills without adding substance, don't have to know much. Compared with other states, New Jersey may well have an especially challenging exam, but that's no solace—a barely passing HSPA score does not mean that a student is ready to take college classes. If graduates choose that path, as nearly 60% do, many of them will find themselves over their heads, funneled into remedial classes and vulnerable to dropping out.

"We have only scratched the surface of what we will become," John says, with his trademark optimism. But with the old guard still firmly in place, focused more on gridiron wins and losses than teaching and learning, just how much can he realistically accomplish?

NUMBER-CRUNCHING

Effective coaching is the cornerstone of John's game plan for making teachers more reflective and students more skillful. Once a week he and his "A-Team" of instructional supervisors—former teachers who distinguished themselves in the classroom and are now coaching teachers and tutoring students—gather around a dark wood conference table in a tucked-away room, laptops to the ready, poised to review a dozen spreadsheets. In 2009 and 2010, when many school districts were using their federal stimulus dollars to buy fancy hardware, Union City built up this cadre of supercoaches. With those funds running out this year, John is campaigning to persuade Sandy and assistant superintendent Silvia Abbato that they must be kept on the payroll.

In this geeky sanctum, statistics are the coin of the realm. "We live and breathe by the data," John says. "We do 'benchmarking' every month [testing students in reading and math] and we can use the results to predict how students will do when HSPA rolls around in the spring." The test scores can be parsed in myriad ways—by student, by teacher, by topic.

This tidal wave of information can overwhelm anyone who isn't a stats-wonk, and so the coaches break down the data into user-friendly chunks. In one instance, a teacher may need to spend time with a handful of kids who are confused about the same thing—how to write that persuasive letter to the school board, for example—while in another case, when most of the students are dumbfounded, the teacher has to find new ways of getting the point across.[8]

Every school in Union City relies on data that tracks students' progress. When Les Hanna at Washington School is going over students' test results with the teachers, her recommendations are based on comparable information. But at the high school the intensity of test-driven practice has been turned up several notches, the calibration of students' test scores has become more fine-grained, the coaches' skills have been more finely polished, and the coaching and tutoring more widely available.

Once a week the math, science, and language arts teachers meet with a coach who specializes in their discipline to talk through their common dilemmas. They noodle about alternative solutions, try them out in class, and discuss their experience the following week. The coaches must be pros in their field, with deep knowledge of the substance of their subject as well as a variety of ways to teach it. They also need the skills of a diplomat who conveys knowledge in a way that high school teachers, characteristically prickly about their autonomy and instinctively suspicious of anyone who observes their classroom, will respect.

The previous year, when Michelle Cowan, a literacy coach, was assigned to work with Desiree Hernandez, she suffered a mini-attack of nerves. By Union City standards, Michelle is a cosmopolitan, a native Californian who went to college in Silicon Valley and came East to earn her master's at Columbia. But Michelle never taught high school students (she was at a middle school when John recruited her) and she wondered whether her new colleagues would take her seriously. Over time, though, she came to understand John's reasoning. "If I'd been from one of the high schools it would have been murder, because of the Emerson–Union Hill rivalry. Coming from the outside allowed me to do what I needed to do. I'm mindful of veteran teachers' sensibilities. New teachers want direction. I tell them, 'I support what you're doing. Let's try this, see if it helps kids.'"

"Desiree is very intense," says Michelle, and that characterization puts matters exceedingly mildly. Over the course of her life, Desiree has navigated hairpin twists and turns of fortune that would have derailed almost anyone.

"There's a point when you realize how messed up your family is," Desiree tells me. "My parents divorced when I was two years old, after five children and twenty years. I lived for awhile with my mom and her new husband, an alcoholic who beat up my mother while I hid my eyes. Eventually he left her." As a nine-year-old, Desiree moved back with her father, a disciplinarian of the old school, and the woman she calls her "step-monster." "When I was nineteen my dad caught me hanging out with friends he didn't like and he hit me with his belt. I ran away and never came back."

Desiree's life turned into the stuff of melodrama—going to college and dropping out to pay the bills; getting evicted from her apartment and moving in with her sister, who paid Desiree's tuition from the earnings of her drug-dealing boyfriend; and dating gang members and hanging out with murderers, "all the people my sister introduced me to. Naïve me—I just thought it was exciting." Eventually she turned things around and saved enough money to graduate from college. During her job interview, Desiree was asked to name her role model. "I am," she replied.

"Students think that teachers have it easy," Desiree says "But when I tell them my story it means 'no excuses—if I could do it then you can too.'"

Even though Michelle didn't know about any of this, she immediately picked up on Desiree's distrust. "When I went into her classroom I felt like she didn't want me there. She didn't understand why I was coming and she was worried that she must be doing something wrong. I asked her if I could observe the class to see how I could help the students. She agreed, and after a few days she said, 'Don't you have feedback?' I told her, 'You're a phenomenal teacher but you're only teaching to the top of the class. What about the kids on the outskirts—they can get through without ever being acknowledged. How do you know how they're progressing?' That wasn't easy to say, but I knew enough about Desiree to know that she cared." For the rest of the year, Michelle says, "the relationship was a dance."

This year she and Desiree are teaching an English class composed of students who are new to the language. "It isn't a dance any more," Michelle says. "We are partners. The first day she said, 'You come up with an open-ended question about the story we've assigned, I'll do the same, and we'll see which one is better.' In fact we came up with the same question. We gelled after that day—now she trusts me."

Michelle's main responsibility is to help students pass the HSPA. Students are constantly being assessed—in addition to the monthly checks, they take two practice exams, devised by the district, that mimic the state test. None of this sits well with many of the teachers, who disdain the near-constant testing as time-devouring and soul-destroying. Heated exchanges about how much time should be devoted to testing have marked some faculty meetings.

"You can do test prep in disguise," Michelle says in response to the criticism, and to some extent she's right. The open-ended questions that ask students to draw on what they've read as well as their own experiences demand serious thinking and logical exposition—just what students should be learning. Desiree has found a way to live with the testing regimen. "I won't HSPA the kids to death but I will show them afterward that the assignment will help them to be successful with HSPA."

During their daily visits, the coaches are observing the content of the lesson—does it get kids thinking?—as well as how it's being delivered—are the students ensnared or dormant? John also makes the rounds, dropping in on as many classes as he can squeeze into his schedule. Pete Kliman, a long-time English teacher, welcomes John's presence. "The first year we were in this building the refrain was, 'At our old school we never did it that way.' Now it's the Bennetti way. I feel like I'm a better teacher—I have clearer expectations—and I'm happier."

"This is John's house," says Michelle. "Even though he's not the principal, everyone goes to him because he's the man with answers. And he never turns anyone away."

THE MAKING OF A TEACHER

The coaches aren't the teachers' only source of help. During the previous two years, assistant superintendent Silvia Abbato contracted with a consulting firm to deliver one-on-one mentoring to interested faculty. No one took greater advantage of the opportunity than a young history teacher named Marc Fusco, who called on his mentor almost as frequently as someone in AA checks in with his sponsor, searching for lessons about life as well as teaching.

No one was more devastated than Marc when the consultants' contract wasn't renewed and he sought out John's support. At a summer workshop, says Marc, "I learned that he was approachable and easy to talk to. He knows what works and holds people accountable for the job they do. And you don't fool around with him when it comes to a game of pool!"

I'm sitting in John's snug, windowless office one morning when Marc shows up looking for advice. Most teachers approach their supervisors warily, and Marc's guilelessness is an attractive rarity. John, the man who "never turns anyone away," agrees to check in regularly with him.

Teaching runs in Marc's bloodstream. His mom and dad are teachers, and so are several aunts and uncles. While it would be logical to assume that his path to teaching was effortless, that isn't so. As a boy growing up in nearby Hoboken, Marc was the classic goof-off, cutting classes and not handing in homework, doing his best to get kicked out of school. He didn't regard college as in the cards because he didn't see the point of getting an education, but two high school teachers changed his mind. Kevin Doyle, his youthful Latin instructor, took a shine to him. "He kept tabs on me, reaching out to my family to get to the core of what drove me," Marc recalls. "'I don't care if you ever learn Latin. I want you to leave with an idea of how to be a productive citizen.'" His history teacher, a no-nonsense, middle-aged man named William Lillis (Marc remembers being told to "do your papers in twelve point font, Times New Roman, not 12.5 Courier New Fusco"), instilled a "romance" with the subject. "When I saw a man who was so rigid crack a smile as I began to excel, my confidence flourished."

In his senior year Marc pulled himself together, boosted his GPA, and went on to New Jersey City University. During a two-year stint as a salesman after graduation, he tells me, "I made a pile of money," but he worried that he wasn't living up to his potential. That's when he turned to teaching. The man who says "I believe in destiny" applied for only one job, teaching history at Union City High.

Like Desiree Hernandez, Marc relies on his personal history to motivate his students. "I talk to them the way I talk to my brother or sister. Other teachers are smarter than me, but they're 'the authority.'" And like Kevin Doyle, his Latin teacher, he is building character. "I want my students to learn how to argue their point, to express themselves concisely, to analyze a situation," Marc says. "Most importantly, I want them to use self-analysis in order to improve upon every aspect of their own lives."

This is Marc's third year in the classroom, his up-or-out year. In June he will learn whether he has gotten tenure, and he's on edge. From the moment I walk into his classroom it's obvious that he's trying his damnedest. A home-made sign on the wall reads: "Vegas Rule/Fusco Rule: Speak Your Mind." Motivational mottoes—"Live the Life You've Imagined," "If you can imagine it, you can dream it and you can achieve it"—are interspersed with banners from an assortment of colleges, mostly local, including New York Institute of Technology and Misericordia.

The first time I see Marc in action happens to be a day when the school's computers have crashed, and with them the lesson he has planned. Because he can't pivot quickly enough, the class turns into a shambles. Only during the final few minutes of the class—only after he has aired a "News Show" that he and several of his students have put together, which features "Mr. Fusco's accessory tips: how you can be dressed to kill without breaking the rules," and delivered a monologue on bullying, sparked by his having witnessed a leader of the senior class, egged on by his friends, picking on a hapless classmate ("you guys need to think about what you are doing" is his wishy-washy bottom line)—does he touch upon the day's intended topic, slavery in the colonies. Twenty students, hunched in their chairs, look dazed and confused.

Over the course of the next few weeks, after many talks with John, Marc becomes determined to be less buddy-buddy and more authoritative. Unfortunately, his students haven't caught up with the shift in teaching style. "Pair up and spend a couple of minutes discussing the colonists' main grievances against the British," he tells them, a technique that John had proposed. ("When you're teaching, how do you know your students are learning? You should give them time and structure to think about the question.") But lots of chatter is going on and no one is discussing the colonists. They don't know what Marc is talking about.

Plainly, Marc needs to polish his craft. But he progresses with surprising speed, and by February his classroom has come to life. These are the days of Arab Spring, and how the events unfolding in the Middle East relate to the American Revolution forms the topic of the day. "What would you be willing to protest for?" Marc asks, and hands fly into the air. The conversation remains grounded in fact as the students shift back and forth between King George and Mubarak, Tahrir Square and Shays' Rebellion. I sit in a few more times during the year, observing a lesson on nineteenth-century restrictions on immigration and another on the roots of the Civil War. Each class comes off a little better than the previous one.

The previous year at George Washington Elementary School, Alina Bossbaly, an acknowledged master in helping kids learn to write, had spent many afternoons in the classroom of her colleague Mary Ann Rick. Mary Ann's kids were having a hard time putting paragraphs together, and she credits Alina for having given her the tools and the confidence she needed to raise her game. Something similar has transpired here—those conversations between John and Marc are paying off.

Teachers like Alina are seemingly blessed with an innate gift for their craft. Talk to Mary Ellen Naumann, the doyenne of the third grade at Washington School, who knew Alina back when, and you'll hear that her talent was evident from her first days in the classroom. The same holds true for John Bennetti. If these teachers keep polishing their craft they're destined to become exemplars. But the transformation of Mary Ann Rick and Marc Fusco shows that good teachers can be made as well as born, that with time and good counsel someone who initially stumbles can become a solid professional.

This is how novice teachers usually find their way, slowly and painstakingly, and with lots of help. Ask teachers about their first year in the classroom and most will cringe at the memory. "I'd cry at my desk every day," I'm told, "and I'd wonder whether I was cut out for this job." If they are fortunate they have someone to turn to. Union City has baked into the system the kind of support that elsewhere might occur only through happenstance. To be sure, it's impossible for John Bennetti to transform every marginal teacher into an effective one by himself, and that's where the coaches step in.[9]

Not all of John's initiatives have fared as well. To counter the impersonality of a megaschool, assistant superintendent Silvia Abbato had envisioned that the new high school would be divided into clusters of 400 students, each led by an assistant principal. The intent was to embed a feeling of intimate connection within gigantism, but in the first year of the school's operation nothing like that was seriously tried and John wants to revive the idea. "I'm working to build a team," he says. "We need to get the assistant principals on board. I want to stretch them."

The clusters have come to life in the bilingual education and special education departments this year, and in a matter of months John has won over the assistant principal in charge of athletics, a thirty-year veteran who, to John's pleasant surprise, comes up with a research-based proposal to yoke athletics and literacy.[10] But the other administrators haven't budged. "They're a 'good old boy' network," he says. In his attempts to woo the assistant principals he's butting heads with bureaucracy—they report to Dave Wilcomes and he has evinced no interest in stretching his subordinates.

Bad Teacher

In altering the academic climate of the high school, John needs to handle another and more serious problem—bad teachers.

One teacher in ten, by John Bennetti's estimation, can't or won't devote the energy that's necessary to motivate their students. Nothing that the school has done for them—coaching, providing data, encouraging collaboration—has made a dent.

Some of these teachers are merely going through the motions, hanging on until retirement. "How can you do new math with an old math mind?": Charlie Brown's lament captures their attitude, and their deadening lectures haven't changed in a generation or more.

Worse still are the teachers who hate kids. They show their hostility by muzzling class discussion, dismissing students' questions as backtalk, and gratuitously awarding bad grades. The steady paycheck, cheap health insurance, and generous pension must be why they remain in the classroom.[11]

One teacher confides that instructing her students, recently arrived in the United States, has proven an exercise in futility. "They won't make it," she tells me. "After all, what can you expect from such kids?" As you would anticipate, she's not putting in much effort. When a delegation of honors students complains about an English teacher who demeans them in class, and gives out Cs and Ds, rather than the As they've always received, John sizes up the situation. The students are right, he concludes, and he takes it upon himself to coach their teacher, regularly sitting in on her classes and discussing his observations with her. He hopes that this show of interest and the suggestions he proffers will bring about an attitude transplant, but half a year later there's no detectable sign of improvement.

Such teachers are murder for an administrator like John, who's trying as hard as he can to bring together the many parts of this academic world—to break down the "Queen Victoria" syndrome, teachers working in unsplendid isolation, by bringing together clusters of teachers; to deliver help wherever it's needed; and to imbed a culture of high expectations among teachers and students alike.

These are the teachers whom politicians and the "no excuses" camp of educators have in mind when they ridicule the profession as filled with louts and layabouts. For the sake of the students they should be fired, but the job security rules in the teachers union contract make dismissal nearly impossible. Statewide, only ten teachers have been fired for incompetency in the past decade. This is maddening—inexcusable, really, because it puts the adults' priorities above the kids' needs.

Union City's strategy for improving the caliber of teaching relies on a system of strong supports, incentives rather than sticks. As the district's enviable track record shows, this model works most of the time, but when it comes to the miscreants a stick would prove handy. Because of a 2012 law, backed by the teachers union and passed unanimously in the state legislature, it will soon be easier to fire bad teachers. Anyone who receives less than stellar ratings for two straight years will automatically be dismissed unless they have shown some improvement.

But that's for the future. As matters stand, John's system-building initiatives are hampered by the unwelcome presence of teachers who ignore his ministrations because they have no interest in doing a good job.

Learning a New Land

The classic rags-to-riches American dream, Horatio Alger's conviction that with guts and hard work anyone can make it, still beckons families who, wanting much better lives for their children, wait years for a green card or else slip across the border. All too frequently, though, their hopes collide with reality as their youngsters are warehoused in the worst public schools and assigned to the worst teachers. Many of them drop out or get pushed out, and they leave school prepared only for the brawn-work and domestic labor that no one else will touch.[12]

Union City has turned this narrative of failure on its head. Over the years it has fashioned a curriculum suited to these youngsters' varied needs, with carefully calibrated steps that lead to fluency, first in a student's native language and then in English.

This process goes most smoothly for children who cross the border when they are very young, because they have the blessing of time to grasp English in a bosomy setting like Hostos or Washington School. Three or four years later they're doing as well as kids born in the United States. But for students who arrive when they're teenagers—about 400 in a high school population of 2,400—it's not so easy to make the grade, both figuratively and literally. They come from a score of Latin American and Caribbean nations, and often their parents have no more than a grade school education. It's estimated that 30% of them have entered the country without documentation and so they live with the constant fear of deportation.[13]

"These kids pose the toughest challenge," Chris Abbato, the knowledgeable, low-key head of the high school's bilingual program (and Assistant Superintendent Silvia Abbato's husband), tells me. Many of them had spent only a few years in school, often sitting on a dirt floor with fifty or sixty classmates and sharing books. Some sixteen-year-olds read and write Spanish at a third-grade level. They can't find their native country on a map. They know nothing about paragraphs or punctuation, fractions or photosynthesis, Abraham Lincoln or Simon Bolivar. Even though their transcripts may state that they've gone to school for eight years and have passed all their courses, this information cannot be relied on, since in some countries officials can be bribed to fake these documents.

Like many immigrants, these teenagers believe they'll be returning home in a few years, but experience shows that most of them will stay in the United States. A high school diploma marks the first step on the path to a decent life, but to earn that degree, and maybe continue on to college, they must squeeze half a lifetime of school into three or four years. They are doing double-work, acquiring a new language at the same time they're being exposed to new subjects.[14]

The education of adolescents with the shakiest skills, Chris tells me, starts with a "port of entry" class. Their progress is constantly being monitored, and those who do well move swiftly into more advanced English as a Second Language courses, then into an English class, taught at a slower pace than regular classes, which is designed to prepare them for English-only instruction. Because they are starting out behind their classmates, their schedules are crammed with the courses they need to cross the finish line. If all goes well, by the time they are seniors many of them will have blended into the fabric of the school.

This step-by-step approach, introduced in the lower grades in the late 1970s, is regularly tweaked. The port of entry program was launched in 2007 and the almost-in-the-mainstream English class, developed by Chris, along with Edernis Garcia, director of the district's bilingual program, began two years later. These innovations have earned the high school national recognition. The Center for Applied Linguistics, a Washington, D.C.–based research organization that aims to improve language teaching, singled out the Spanish-to-English transition program and the port of entry initiative as among the nation's best.[15]

But the mandarins in Trenton don't care about such kudos. For the high school to be free from the stigma and scrutiny that accompanies the designation "in need of improvement," at least 10% more of these English language novitiates must pass the HSPA, which is given only in English. Their teachers feel the test pressure especially acutely because these students haven't ever made such rapid progress. One reason, says Chris, is that most of the native Spanish-speaking teachers, whom these youngsters see during their very first years, emphasize conjugation and memorization drills, not higher-order thinking.

The bilingual program used to be treated a stepchild, the teachers tell me. No attempt was made to integrate what they were doing with teaching elsewhere in the school; unless trouble arose, they were left to their own devices. But if the HSPA scores are going to get better, this situation must change—the teachers can no longer inhabit a separate world, with its own distinctive practices and expectations. They have to become integrated into this complex organization, adopting its approach to teaching and learning. They need to embrace the "high standards" expectation, set by Sandy Sanger and Silvia Abbato, which pertains district-wide. For this to happen, John and the coaches must convince them that they can push their students, even those who come to them essentially unschooled, to become problem-solvers.

Seven teenagers slouch in a semicircle in Angelina Martinez's port of entry Spanish-language class. "It's a rough group," Angelina tells me, surreptitiously pointing out a boy recently arrested for sexual assault. While all of the sixty-six new port of entry students need extra help, this class is the furthest behind and these students are the hardest for the school to reach. Although some of them are sixteen and seventeen, the school treats them as ninth graders, and while that affords them a realistic chance to graduate the fact that they're several years older than their classmates invariably stirs up social tensions. To make matters worse, they are just learning what it means to be a teenager in this city. The gangs hover, holding out the beckoning promise of belonging to something.

Much of what Angelina does, whether it's teaching a history lesson about Latin America or reading a book on salsa dancing, is tied to her students' Hispanic roots. Hanging on her classroom wall are their hand-drawn family trees, some of which reach back three generations, their branches spreading wide to make room for all the uncles and aunts. Every week she scours the local Spanish-language papers for easy-reading items that might interest these students.

Laura Maczuzak, who is introducing a class of eleven port of entry students to the rudiments of English, could almost pass for one of the kids. When I walk into her classroom she is working her way through the words that describe different facial features. "What is hair?—show me. Does anyone in the class have red hair? How about a moustache? Dimples? I'm the only one with wrinkles," she jokes. When she asks who has a scar, every hand pops up—in this class, everyone bears a scar on his face.

If they stay on track, these teens will be taking Sophie Karanikopolos's English class, one of the new, almost-mainstream classes. This is the last time they'll be treated specially because they are native Spanish-speakers; next semester they'll be in a regular English class. It's October, which Sophie, mindful of her students' *True Blood* fixation, has turned into Gothic romance month, and the students are reading Edgar Allan Poe's "Telltale Heart" and "The Pit and the Pendulum."

A year earlier, in an English as a Second Language class, they would have parsed the text line by line to check for comprehension. Here they are dissecting Poe's use of suspense, and unless you'd been told, you would never suspect that this isn't a typical English class.

Like Chris, who doubles as the guidance counselor for these kids, Sophie pushes her students to "think college." She and her colleagues prep them for the SAT, which all of them take, and help them fill out their college applications. "I tell my students 'if college is what you want, then we'll get you there.' Undocumented kids too—even though they'll have a very hard time getting scholarships or loans, I say that 'if you have the motivation we'll figure out a way to deal with the money issues.'"

"I love these kids," says Sophie. "They are so needy and so appreciative. They're like our own. We keep helping them three, four years out—we don't let them go." Nadia Mosbet, who teaches another section of this class, calls the bilingual program "the best-kept secret in the school, the best place to be teaching. The kids love you unconditionally. They're interested in learning, and they have so much respect and admiration."

These teachers receive daily doses of encouragement from their coaches, who apply the same techniques that Michelle Cowan has used with Desiree Hernandez, sometimes teaching together and sometimes watching how a lesson is taught. "We are turning them into test-takers," says Sophie, with decidedly mixed feelings. "They know the format and the speed. And they're gaining confidence. 'Miss, we're going to pass,' they say. 'Miss, we're good.'"

Sophie understands how much the test results will affect the school's fortunes, and her students' fortunes as well, and she acknowledges that high school graduates should know how to write a coherent five-paragraph essay. But she worries that reading and writing are being reduced to a creativity-killing formula—introduction, transitions, three or four paragraphs, conclusion.

"I'm working so hard to get a kid who a couple of years ago couldn't say 'hello' in English to pass," says Nadia Mosbet. "I'm singing and dancing on my head."[16]

Among all the students at Union City High, those whose education begins in a port of entry class like Angelina's are the likeliest to drop out. If the past is a reliable guide, Chris tells me, only about half of them will graduate. He badly wants to break this pattern, and with a $4 million grant from the U.S. Department of Education the high school is joining with Saint Peter's University, a few miles away, to give them a solid reason to stay in school.

The district already has formed partnerships with nearby community colleges and state universities that give high school students college credit for courses they take on campus. Now it is reaching out to bring a private school into its orbit. When this venture was announced, students queued up to be selected. No wonder—over the course of the next three years they will be tethered to Saint Peter's, with field trips and classes on the campus, and when they graduate from high school they can enroll there. For teenagers who, just a few years earlier, didn't know a word of English that's a powerful lure.

Respeto

The students at Union City High sometimes behave like college freshmen, as in a seminar where they're parsing Toni Morrison's *Beloved*; and they can be boisterously jokey with their teacher, who may have to dial down the energy level. But there's none of the note-swapping, gum-chewing, wise-cracking, talking-back rudeness you'd anticipate if your opinions about high school have been shaped by movies like *Bad Teacher* or TV shows like *The Wire*. The worst you're likely to encounter are a few kids, their eyes closed, their heads nestled in their arms, and it's not much of a stretch to suppose that they have been working at McDonald's, flipping burgers until midnight to help pay the rent.

This attitude of respect—*respeto*—is pervasive in a city where almost all the students are immigrants or the children of immigrants accustomed to accepting authority. Even the gang leaders behave themselves when they're in the building, Dave Wilcomes tells me. A team of educators who spend several days at the school makes the same point, and so do alumni from the Class of 1961, self-described "geezers" who compliment the students for being helpful and polite during their visit. "If you care for them," says Desiree Hernandez, "these kids will break their backs for you."

Make no mistake—Union City High isn't heaven and these kids are no angels. You can see students pushing and shoving in the halls, food fights occasionally breaking out, rules about school uniforms being ignored, students being bullied, insults like "faggot" casually lobbed. Gangs lurk a block or two away and the police department maintains a presence on the campus. "A kid might get into a fistfight in the cafeteria or right outside the school, and he'll get suspended," John tells me. "But those incidents are few and far between—there might be twenty-five of those knuckleheads. And there's an unwritten rule that this doesn't go on in the classroom. Put that in context—there are no metal detectors here, no police with drug-sniffing dogs, no one's carrying heat. The most common problem is when a kid won't put away his iPhone."

This is trivial stuff compared with life in many urban high schools, where knives are as common as backpacks and hazing is taken for granted. Officials at one Jersey City high school are so fearful of internecine warfare or assaults on teachers that they shoo students off the premises at 3 o'clock sharp. Nor does suburbia guarantee security. At Berkeley (California) High, which enrolls more than its share of prodigies as well as students who are reading at the seventh-grade level, academically minded youngsters used to stay clear of the bathrooms, fearing that they would be robbed or beaten up. (Wanting to see for myself the situation at Union City High, I make it a point to use the boys' lavatories, not the faculty bathroom, and they're as peaceful as any shopping mall restroom.)

Dave Wilcomes tells a story about taking a girls' basketball team to a game in Basking Ridge, a posh village nestled in the somnambulant countryside. Nervous school administrators there had summoned the police for backup, but the game went off without a hitch. "For Latinos, your kids are great," the Ridge High principal told Dave, meaning it as a compliment. "They're not 'Latinos,'" he replied. "They're kids, and they can succeed just like your kids."[17]

John and the teachers are capitalizing on *respeto*, using this habitual deference to authority to prod students into engaging more deeply with their schoolwork and paying more attention to their futures. From what I can see, it's working. I never meet a student who tells me that he doesn't care whether he passes the HSPA—quite the contrary—and any time I ask students what's going on in class, they do a solid job of explaining.

One afternoon I'm in Joe Chung's eleventh grade chemistry course while the students are conducting an experiment to determine whether Coke or Diet Coke floats atop the other. Working with different mixtures of the two sodas, they are measuring the densities of water and sugar, and then graphing the results. (They find that Coke sinks to the bottom because sugar is heavier than sweetener.) In an aside, Joe tells me that several of these students have been diagnosed as "special needs" youngsters, but while they're getting some extra help they are carrying out the same project. When I ask one of them to clarify the research he nails it.

More than *respeto* or good teaching is at work here—the spare-no-expenses school that Brian Stack's political skills made possible is paying off, just as everyone hoped—*if we build it, they will learn.*

"These are dream labs, Nirvana," says science supervisor Ron Ciriani, "much better than at the community college, where the kids get just one lab period a week. Here there's no lab period because all the science classrooms are labs, and no lectures. A few years ago these kids would have been in a rote memory class. This turns them on."

March Madness

March madness, which usually refers to college basketball's championship competition, takes on a different meaning at Union City High. As ever, it's the moment when students will be taking the big test. But this year there's something more—the state is sending a team of educators to do a three-day soup-to-nuts review. To be free from such micromanaging the school must do well on both the HSPA and the evaluation.

In midmonth the school puts on a pep rally. The bleachers that curve around the athletic field are overflowing and the students whoop it up as the band blares, the cheerleaders hurl their batons, the thespians perform skits, and the dance team goes through its syncopated routine. But while this looks like other pep rallies, no big game is looming. The adrenaline rush is meant as a sendoff for the junior class, which will take the HSPA for the first time during the coming days, as well as for the seniors who haven't already passed it.

The pep rally is just one indication of how much rides on this test. Another sign is the visible weariness of John and his team, as they concentrate more and more on moving the needle. The coaches are spreading out across the school, conducting question-by-question reviews of the results on the district's simulacrum of the HSPA, holding sessions with small groups of students to make them more adroit test-takers, and jointly teaching English and math classes, spooning shrewdness about test-taking into the lesson plans.

Meanwhile, the outside reviewers dispatched by the state have arrived in force. They sit in on classes; talk with teachers, students, and school officials; and survey the staff. They analyze reams of material, everything from lesson plans to the school's handbook, students' portfolios to notices sent to parents. This review is meant to judge the quality of instruction, with an eye to improving student outcomes. It's another instance of the Collaborative Assessment for Planning and Achievement, or CAPA, that Washington School went through two years earlier—a price that any school "in need of improvement" must pay.

Because several Union City schools are in the same boat, these reviews are familiar. But this is the first state assessment of the new high school, its first external audit, and close attention is being paid. Half a decade earlier, a CAPA team visited the old high schools, and at times the veneer of professional courtesy had cracked. Together with Assistant Superintendent Silvia Abbato, his longtime mentor and collaborator on matters academic, John has labored for months to make sure there's no repeat performance, meticulously analyzing the evidence that shows improvement since the school's opening.

When the assessors depart they're effusive in their praise. But for CAPA, as for the test scores, the results aren't in, and uncertainty will hang in the air for months to come.

BEATING THE ODDS

In June, celebrations break out and champagne corks pop—it's a trifecta.

First comes word that the high school has aced the CAPA review. "The merger of the two high schools has created an educational institution that uses data to drive instruction, intense and cohesive professional development to refine teacher skills, and continuous monitoring to support and ensure implementation of the instructional program," the report gushes. "The school is a model for an instructional facility that is designed to focus on 21st century teaching and learning."

Shortly afterward the HSPA test scores arrive, bringing more cheer. The school has done so much better that it is off the state's watch-list. What seemed nearly impossible in September has actually come to pass nine months later.

"We get to know the kids intimately—what their strengths and weaknesses are—and we work with them individually," says John, summarizing his approach. "Assessment leads to support. We give every kid who isn't doing well what they need academically. Solid assessment is the starting point, the basis for targeting our support. And we look at the big picture, at how these kids are doing overall, what problems they might be having. We keep our eye on the ball."

There's a third milestone to celebrate: a new graduation record. Among the students who started Union City High four years earlier, 89% earn their diploma—that's 6% higher than the statewide average and 11% higher than the national average.

What's more, 100% of the seniors are graduating. More than 80% of them passed the HSPA and almost everyone else passed the alternate exam. It took a special appeal to the state to get the last two students through, but a portfolio of their written work did the trick. For the first time in the annals of Union City, all the seniors walk across the stage, shake the principal's hand, have their photos taken, and receive their diplomas.[18]

It's standing room only for the graduation ceremony. Amid the round of valedictory addresses, a senior named Hamlet Diaz steals the show. Hamlet, a blind student, knew no English when he came to Union City from the Dominican Republic as a boy. He speaks movingly about how he learned to read and write in Braille—how he was able, with lots of help along the way, to make it.

Three times the young man receives a standing ovation. Sandy Sanger is crying. Dave Wilcomes is sobbing. Massive linemen from the football team, sitting shoulder to shoulder, have tears in their eyes. You can't find a dry eye in the house.

Silvia Abbato was Hamlet's elementary school principal. "We're working on getting him into college," she tells me. "It's not easy because he's illegal, but we'll figure it out."

WHERE FUN COMES TO DIE (AND BE REBORN)

George Washington Elementary School—Reprise

The first months of 2011 bring ugly weather, the worst in modern memory. Freezing rain buckets down, streets become slick and menacing with ice, sleet rattles against windows, gusty winds upend trees and telephone poles. Blizzard follows blizzard, three major snowstorms in rapid-fire succession that knock out electricity in millions of homes across the region, prompting the governor, no friend of Washington, to seek federal disaster relief.

Even though the mayor has the snowplows on constant patrol, Union City, like many other communities, is immobilized, and for six days the schools are shuttered. Despite this lost time, there's no talk of postponing the high-stakes exams that the third through sixth graders at George Washington Elementary School will be taking during the first week of May. The grind of test preparation will have to be accelerated.

"While you might think that teachers like these snow days," Alina Bossbaly tells me, "they are just putting us further and further behind." The kids return from Christmas vacation chattering about their presents, the LEGO bricks and Lalaloopsy dolls, but the playfulness that characterized the weeks before the holidays is about to give way to a more rigorous regimen.

Early in January, with her youngsters still feeling restive after the break, Alina gives them a talking-to about how they have to become more mature in the new year. Speeches like these usually turn out to be exercises in futility, especially when they're delivered to eight-year-olds, but this time something sticks and over the following weeks these kids buckle down. The third grade teachers—the Dream Team—can see the unfolding transformation. They had wondered whether this year, with its combustible mix of children, would be the exception to Alina's unbroken twenty-seven-year record, but they're reassured by what they are now witnessing.

The students in Room 210 no longer fidget when Alina reads aloud, and when she gives them her narrowed-eyes look they become church-mouse quiet. A glance suffices to awaken a child from his reverie. The kids have the hour-by-hour routine down pat. They know which day they're supposed to go to the classroom's well-stocked library or listen as the stories of the week are read aloud or tackle an assignment on the computer.

What's more, evidence of learning is everywhere. The youngsters are writing longer papers and drawing on a richer vocabulary to express themselves. "They will go from words like 'great' to 'ecstatic,'" says Alina. "They will learn a lot of 'excitement' words because that is who I am." "What if?" essays (speculative essays, in test-talk), a new style for them, give them running room for their imagination. They edit one another's papers, and when they read them aloud the rest of the class often awards them 4s and 5s, the top grades on the big state test and a token of their high hopes.

In math as well there are signs of solid progress. The coin-counting and numerical calculations that comprise "Every Day Counts" have become so ingrained that the children complete the tasks largely on their own. Alina's "pie" places a lot of emphasis on helping and sharing, and when these kids need assistance their seatmates come to the rescue. They are learning how to multiply and divide, not by rote formula but by using blocks to visually understand the operations.

The kids' individual folders, which contain the best of their schoolwork, keep getting fatter, and the work keeps improving. I'm especially struck by the lollapalooza leaps like those initial essays that, unbidden and unexpected, Matias and Andres wrote in English during the weeks leading up to Christmas.

This evolution has been hard-won. "This is one of the toughest classes I have ever had," Alina tells me. They crave lots of mothering from Alina, and some of them seek out fathering as well. Every time I visit, Joaquin and Andres rush over to me. "Be my father!" they implore, each of them holding me tight.

Helping these students to master the reading assignments is also proving unusually difficult. The wide range of brainpower and fluency in English (six of the youngsters have been in the country less than two years) has led Alina to split the students into four separate groups, each with its own handcrafted reading and writing assignments, and so she's constantly on the move, darting from one table to the next.

"I'm teaching four of the kids to fly, showing four of them what life in Union City is like, moving four quickly to the mainstream," she says.

Still, Alina remains the unflagging optimist. "In the long run you say, 'Wow! Look at these kids!' I believe all of them will make it. They will be Bossbaly-ized. They will care, respect, and love one another as proud members of the community"—"slices of the pie," as she says—"and most of them will pass the ASK," the state's Assessment of Skills and Knowledge that they will take in the spring. "In September everyone was at a different level—there were people who knew no English, people who knew lots of English—but now everyone is on track."

These youngsters present an array of pleasures and puzzles. Joaquin, a bundle of complexities who has taken up much of Alina's time since the first day of school, persists in trying her patience. He pops out of his seat like a jack-in-the box, sits back too far and crashes to the floor, spends time on the computer when he's supposed to be elsewhere. But he also displays an original mind, a newfound talent for writing, and an immense heart. "I don't want a thing," he writes in a journal entry about what's on his Christmas list. "I want love for my family."

Matias, Andres, and Roberto, seated next to one another, are all on the glide-path to mastering English. Matias, the Dominican charmer with Bing Crosby ears who caused so much trouble the year before, has become a rock star. He's making great strides, especially in his newly acquired language, and his charisma stamps him as a class leader.

"Matias is the kind of kid that makes me love teaching so much," says Alina. "Last year he couldn't even write his name and he was a real handful," but he has spent a second year in her classroom, catching up and calming down. "The women in the cafeteria talk about his metamorphosis," says Alina. "They call him 'el caballero,' the man. Last year his mom hated me because she thought I was working him way too hard, but that's all changed. Now she loves me." When I meet Matias's mother, she has only the nicest things to say about Alina. "We work together," she tells me, speaking in Spanish. "I want my son to study so that he can be what I can't be."

Andres remains high-strung and hyper—"Flash" is what his second grade teacher, Maria Casanovas, had nicknamed him. Pushed hard by his mother, who checks in with Alina several times a week, he's a perfectionist who goes into meltdown mode whenever he makes even the smallest mistake in math.

In December, months before Alina thought he was ready, Andres insisted on writing all his papers in English. He wanted to keep up with Matias, and Alina felt she couldn't say no without doing emotional damage. For the moment he is relying on Spanglish, inserting Spanish words when he doesn't know the English equivalent, but Alina is unfazed. "He'll get there," she says. Roberto is chugging along. A paper written in mid-February about how to grow plants contains his first sentence in English: "Use a little bit of water."

Mauricio, who has been diagnosed as a "special needs" student because of his unpredictable mood swings, has his out-of-control moments. But those episodes come less frequently than they did in the fall, as the efforts of a behavior management specialist, provided gratis by Union City, are starting to pay off. When Alina asks the students to grade each other's papers, he invariably gives them a "5." "You're so generous," Alina tells him. "You should be one of the judges."

Isabella poses a more pressing problem. Her family is living through convulsive changes—they've lost their house, her father can't find work, and her mother, the mainstay of the family, has been in and out of the hospital—and while she's as sweet as ever she's falling further behind.

The kids who came to the United States most recently are progressing at different rates. During much of the fall, Ariana, the class beauty, didn't want to exchange her middle-class world in Venezuela, where her Montessori academy had a swimming pool, for gritty Union City and Washington School, where there's barely a playground. She kept her distance by maintaining an air of superiority, but now she is emerging from her shell. While she can still be pouty—"she'll need Botox when she's thirty," Alina jokes— smiles break through more often. Her writing in Spanish, initially disjointed and herky-jerky, has become leagues better. Early in the year she wouldn't have anything to do with English, refusing to utter a word and shutting her ears whenever Alina would read aloud, but now she's beginning to try it out.

Santiago, who arrived from the Dominican Republic a few months ago, is this year's Matias, a child who has had little schooling. He has picked up the rhythm of the class, and there's no doubt about his intelligence. But several times he doesn't turn in his homework, and for that he's temporarily banished from the room. "He's getting the message that this is unacceptable," says Alina.

Clara has been having the hardest time adjusting. She's younger and more immature than her classmates, and when she doesn't understand the lesson she throws a tantrum. In February her family moves to a neighboring town, and she's gone. Alina fears for her future. "She won't get the kind of attention she gets here. She might wind up in special education, and that would be sad, because she's a bright girl who just needs to catch up."

In the corridor outside the classroom, paintings in the style of Paul Klee are tacked to the bulletin board. When that project, completed in the first weeks of winter, grabs the kids' imagination, Alina tells them to find out everything they can about the painter's life, and those write-ups are clipped to the paintings. "That isn't in the curriculum," she says. "I'm taking advantage of the kids' energy."

A month later, the youngsters are entranced by *The Magic School Bus on the Ocean Floor*. It's one of a series of immensely popular books that describe the adventures of Valerie Frizzle and her class, who board the bus for trips to everywhere from the farthest reaches of the solar system to the inner workings of the human body. On this particular bus ride, Alina's kids are discovering the undersea world. They write about how animals in the sea move—the whale, which swims by flapping its tail up and down, and the jellyfish, which opens its body like an umbrella. They draw pictures to illustrate their accounts and then go online to devise habitats for different marine creatures.

Alina loves this kind of teaching, where science and reading and art connect. "I hate the old-fashioned separation," she says. "That's for high school."

Good teachers behave this way. They tie together multiple ways of comprehending the world. They seize the moment, capitalizing on their students' excitement, instilling the sense that learning is an adventure to be savored and not a grind to be endured. Alina relishes these times, because she's about to have far fewer opportunities to be so ingenious. More and more the state test looms, cabining teachers' originality. "Those tests make a lot of us more boring," she tells me, but she does her best to resist. "I have to find the fun in whatever I'm teaching."

PRESSURE TO PERFORM

The standing of Union City's public schools rests heavily on the fact that the district's overall performance in the testing sweepstakes surpasses the other poor cities in the state. But that perch is insecure. To stay atop the heap, several schools, including Washington, must work their way off the state's watch list by boosting the number of students who pass the New Jersey ASK, the state's math and reading tests.

To improve the odds, the school system has devised its own practice tests that parallel the state exams. Teachers are expected to use the results from the practice tests in forming their lessons, concentrating on students' weak spots. While many teachers chafe under this constricted focus, they do their best.

In February, the third grade teachers are informed that their students fared poorly in math on the first practice exam. Outwardly they're not fazed. "You can throw out those early scores," they tell the principal, Les Hanna, who reviews the results with each of them. "We hadn't done geometry yet— it's the same story every year." Nonetheless, the weak scores remind them that they must pick up the pace, making sure they touch on everything, even at the expense of gaining insight.

On the language exam, many of the third graders can't make sense of the nuances of nonfiction passages describing how to make bark and leaf rubbings or how animals use camouflage. "They're not exposed to English outside of school," Alina laments, explaining this perennial weakness, but she knows that what's wanted are better results and not explanations.

Although the big test is more than two months away, the effects of the pressure are starting to show. The third grade teachers look pallid. Deep purple circles, telltales of lost sleep, shadow their eyes. Alina comes to school one morning barely able to speak, her normally high-pitched voice reduced to a squeak. "I'm overdoing it," she acknowledges. "We are working way too hard."

As if their regular 7 A.M. to 3 P.M. schedule wasn't sufficiently taxing, these teachers are now staying after school three days a week to run test prep classes. In the elementary school version of triage, the sessions are offered only to "cusp" kids—that is, the youngsters whose scores on the practice test show that they have a very good chance of passing the test.

It feels wrong, even immoral, to deny the same opportunity to children who, while likely to make great gains with extra help, probably won't meet the state's definition of "proficiency." Relying on this criterion makes Les uneasy, for she sees herself as a caregiver, not a bureaucrat, and it also troubles the teachers, who think of their school as a nurturing place and not a sorting machine. But the school has been given little choice. When the state education department decides whether a school has done well enough to be freed from micromanagement, it only takes into account the number of students who pass the test. How much improvement they make from one year to the next, though obviously important, isn't of interest to the state officials. This makes for bad pedagogy and dubious ethics as well, but if Washington School hopes to stand on its own it must focus on the youngsters at the borderline of passing.[1]

From early March until exam time, Alina spends most afternoons away from her own classroom, leaving a soft-spoken young woman from Venezuela, a college math major, to teach that material. Alina has stepped up the time she's spending with Jennifer Mondelli, the young fourth grade teacher.

"If you could be any animal for forty-eight hours, what would you be?" That's the writing assignment Alina has given Jennifer's students, and she asks them to analyze Matthew's paper (he wants to be a python). She is relying on this single example to teach the craft of writing—more precisely, writing as the state's test-makers comprehend it. "Go back to the standards the judges use," she tells them. "Don't forget the brownie points," the vocabulary words that will make the judges take notice, she adds, turning the class back to Jennifer and assuming the observer's mantle.

By now, science and social studies have largely been banished, replaced by *Motivation Math*, a drill-and-kill text meant to push students over the test hurdle, and *New Jersey ASK Coach*, dessicated exercises that do the same for language. In Alina's class, one lesson focuses on distinguishing main from supporting sentences, main from supporting themes. The kids are nodding off, their heads resting lifelessly on their desks. Trying to breathe life into the class, Alina has them read an article describing the flags of different countries, and they are able to disentangle the main theme, that a nation's flag changes over time.

"We're hyperventilating," says Alina. "Time goes so fast." In mid-April, two weeks before the state test, the scores from the second practice exam have arrived. While the third graders are doing better, that doesn't allay the teachers' mounting anxieties. "There's so much to cover in math," Alina laments.

Eight- and nine-year-olds are expected to know so much more than we did when we were that age. On the math test, they must find patterns in number sets, represent data in the form of a graph, and calculate probability. They are expected to master rudimentary geometry—calculate the area and perimeter of a pentagon—and even simple algebra: "What does K equal in the equation 6 + K=18?" In the reading and writing test, the youngsters have to produce three essays on topics such as: "Describe a time you had to do something challenging and compare your task to the experience of a character in a story you read." Alina wonders whether her students will use the mechanical format that the state is looking for—to include an introduction, transitions between paragraphs and a conclusion; to write three- and four-sentence paragraphs; to use the multisyllabic Latinate words that the exam readers reward—within the span of just thirty minutes.

TRAPPED

Every teacher I talk with at Washington School sees herself in the same rudderless boat, swept along by the relentless current of testing. "We feel trapped by the test," says Mary Ann Rick. "This year I didn't do an experiment on plant life that I've always done because the kids aren't tested in science and I felt too much pressure." Jen Shuck's third graders—a lively bunch who, earlier in the year, had wondered aloud whether I found them "scintillating"—are "really scared they won't pass," she tells me. In a writing assignment about their test-day fantasies, one youngster imagines that "suddenly the lights were turned off. When they were turned on, the booklets were gone," while another dreams that "a parade passed by but I was focused and worried."

Sue Emmerling, Alina's alter ego in the fourth grade, is the kind of teacher you wish you had, brimming with ideas calculated to enthrall her youngsters. In her mind, the state test devalues everything she has learned about how to reach urban kids over the course of three decades in the classroom.

"The expectation is that ten-year-olds can write five paragraphs in half an hour, solve complicated math problems and have a wealth of knowledge about science, and do it all entirely on their own. But these youngsters freeze up under stress—one word on a question can throw them off—so it's important to get them to relax. I encourage them to think out loud, to make a mistake, but on the test there's no brainstorming with classmates, no chance to think before they write. We work together on projects so that the youngsters can share knowledge and the weaker students can learn from the others. Why give them a test that's the opposite?

"You could have a ball with these kids," Sue adds, "but they won't let us. We have to direct their energy another way."

Two weeks before the New Jersey ASK, a standard-bearer from Standards Solution ("From classroom formative assessments to high-stakes testing, Standards Solution assists hundreds of schools in meeting their assessment goals each year" is the company's marketing pitch) delivers a primer on test-taking to Sue's class. My presence makes the consultant visibly nervous. "This is all proprietary material," she admonishes me.

"The exam is just a cat-and-mouse game between test designers and test takers," she tells the students. "You should read multiple choice answers from bottom up, because the examiners know that kids skim 'd' and 'e.' And look out for the killer question—the stinkin', thinkin' question—between items five and eight. Skip it if you don't get it right away." The kids, who giggle at the tintinnabulation of "stinkin', thinkin'," may be absorbing some of the pointers.

In hiring this company to spend time with the fourth through sixth graders, the youngsters who are most likely to fail the ASK, the school district is behaving with its patented pragmatism—if you know the tricks of the trade, your score is likely to improve. But are these really the skills that ten-year-olds should be learning? Is this the mindset they should be acquiring?

Since second graders don't have to take this test, you might think that their teacher, Maria Casanovas, would have an easier time, but she's feeling the heat as well. Her eight-year-olds must take a practice exam that's constructed along the same lines, with open-ended essays to draft, two paragraphs in less than half an hour; multipage readings to unravel; and graphing problems in math to solve. Union City treats the test results as a distant early warning signal. "We're told that 'this is what you need to concentrate on,'" Maria says. "It's push, push, push."

Escaping the Hammerlock

Les Hanna has lived through a rough year. Her husband Richie, Union City's school superintendent in the 1980s and a generation her senior, has been laid low by a string of maladies. Not so long ago Richie was full of restless energy, but now he's homebound. Les has weathered more than her share of ailments as well. Through much of the year she has been the consummate professional—able to shelve her troubles when she's at school, radiating her trademark ebullience—but now she sounds frazzled.

"I'm worried that testing, testing, testing has taken over the nation," she tells the teachers, while going over their students' scores on the practice exam.

At the face-to-face meeting in February, her second opportunity to sit down with the district's senior administrators and review what's happening at the school, the New Jersey ASK is on everyone's mind. "Washington School is right on the cusp," Les says, borrowing the term used to describe students whose scores put them on the verge of passing. "If we continue to improve, we can get out of the hammerlock of state oversight." What's particularly encouraging is the fact that the fifth and sixth graders are improving—on the district's practice test, their scores went up by nearly 8%.

"The teachers are tense," Les adds. "They hate to leave out science." Assistant Superintendent Silvia Abbato hastens to reassure her. "They don't have to cut out science. There's an easy connection between science and math, science and reading." While that's true enough, doing a science experiment, not just reading about it, takes time. That's why Mary Ann's third graders won't be making daily observations about how plants grow.

"We're in test mode from January on," Les tells me. "We're totally geared toward the ASK. That's demoralizing for us—imagine what it's like for the kids. These children used to have plays, more art, more phys ed, but that's all gone because of the test. You want kids to have some fun in school, not be gloomy because they're doing the same thing, again and again."

The Pros and Cons of High-Stakes Testing

It is tempting to join this full-throated chorus of complaints, to damn testing as the killjoy of American education, but the reality is more complex. Testing can be a force for good, especially for the have-less kids on whom schools have too often given up—everything depends on what's being measured and how much weight that attaches to the results.[2]

High-stakes exams contributed to making Union City's schools better, from the late 1980s, when the threat of a state takeover because of students' dismal test scores forced major changes, until now, when only a few schools remain on the state's watch list and the district has become a model of steady improvement. But in the meantime educational policy has shifted from one extreme to another, going from a near absence of accountability in the old days to today's truncated understanding of what schools should be held accountable for.

The No Child Left Behind Act proclaims that all children must be "proficient" by 2014, as if saying it will make it so. But instead of setting a national standard for what all children should know—a sensible idea in a highly mobile nation—the statute lets each state decide for itself what "proficiency" means. That's a guarantee of inconsistency, since what suffices in one state doesn't necessarily satisfy the expectations of another. What's more, many state tests rely almost exclusively on multiple-choice exams, which are easier to grade, and measure only the most basic of skills—the ability to regurgitate facts learned in isolation and apart from real-life contexts.

To prepare students for this kind of exam, school districts often depend on scripted lessons—direct instruction, it's called—with the teacher posing the questions and the kids parroting the answers. But these students flounder when they're asked to solve a problem and not recite a fact. That's likely the reason why, on the Program for International Assessment, known as PISA, American high school students' rankings have fallen to seventeenth in reading, tied with Poland and Iceland, and thirty-second in math, behind Hungary and the Czech Republic.[3]

These often-cited national figures conceal big differences among the states. If New Jersey were treated as a nation, it would rank far higher—fifteenth in math and fifth in reading—and its scores on the National Assessment of Educational Progress, known as NAEP, are among the best in the country. A key reason is that, from the practice test that second graders take to the exam that high school students must pass in order to graduate, New Jersey, unlike many states, expects its youth to think and not just memorize. Writing "what if" essays, deciphering complex readings, handling word problems—these are the staple items on all the New Jersey tests.

Teaching to the test comes in for a lot of criticism, much of it justified, but teaching to *this* kind of test means readying students to become problem-solvers. The Lewis-and-Clark voyages of discovery in preschool, the learning centers in elementary school, the Socratic method in high school—all these approaches sharpen students' minds, and in a state like New Jersey, they give students a leg up on the make-or-break exams.

In states where basic skills are all that's asked for, students whose teachers cling to tradition, spending class-time lecturing or drilling them, will do fine—that is, until they take the NAEP or a college entrance exam like the Scholastic Aptitude Test (SAT). In New York City in the early 2000s, school chancellor Joel Klein was hailed as a miracle worker when students' scores rose astronomically on the state test, but these same students didn't fare nearly as well on the NAEP and SAT.[4]

New Jersey–type tests of thinking call for genuine proficiency in reading and math, and if that was all we cared about, the critics would be silenced. But we actually care about a lot more—we want students to be well-versed in science and history, geography and foreign languages, art and music; and we want them to become engaged citizens as well.[5] The enormous importance attached to the state tests pushes those subjects, and those ways of thinking, to the periphery. In all the Union City schools and in schools across the country as well, this is why, come spring, an extraordinary amount of time is spent rehashing the three R's. Whether proficiency is being judged thoughtfully or foolishly, it's too much time.

This suffocating pressure explains why Washington School changes its character during the months leading up to those exams—why a school where learning is fun turns into a school where fun comes to die. It's why *Motivation Math*, a book whose dryness gives the lie to its title, and *New Jersey ASK Coach* sit on every child's desk. It's why brainstorming, with kids sparking ideas among one another, gives way to timed practice tests. It's why plays are no longer being mounted, why kids have only one hour a week of gym, and why math problems and three-paragraph essays, not art or music, are what's on tap after school. It's why Mary Ann Rick feels that she can't ask her third grade students to perform a science experiment.

What's wrong about this understanding of what matters in education goes beyond its intellectual narrowness. Anyone who has spent time in a classroom knows that education means more than mental gymnastics, and that a teacher's mission involves more than honing the minds of her students. A youngster's sense of her own worth and potential; her capacity to form friendships; and her willingness to wait her turn, help her classmates, and contribute to the group figure significantly in the equation.[6]

Students who have honed what psychologists call "social-emotional skills" are likely to do better on the high-stakes tests than socially isolated youth. What's more, by the time they reach eighteen, they are less likely to have gotten in trouble with the law or become pregnant, and less likely as well to smoke, drink, or do drugs. This is why Nobel Prize–winning economist James Heckman, the antithesis of a softie, stresses these "soft" skills as essential to students' success. It's the reason highly regarded schools like the KIPP academies are reviving character education, which until recently was derided as mushy. It's why dawn-to-dusk, six-days-a-week, twelve-months-a-year community schools are flourishing. And it explains why Alina commits so much of her energy to "Bossbaly-izing" her kids, enticing them to become a "slice" of the Room 210 "pie."[7]

There's an important place in education for tests of literacy and numeracy. When well-designed, they assess the skills of critical thought; and when the results are used in figuring out what kinds of help would be most valuable to students and teachers, they represent a force for good. But these exams have to be kept in their place, and the Union City story illustrates how, in fetishizing them, we have gone wrong.

The New Jersey Assessment of Skills and Knowledge begins on May 2, the Monday after a weeklong vacation. When the third through sixth graders arrive at school, they enter a denuded and barren landscape. Everything that might conceivably spark a thought has vanished. The classroom walls, usually festooned with their own work, have been stripped bare. The Word Wall is gone and so is Every Day Counts. Even the classroom clock has been hidden under a sheet of butcher paper.

Many of the teachers at Washington School cook breakfast for their kids on test days, hoping that this homey touch will calm their nerves, but that's the extent of what they are permitted to do. At a somber teachers' meeting a few weeks earlier they were admonished that a breach of security—anything that even hints of cheating—means instant dismissal for the teacher and harsh penalties for the school system. If just one youngster cheats, the test results for the entire district may be invalidated and all the students forced to retake the exam.

The teachers are told that they must secure the exam as if it were a classified document: "If there's a fire, be sure to safeguard the test." To hammer home the seriousness of these instructions, the teachers are obliged to sign a "security test agreement" that bristles with legalese. No one wants a repetition of the Atlanta testing scandal, where widespread cheating by teachers and principals made a travesty of seemingly miraculous test results, embarrassing the superintendent, or the imbroglio in Washington, D.C., where suspiciously high scores in forty-one schools threatened to tarnish the image of celebrity superintendent Michelle Rhee, a leader of the "no excuses" movement.[8]

It's Raining Love

Testing consumes the better part of four school days, and in Room 210 the day afterward a band of worn-out and brain-dead third graders slump in their chairs. Alina asks them to describe their reactions to the exam. We had to write too many essays, they complain, and the readings were too long and complicated to absorb. But they feel more confident about math. "The entire math test had things I had learned from my teacher," writes Matias. "I was tempted to copy," Andres writes—perhaps the maternal pressure has gotten to him—"but I found the math easy." So did Joaquin, who dismisses the entire experience as "boring."

In every classroom the tension recedes during the days following the test, and the feeling of relief is almost palpable. April has been the cruelest month, but finally spring is busting out. The results won't be known until August. Meanwhile, the teachers replenish their storehouse of creativity and the students come alive again.

The kids in Room 210 won't be doing any more fraction drills or formulaic papers. With *Motivation Math* and *New Jersey ASK Coach* boxed up and stashed away, Alina can resume the kind of teaching she loves. Science makes its return, with an experiment that calls upon the students to compare how plants grow in soil, gravel, and sand. Everything comes together in this project—the kids paint and design boxes for their plants, search the web to find their habitats, and then write up the results, using the scientific method they've been taught ("gather the data; form a hypothesis . . ."). Later, compasses and notepads in hand, they draw a map of the school, and then head outside to map the surrounding neighborhood.

When Alina distributes iPods, something that few of her students have ever seen, the kids listen to rap and Latino folk songs and pop tunes, each in her own cocoon and each tapping out her own beat, finding the poetry and meaning that lodge in the lyrics. Alina uses one of the kids' favorites, a cleaned-up version of Katy Perry's "Hot N Cold," to teach antonyms, and "Yellow Submarine" launches a lesson on the culture wars of the 1960s.

"Imagine that many parents didn't allow their children to listen to the Beatles?" Alina tells the students, who can't understand what the fuss was about. When the girls gush over George and Paul, and the boys get into Ringo's drumming, Alina has them write about their favorite Beatle. They don't have to obsess about the number of paragraphs in their essays.

Stop by Washington School any afternoon in May and you're likely to hear dance music seeping from under the classroom doors and echoing in the corridors. Everyone is getting ready for the schoolwide multicultural extravaganza that caps off the year.

Alina remains a party girl at heart, who loves to dance till the wee hours—she'll break into a swivel-hips rumba to punctuate a story she's reading—and she's in her element. She devotes hours to choreographing a hyperflamboyant routine for her students, finding just the right music, making the costumes eye-catching, and assuring herself that her kids have their routine down pat. Most of Washington School's teachers are doing the same for their youngsters. "These families can't afford dancing lessons for their kids," says Alina, "so this is their one chance to perform."

On June 9 the gym is festooned with red, white, and blue bunting, and balloons fill the basketball nets. On one wall hangs a mural, painted by the class of 2006, which depicts George Washington admiring his namesake school. It's brutally hot—at 9 A.M., the temperature inside the gym is 101 degrees and climbing—and although three large fans, rented for the occasion, are turning and the windows have been opened wide, the air is moist and still. The bleachers are packed with parents and grandparents, who fan themselves with their programs. The kids are at full throttle, whistling and stomping so hard that the bleachers shudder.

When the youngsters file in for the opening ceremony, hoisting flags from more than fifty lands, a roar goes up for the Dominican Republic flag and another for the banner from Puerto Rico. The longest, loudest cheer is heard when the flag of the United States, their new homeland, is unfurled. Alina had asked Joaquin to carry the Chilean flag, but he demurred, complaining that it weighed too much. The real reason for his reluctance, Alina realized, is that his grandfather, who emigrated from Bolivia, will be in the audience, and for Joaquin to be representing Chile, the land of his absent father, wouldn't sit well. "Would the Bolivian flag be lighter?" Alina asked him, and that's the banner he's holding. "There you go again—spoiling Joaquin," chided third grade teacher Marilyn Corral, Alina's good friend and Cuban soul sister.

One razzle-dazzle number follows another in rapid-fire succession. An exuberantly costumed gang of kindergarteners bounces to a Trinidadian song about a tiger racing after a rabbit. Wearing jeans and carrying bandanas with the red and green colors of the Portuguese flag, a class of fourth and fifth graders performs "Danza Kuduru," carrying it off with the gusto of a halftime show, and then a band of sixth graders, Cossacks for the morning, stomps to the insistent drumming of "Rasputin." Jen Mondelli's fourth graders find the beat of "Eh Cumpari," a tune you'd hear at any Italian wedding, and Marilyn Corral's youngsters, splashily Cuban in attire, do a fancy-step routine to "We No Speak Americano." Irene Stamatopolous is leading her third graders in "Opa," her blonde mane flying, while the kids whirl in the blue and white of Greece. And sixth graders are rocking to pop star Miley Cyrus's "Party in the USA." "Welcome to the land of fame, excess / Whoa! Am I gonna fit in?" the lyrics begin, a question that many of these kids, fresh off the plane, have surely asked themselves.

The finale belongs to Alina. She has picked an unabashedly romantic Puerto Rican song, "Llueve El Amor" ("It's Raining Love"), and her choreography extracts every ounce of passion from the music. The kids are pantomiming the joys and emotions of love, and when the boys doff their caps, out flutter rose petals that garland the girls. As the last notes reverberate, they fall to their knees, smitten.

The histrionics bring the crowd to its feet, and everyone is standing when the sixties standard, "Put a Little Love in Your Heart," starts to blast from the speakers. The kids have come back on the floor, dancing and singing, and some of the parents and grandparents are jitterbugging in the bleachers. Alina is down there, and so are Les and Martha, and so is the rest of the Dream Team. They start a conga line, waving their arms and swaying together, and as the line grows longer it snakes across the floor.

I watch all this, taking it in, and then, without a moment's thought, I bolt out of my seat and run down the bleacher stairs to join them. On the gym floor, sweating buckets, I'm swaying along with everyone else on that conga line.

8

THE ODYSSEY CONTINUES
Union City School System,
One Year Later

The school year never really ends for Sandy Sanger and Silvia Abbato. The trifecta of good news from the high school gave these two administrators something worth celebrating, but there's always work to be done. After a long July Fourth weekend they're back at their desks.

The summer of 2010 was an especially trying time, with budget cuts to inflict and massive audits to prepare for. But because of yet another ruling in the long-running *Abbott* litigation, things are looking up a year later. That lawsuit, originally filed in 1981, has dragged on for three decades. Ray Abbott, the lead plaintiff, was a young schoolboy when the case began. Now he is in his thirties, an ex-convict trying to repair his life. In the Court's twenty-first decree, handed down in May 2011, a bare majority of the justices concluded that the 15% cut in the education budget passed by the state legislature will inflict a "substantial and consequential blow" to the children in the state's thirty-one poorest urban districts—the "*Abbott* districts." The Court ordered the lawmakers to come up with an additional $500 million, and so Union City will have more money to spend this year.[1]

In July, the school district has twenty million unanticipated dollars in the bank. But there's a catch. Governor Chris Christie loathes the *Abbott* case, which he has repeatedly attacked as "the Supreme Court's grand experiment with New Jersey's children." The governor has done more than bluster—he refused to reappoint a justice because he was an *Abbott* supporter. With several judicial vacancies to fill, Christie is attempting to refashion the court to his liking, and his nominees are seen as sure bets to reverse the 2011 ruling. For Union City, this imbroglio means that the $20 million must be treated as a onetime windfall.[2]

Sandy is left puzzling over how to spend the money without making commitments that must be undone the following year. Some of the money, he decides, will go toward maintenance, some to technology. Characteristically, much of it will be invested in people, especially in the coaches that have had such an impact at the high school.

A July 6 letter from the New Jersey Department of Education contains the sweetest news—Union City has fared well on the QSAC (Quality Single Accountability Continuum), the system-wide evaluation that had consumed so much time and generated so much paperwork. That's an unheard-of accomplishment among inner-city New Jersey districts, another vindication of the district's strategy of continuous improvement. "Congratulations on this accomplishment," reads the missive from Chris Cerf, the state's education commissioner.

But as with everything in the accountability-driven world of public education, the relief is only temporary. In just three years, Union City will have to go through this wringer again.

JOHN'S HOUSE

At the high school, expectations are running high because John Bennetti is now running the show.

"I was tired," Dave tells me a few months later, explaining his last-minute decision while catching up on all the house repairs that he'd neglected. "The last two years took their toll. I just couldn't gear up for another year." What goes unmentioned is the fact that, in a survey of teachers that the CAPA reviewers had conducted, he and his assistant principals were singled out for criticism, while John and the coaches came in for unstinting praise.

"This is John's house," Michelle Cowan had said the winter before, but until now that "house" had a co-tenant who held different views about how to run the school. Although shared governance was the plan, frustration was unavoidable, but now John has a free hand, as the old-guard assistant principals have been shipped to other schools. "We've given him a great team," says Sandy Sanger. "It's up to him." The day before classes begin, Sandy comes by to give the teachers a we're-in-it-together pep talk. "Everyone is part of the same mission. The banana that leaves the bunch gets skinned."

An army of scholars has written reams about what it takes to be an effective high school principal. Here's a laundry list of what they've come up with. Confronting "intense pressure to improve student learning," a principal must be "focused on academic performance," able to build "leadership structures that support schoolwide use of data," and understand "how leading and managing for instructional improvement gets done in their school and in turn use their diagnoses as the basis for mindful design and redesign." If that's not enough, a school leader "needs to be visible, accessible and provide for personal involvement of students and faculty," having learned how "to manage a network of relationships among people, structures and cultures," all the while "embracing change as exciting rather than threatening."[3]

In short, this paragon must possess the patience of Job, the wisdom of Solomon, and the people skills of Dale Carnegie.

That's an impossibly tall order. But it's a fair description of how John regards his assignment. He looks forward to putting in place the big ticket items that he has had in mind since the school opened. In his punctilious way, he has thought through everything that must happen if the high school is going to accelerate from good to great.

But life, the great prankster, can waylay such best-laid plans. On the night of September 14, 2011 less than two weeks after the opening of school, Mariah Santiago, a seventeen-year-old senior at Union City High, is killed when her boyfriend loses control of his Chevy Malibu and smashes head-on into a utility pole. Kind, joyful, outgoing, nice, no-drama, popular—that's how friends and teachers describe Mariah to a *Jersey Journal* reporter, and as word spreads the next morning, disbelief gives way to trauma. Guidance counselors patrol the halls, talking with tearful students. People at the central office are in shock as well. Everyone there knows Mariah's mother Angela, who has been a clerk in the district's special needs department for years, and they've heard countless proud-mother stories about her only daughter.

With Mariah's death, John's grand ideas must be set aside for the moment. This moment tests both his leadership and his character. A memorial service will be held the following week, he decides, and then he does something that the old guard wouldn't have considered—he trusts the students to take the lead. "They set up the entire service. They determined who should speak, they arranged for the flowers and the singers, got the technology working, organized the teachers, reached out to the parents," John recalls. "At the service I said: 'This is something no principal ever wants to go through, but it's one of our best moments, the entire community coming together.'"

The teachers and coaches at Union City High already knew that John was the go-to man when it comes to academics, but they hadn't realized how easily he could connect with students. "As the guy who was just responsible for instruction I felt a little isolated," he says. "I didn't have much contact with the students." Now his favorite part of the day is hanging out in the cafeteria, playing Spit with the kids.

Like Les Hanna at Washington School, John Bennetti is replacing a principal who had a hard time relating to many of the teachers and students; and like Les, he's working to shape a new culture. That's not something you announce—it emerges in the accumulation of small but meaningful changes that, taken together, comprise a community.

During the first week of school, John lays out what he calls the five "nonnegotiables," among them no cursing, no lateness, and no violations of the dress code. Break those rules, he says, and discipline will be automatic. But unlike Dave, who would set down the law, no questions asked, John explains why these rules matter. He ties everything to a single theme—pride and respect in "our house," the Union City High community—that's attuned to the community culture of family, unity, and *respeto*. "Cursing doesn't showcase our talents. Breaking the dress code means we're setting a tone that unity isn't important, coming in late means missing opportunities to learn." Bullying is high on his list of nonnegotiables: "We are about caring and supporting."

The students pick up on John's sincerity, and their behavior markedly improves. The year before, an average of 8% of the students showed up late; this year the figure plummets to 1.7%, and the laggards usually arrive less than five minutes after the school bell rings. Similarly sizable declines are recorded in fighting and bullying. John harbors no illusions that the school has become a sea of tranquility. He has assigned a tough-nosed assistant principal—"a pit bull with a heart," in John's thumbnail description—to manage discipline.

The principal's door used to be closed to students, except on specified occasions, but John makes himself available—and what's more, he listens. When a delegation asks for more vegetarian items on the menu, he directs the cafeteria to add more salads. Fifty kids submit a petition for a stepping club, a syncopated, hard-pounding dance routine, and they secure a coach, Carlos Sosa, a gym teacher who had been a stepper himself in college. "They're psyched," says John. "They're here at 7 A.M. to practice and the coach is volunteering his time." In past years, every activity that a teacher undertook had a dollar sign attached. When John describes Carlos's good deed in one of the email updates he sends out daily, he's telling the staff that he can't do it alone, that they're an indispensable part of the change.

"I'm open to anything," is John's stock response to students' requests. "Get yourselves a faculty adviser and I will put you on the map." By Christmas vacation there are forty-six clubs, many of them new this year, among them a crocheting club and an English honors society. "The list keeps growing," he says, "and I keep saying yes."

Until he became principal, John couldn't have cared less about school sports. "For me, academics always substituted for athletics," he tells me, a bit abashed at how wonky that sounds. But now he's running a school where a quarter of the students compete in a sport, and he plunges in enthusiastically.

When he places an order for Soaring Eagle souvenirs, including an oversized eagle talon claw, Silvia Abbato, recalling Dave Wilcomes's passion for football, gives him a jokey warning against going over to the "dark side." But the new principal won't live or die with the fortunes of the football team. He's impressed by research that shows how athletics can further his aim of building a strong community and motivating students to do well in school. Together with the assistant principal who runs the athletics department, he's formulating a plan that meshes sports and coursework.[4]

As you'd expect, academics top John's priority list. The old-guard assistant principals regarded themselves as bureaucrats; their replacements are educators in the Bennetti mold. Armed with protocols that he has prepared, they are spending lots of time in the classrooms, observing lessons and talking with the teachers, augmenting the work of the coaches. John has asked the teachers to make sure that students who are neither brainiacs nor in trouble don't slip off the radar and also to spot kids who are showing the first signs of trouble, like someone whose grade drops from B to C, before they get into hot water.

Doing better on the New Jersey HSPA, the state's graduation exam, has been the clarion call at Union City High, and John was the loudest crier. Now that the school is no longer labeled as "in need of improvement," though, he wants the teachers to think beyond getting the students to pass HSPA and graduate from high school, asking themselves what academic rigor really means. "There should be more courses that prepare students for college, not simply more work but higher-quality work," he tells me. "And I don't want teachers in regular classes to be thinking: 'This isn't an honors class. We can't challenge the kids.'"

When the high school was being planned, Silvia Abbato, who shepherds academic initiatives district-wide, decided that the curriculum should be as cutting-edge as the building. That's how Mandarin Chinese entered the picture. "I was reading about rich school districts and progressive charter schools that were offering Mandarin," Silvia tells me. "Our students are already bilingual in English and Spanish—imagine their prospects if they become fluent in Mandarin as well." Forensics was added for similar reasons. "These kids grew up on all the *CSI* TV shows—this was an innovative way to get them excited about science."

Nadia Makar, a redoubtable septuagenarian who immigrated from Colonel Nasser's Egypt more than half a century ago, has shown just how far the best Union City students can go. Year after year, under her tutelage, their research projects win statewide science competitions; and year after year, three or four of them receive full scholarships to Ivy League schools. "My mission is to show the world that these kids can do it, that you can't write off a whole class of kids," she says, and she devotes nights and weekends to work with them. "There are so many success stories—they keep me going." When the state's number-crunchers raised petty objections to Nadia's initiatives, Silvia came to the rescue. "A few years ago an auditor questioned why we spend $1.10 for posters in science fairs," Silvia recalls, still amazed at the picayune probing. "They don't understand what it means to be poor. I told him that it's better to spend that $1.10 than to have the kids use ShopRite cardboard boxes and lose the competition."

What the high school could use is someone like Nadia Makar to champion the nonscientists. By proposing to double the number of students enrolled in the honors and Advanced Placement classes, John is moving in this direction. Rather than relying solely on grades in determining who should be admitted, he has asked the teachers to take into account students' commitment and perseverance, the character traits that spell success. "You don't need a 95 to do well," John argues. "A kid with an 85 but excellent study habits can also make it in those higher-expectations classes."[5]

If Union City High is going to move from good to great, then students' attitudes about college, their widely held belief that Hudson County Community College or New Jersey City University is the best they can aspire to, must also be confronted. In fall 2011, only seventy-seven juniors out of a class of 800 take the preliminary scholastic achievement test, the PSAT, the training-ground test for students who will be applying to top-tier schools. In a year or two, John wants every student to take that test. Even more ambitiously, he'd like to make it the measure of the school's accomplishments. "The discourse among students shouldn't be 'I have to pass HSPA' but 'I have to get into a good college,'" says John, and he makes this a theme of his conversations with students and teachers. One year later comes national recognition that greatness may be at hand—a study of 22,000 high schools, conducted by the American Institutes of Research for *U.S. News & World Report*, ranks Union City High among the top 12% in the nation.[6]

High school teachers can be a stiff-necked bunch, but the teachers I talk with speak about their new principal with the veneration normally reserved for minor deities. "The atmosphere is much more positive," Pete Kliman, a veteran English teacher, tells me. "With Dave, the attitude was 'I want to be sure you're working.' He didn't get involved except when there were problems. This year there's much more approval. Everyone is more engaged."

Michelle Cowan, who now runs the language arts coaching program, sees the school "taking off in a new direction. Everything John does is thought out, planned, precise. He hates 'loosey, goosey,' and people like that." Marc Fusco, the history teacher who, the year before, buttonholed John for hours-long tutorials on teaching, was awarded tenure in June. "I love the feel of the building now that Mr. B. is running the ship," he effuses. "There is much more of a community feel. The building looks different too. It's truly a celebration of education."

"John is just fun to work for," Marc adds. "He is the man!"

No one can predict how long John Bennetti's honeymoon at Union City High will last. Eventually the teachers may weary of the expectation that they'll keep pushing themselves and the students will realize that even the most responsive principal can't give them everything they want. The killing schedule, twelve-hour days and six-day weeks, can grind down even someone as energetic and driven as John.

"The big-picture work is just starting. I won't even think about leaving until we're sailing," he says, when I pose the question. Characteristically, John the planner is already starting to contemplate what comes next. He is grooming his assistant principals and coaches to become the next generation of leaders—just as, early in his career, Fred Carrigg, Silvia Abbato, and Sandy Sanger readied him for these responsibilities. But in the first year of the Bennetti era there's not the slightest hint of disillusionment or departure. John is the man.

At the first pep rally of the 2011 football season, hard on the heels of two blowout victories by the Soaring Eagles, 3,000 students, including 600 youngsters from the ninth grade academy, cram the field to cheer on the team. It's the biggest crowd ever to gather at the high school.

"Bennetti, Bennetti, Bennetti!" the cry goes up. No principal expects this kind of accolade, and when John acknowledges the cheering he is blinking back tears. "I love these kids," he tells me. "They have such great potential. At that moment I was filled with a very surreal feeling that this is what I was meant to do in my life."

There's Always Next Year

At Washington School as well, the grind never ceases. Principal Les Hanna tackles her biggest problem, the fourth grade, by shifting Stacy Eccleston, the teacher whose fill-in-the-blanks science lesson came straight out of the 1950s, to the second grade. "Stacy didn't fight me," says Les. "I told her, 'You're a great teacher, but you haven't worked out. The change will be good for you—you know the second graders.'"

Les is right in her calculation, for Stacy blossoms in her new assignment. Second grade teacher Barbara Prieto switches places with her. "Last year the fourth graders were out of control—they became little bullies," says Les. "That can make a teacher's life miserable and she'll react accordingly. Barbara's not only a good teacher, she's a disciplinarian. She ran second grade like boot camp." The switch also alters the relationships among these teachers, bringing an end to the factionalism, and that can only benefit the kids.

A month into the summer, consumed by work and her husband's protracted illness, Les still hasn't taken a break. "You're working too hard. You've got to get away," her son, Richie Jr., who teaches history at Union City High, tells her. She's rejuvenated when the family heads for their vacation home on the Jersey Shore, a few blocks from Sandy Sanger's place. "Being a water bunny at the beach immediately gets me in a better mood," she says.

"This year I want to get more into the classrooms, to observe what's happening on a daily basis," Les tells me. "I'd like someone else to do the paperwork, so I can really be an educational leader." Happily for her, John Coccioli has retired, and so she'll get a new assistant principal. She has been lobbying on behalf of Martha Jones.

In many ways Martha looks like the perfect fit. The transition would be effortless, since the two women have worked together for years. Though Martha's title is "bilingual specialist," nothing more, she has handled everything that Les has asked of her—helping to prepare for the face-to-face meetings, drafting reports for the district administration and the state education department—without a murmur of complaint. Martha and Les exude warmth, and the intimate gesture—the arm around a child's shoulder, the hug for a nervous mom—comes effortlessly. Together they personify the culture of *abrazos* that defines Washington School.

But Sandy chooses a young eighth grade math teacher named Mike Cirone to fill the position. At the middle school where he had taught, Mike was known as a hard worker and a good citizen. The superintendent envisions that Les will continue working with teachers in the early grades while Mike devotes his time to the fourth, fifth, and sixth grades. That was supposed to be Coch's bailiwick, but he never really functioned as an academic leader, and Sandy expects Mike to fill the void. "Martha and Les are great," Sandy tells me, "but they are very much alike. Bringing in Mike introduced a fresh way of thinking."

Mike is not only an up-and-coming educator. He also has a keen appreciation for political life in the community. "I always did politics," Mike tells me, "door-knocking, working at headquarters, helping with events. Politics controls the climate and culture of education. If you choose to get involved you have some measure of influence." In Union City, politics is imbibed with mother's milk. In earlier years, most notoriously during the long-knives fights of the 1980s, it effectively determined who was promoted and who was punished. In the past, this is how hacks got ahead, but most of the hacks have now retired and talent has become the essential factor in the equation. These days, when administrative vacancies open up, incompetent loyalists need not apply.

Ten days before the start of the school year, Les is felled by pancreatitis and rushed to the hospital. While she badly wants to be standing on the front steps for the first day of school, greeting parents and kids, her doctor orders her to spend six weeks recuperating at home. Suddenly and unexpectedly, Mike finds himself thrust onto center stage, in charge of a school he knows almost nothing about, and he's understandably nervous. "For the first few days after the operation he kept asking me questions," says Les, "but I was exhausted. 'Honey, it's your responsibility,' I told him."

Mike's hard work during those make-or-break first days of school wins over the teachers. Even as he surfs the waves of paperwork he finds ways to make himself useful, whether it's moving boxes of books into classrooms, asking teachers how he can help out, or meeting the kids for whom Washington School will be their first experience of an American school.

"Here you need to understand the nitty-gritty," he tells me. "You need to be sure that the parent who's picking up a child after school doesn't have a restraining order against him or doesn't come drunk." Mike knows what he'd like to see happening in the classrooms, "but if teachers don't know you they don't trust you."

"Slow down," Alina Bossbaly advises him, like a *mamacita* calming her overexcited teenager. "You don't want a heart attack before you're forty."

"It's hard to be an academic leader when there are only two administrators for 800 kids," the newly minted assistant principal muses. "It's easy to become a plant manager." But he knows that if the school is going to make it and if his career is going to go anywhere, he must do far more than manage.

Les and Mike have their work cut out for them, because the school did not fare well on last spring's high-stakes tests. While the sixth graders' scores improved, fewer students overall passed than the previous year. What's more, the Dream Team, whose third graders had chalked up spectacular test scores in previous years, looked like mere mortals. Only 68% of their students passed the reading test, down 11% from the previous year. And fewer than half of the recent arrivals whom Alina taught, the youngsters who took the reading exam in Spanish, were proficient.

Despite the temptation to find excuses for failure, these teachers are inclined to blame themselves—they ask themselves where they went wrong, where they let their kids down. But the odds are excellent that their concerns are misplaced, that they did as good a job as ever and that happenstance, not competence, offers the best explanation.

Scores on an achievement test like the New Jersey ASK are affected by what statisticians call "noise," unexplained variations from year to year. Those variations might be caused by any number of things—days lost to snow or a flu outbreak, unseasonable weather, or the din from construction outside the school on test day. Despite the claims of the "no excuses" crowd, who insist that good teachers are all that's required for students to do well and that test scores represent the most reliable metric of success, testing remains an imperfect science. A teacher like Alina, who ranks among the most effective one year because her students' test results have improved a lot, may well find herself among the least effective the following year, and it strains credulity to conclude that in twelve short months she has forgotten everything she knows about teaching.[7]

At Washington School, the kids themselves are different from previous classes, and that may partly explain the drop in test scores. The year before, as second graders, their scores on the state's practice exam were considerably lower than those of their predecessors. Even if they had made outsized gains in third grade, they might well have fallen short of scoring 200 on the ASK, the magic—and arbitrary—number that divides the proficient from the merely partially proficient.

Nonetheless, the bottom line is that Washington will remain on the state's watch list for another year. "Les was bitterly disappointed," Silvia tells me. In these circumstances, she adds, some administrators need a kick in the pants, while others, like Les, need a dose of reassurance.

"Change has to be gradual," says Silvia, describing how she sees her job. "It's like how you teach a child to swim. You don't start by putting him in the deep end of the pool. First it's feet in, then make bubbles, then learn to float, finally learn to swim. It's the same with the state assessments—accomplish something, then move onto something harder. That's what we tell the principals. That's how you build trust."

"You can't hit it out of the park every year," Silvia explains to Les. She focuses the principal's attention on the fact that students who have been going to Union City schools for at least three years usually do well on these tests. It's the newer arrivals who have the biggest problems, and there are an unusually large number of students who recently came from other cities or other countries.

Washington School isn't the only Union City school to report lower test scores, and Union City isn't the only district to report such a decline. Similar reports have been coming in from across the state, and the reason has nothing to do with the students or the teachers. "Proficiency" means whatever the state decides, and Trenton has decided to tighten the screws. Students who would have barely passed the year before have failed this year.

There's always next year, as Silvia reminds Les. If the scores on the 2012 tests are good enough, Washington will finally rid itself of the "need of improvement" curse—at least for the moment.

ALINA'S NEW LIFE

Another big change has occurred at Washington School, and this one stuns everybody. After teaching for twenty-eight years, Alina Bossbaly, the mainstay of the third grade, is giving up her classroom to take on school-wide responsibilities.

Silvia, who has known Alina since they started teaching, frequently urged her to make the move, but she never wanted to go. "I am an asset by being a simple teacher to my students," she kept replying to Silvia's importuning. "And I mentor the girls," she would add, referring to the other third grade teachers. A few years earlier, she had reluctantly agreed to leave the classroom, only to decide after several sleepless nights that she had made a terrible mistake. That time, she persuaded Silvia to let her stay in her classroom. But after agonizing during the humid summer months, she has said yes.

These days you'll find Alina everywhere. She is helping Martha, who has received a well-earned promotion and now runs the school's bilingual program, in testing the new arrivals, making sure that they're placed in a class that matches both their fluency in Spanish and English and their academic skills. She is coaching several teachers, showing them how to turn their students into avid writers, just as she did a couple of years earlier for Mary Ann Rick, her fellow third grade teacher, and the previous year for two of the fourth grade teachers.

Alina has hardly forgotten about her last class, the kids who were in Room 210. She's their mother hen. Matias, the boy whose transformation from troublemaker to leader reminded her why she wanted to be a teacher, is flourishing in the purposeful cacophony of Sue Emmerling's fourth grade class, where he's speaking and writing entirely in English. The year before Matias had said he wanted to be a policeman or a star on the Lakers. Now he tells me: "I want to be a writer, just like you." But Joaquin, the irresistible and sometimes infuriating boy who had become almost a son to her, has not fared well with a tough-love teacher. "Maybe I did spoil him too much," Alina muses.

In 2011, a year after a Rutgers University freshman, driven to desperation by homophobic taunting, committed suicide, the New Jersey legislature passed the Anti-Bullying Bill of Rights. It's far and away the toughest such law in the country. Zero tolerance is the rule—every allegation, no matter how seemingly trivial, must now be reported, a report must be drafted, and the parents must be notified. Alina has become the school's go-to person on bullying. She goes from classroom to classroom, talking about the do's and don'ts—no more calling a classmate "fatso" or "queer," no more malicious Internet gossip. She wants kids to feel they can speak up for themselves and for others. "This isn't a school rule," she tells them. "It's the law."[8]

Although the new legislation has sparked controversy, with school administrators complaining that they are spending all their time on the paperwork, Alina loves this aspect of her job. Doing what she can to stop bullying plays straight into her commitment to bring every student into the community of Washington School—to instill *respeto*; to make each one of them, in her familiar phrase, a slice of the pie. "I believe that if we start in first and second grade, the things that happen in high school won't be going on."

"It's really exciting," Alina tells me, reflecting on her new life. She's perpetually on the run, up and down the stairs a dozen times. At the end of the day she's wiped out, ready to put her feet up and enjoy a glass of wine. "I thought it would be different," says Jesus, her ever-patient husband, but Alina doesn't know how to run less than full-out.

"There's something new every minute. The classroom was fun, but I'm more beneficial now because I belong to the school, not Room 210," she says. "Everybody knows Mrs. Bossbaly. Everyone can have a piece of me."

"One thing will really disappoint me," she adds, "if the Dream Team doesn't stick together." Her replacement, Marisol Hernandez, had been teaching students who only spoke Spanish. Here, some of her students know no English and may not have studied much Spanish in their home country, while others are almost ready for English-only instruction. She needs to teach them in separate groups, just as Alina did, switching constantly between Spanish and English. That's no mean feat, and the fact that Marisol was handed her new position with little time to prepare makes her assignment even harder.

Alina spends a lot of time with Marisol, showing her some of her favorite student projects and tutoring her in everything from setting up learning centers to motivating budding writers. The other third grade teachers are pitching in as well. "Since Alina left I've felt like I had to step up—to be less on the periphery, to take more responsibility," says Mary Ann. (During the summer she got married—she's Mary Ann Hart now—and she's over the moon.)

Before Alina moved on, the Dream Team had stayed intact for half a dozen years; this kind of stability isn't common in education, where half the teachers quit within five years. The fab five have come to know one another very well, to make the best use of their distinctive talents, and the change in chemistry comes hard. "They want Marisol to be me, but she's not me," Alina complains. "And they're not letting me move on and be me."[9]

"I lived teaching at its best," Alina tells me, reveling in the days before being proficient on a high-stakes test came to be equated with student learning and the metric for judging teachers and schools. "I loved what I did. I wanted to get up every single morning. I feel sorry for the girls. They will never get the pleasure I got out of my thirty years because of all the state and federal requirements. We should be teaching kids how to enjoy a novel, how to do math problems—lighting a fire, not filling a pail. You should read what the children write on their practice exams: 'We started our theme on x and y, this depicts one and two.' C'mon—whatever happened to creativity?"

But it isn't in Alina's nature to remain pessimistic for very long. "There's no school district that's better to its students than Union City," she says, with the fierce pride of someone who has belonged to this community ever since she came to the United States forty years earlier. "Even with all the test pressure, we are still giving our kids what they need—the love, attention, culture, health, caring about parents, emotional well-being, creative spark.

"When I retire I am going to be an advocate for enjoying learning. You know me—I won't shut up!"

9

WHAT UNION CITY CAN TEACH AMERICA

Nationwide, Slow and Steady Wins the Race

What works there can't work here—we're different because [fill in the blank]: Skeptics will dismiss the narrative of Union City's accomplishments as a one-off—a remarkable story, granted, but one that's as rare as the Hope Diamond, and for that reason irrelevant anyplace else.

Confronted with an exemplar, rejection is the knee-jerk reaction among leery practitioners. As Harvard education professor Richard Elmore acidly observes, "educators are fond of responding to any piece of research that demonstrates a promising approach, or any seemingly successful example from practice, with a host of reasons why 'it'—whatever it is—would never work in their setting." Among the doubters, that's tantamount to a death sentence. "Public education," Elmore adds, "is astonishingly, perversely, and ferociously parochial and particularistic; all significant problems are problems that can only be understood in the context of a particular school or community; no knowledge of any value transfers or adapts from one setting to another."[1]

This time the naysayers are flat-out wrong.

Let's be clear—no other school district has exactly the same portfolio of dilemmas and opportunities as Union City. On the one hand, few communities are as poor or as crowded or as crammed with immigrants; but on the other, few can claim an ally as commanding as Mayor Brian Stack or spend as lavishly on their students. It turns out, however, that these differences matter far less than the "not-made-here" skeptics presume.

Three change-minded school systems—very different from one another and from Union City as well—illustrate this point. All three approach the challenge with a Union City–like absence of superstars and fireworks, and all three are succeeding. They are steadily rewriting the script for poor and minority kids, boosting achievement and closing gaps, relying on strategies as research-tested and securing results comparable to Union City's. Yet each of the three is missing one or more of the elements that a skeptic might claim are the impossible-to-duplicate preconditions of Union City's success—its small size and homogeneity, its money, its political support, and its students raised in a culture of *respeto*.

The school systems in Montgomery County, Maryland, a district far larger than Union City with a populace that's as socially and economically varied as Union City's is homogeneous; in the recession-decimated farm town of Sanger, California, with half the per-pupil funding of Union City; and in the sprawling, featureless suburb of Aldine, Texas, united mostly by its poverty, are raising achievement levels for all students, with the same slow-and-steady approach that works so well in Union City.

Beyond their confines, the public has never heard of these places, and it's easy to see why. Journalists thrive on color, and in these locales there's nothing sexy to report—no bigger-than-life figure like Geoffrey Canada at the Harlem Children's Zone; no overnight progress after the mass firing of inept teachers, as was said to have happened in Washington, D.C. when Michelle Rhee ran the show. If you consider the volume of grunt work in the Union City superintendent's office, Thomas Edison's whiskery maxim about the 99%-to-1% ratio of perspiration to inspiration sounds about right.

This seeming ordinariness, the absence of drama that would garner headlines, partly explains what makes these districts so good—instead of courting attention, they're minding the store.

DIVERSE COMMUNITIES, SIMILAR RUBRICS

With an enrollment of 15,000 students, Union City is small by metropolitan standards, and that scale makes it a relatively manageable system. What's more, the almost entirely Latino population of the city forms a cohesive community. But as Montgomery County, Maryland and Aldine, Texas show, neither smallness nor like-mindedness is an essential ingredient of success.[2]

The public schools in Montgomery County, which borders Washington, D.C., to the north, are blessed with generous funding, but there the similarities with Union City end. Its enrollment is ten times bigger and infinitely more varied—half the students, mainly white and Asian, come from privilege, while the rest, African American as well as Latino, live on the edge of poverty. The school system is doing well by all of them.[3]

In the verdant enclaves of this suburb, multimillion-dollar estates are scattered across the landscape. The residents include some of Washington's power brokers, the lobbyists and lawyers who run the town, as well as the CEOs of international corporations like Marriott, Lockheed, and Discovery Communications that have their headquarters here. It's an intellectual hub as well—30% of the adults have postgraduate degrees, more than anywhere else in the nation. Renowned scientists work at a host of government agencies based here, among them the National Institutes of Health, the Department of Energy, and the Food and Drug Administration, as well as at biotech firms that cluster in the East Coast's answer to Silicon Valley. The only poor people you're likely to encounter are nannies and gardeners.[4]

Travel just a few miles, though, and you enter not just another neighborhood but another world. This isn't the inner city—there are no gutted buildings and boarded-up windows—but appearances can mislead. Inside the tired-looking multifamily homes, the laundry hanging on the front porch, a dozen people may be jammed into a three-bedroom apartment. In this part of town one family in six is certifiably poor and the rest are barely making ends meet. The recession bludgeoned these families, and in the past few years there has been a 60% increase in applications for food stamps.[5]

Two school systems within one—that's what Jerry Weast found when he became superintendent in the summer of 1999. Montgomery County had long been rated the best academically among the nation's big school systems, but the glowing overall figures camouflaged an achievement gap that could more aptly be labeled a chasm.

One explanation for this gap was the district's funding formula. Every school, whether in a rich or poor neighborhood— "green zone" and "red zone" neighborhoods, the superintendent labeled them—received the same amount of money for each student. To Weast, this superficial equality actually shortchanged the kids from the red zone, who needed the most help.

The superintendent had to do lots of persuading to convince well-to-do parents that money should be diverted from their schools and funneled to the poorer schools. The case he made combined an ethical claim—doing something extra for these students is socially responsible—with an appeal to self-interest. A good school system increases property values, he reminded them, and you can only have a good system if all the students are doing well. Ultimately, the school chief staked his reputation and his job on the promise that everyone, not just the poor and minority students, would be better off. "I'll raise the bar *and* close the gap," he vowed.

As in Union City, the process of change began—for research-proven reasons—with the toddlers, but where Union City reached out to include every mom-and-pop daycare center in the city, Montgomery County opened new prekindergarten classes mainly in the red zone. As in Union City, it was essential to develop a district-wide K–12 curriculum, with instruction carefully aligned and sequenced across grades and schools. A commitment to monitoring and coaching teachers was also a must. Initially, these changes didn't go down well among teachers who had been free to teach as they pleased. Because Montgomery County is a big district, it is harder for the superintendent to get the word out and build confidence, but by spending endless hours in the schools, Weast and his staff made sure that the changes would stick.

Some innovations, like a direct teaching, with its Q-and-A format, were introduced only in red zone schools. Critics argued that this pedagogy muffled creativity, but the administrators countered that it was working, and rising test scores made out a decent case for Weast's approach. Other initiatives, such as smaller class sizes and in-house coaches for struggling teachers, were initiated in the red zone and later implemented in every school.

The size and diversity of Montgomery County doubtlessly affected Weast's strategy. Still, it followed much the same course as Union City: setting high expectations for its students; sticking to its long-term goals; developing a uniform curriculum; expanding prekindergarten ("it's at the top of my list of priorities," Weast tells me); emphasizing early reading; strengthening ties among teachers, principals, and administrators; and making sophisticated use of data to figure out what kind of help would benefit students and teachers the most. And as in Union City, the approach worked. In 2003, only half the district's black and Hispanic fifth graders passed the state's reading test; by 2011, 90% did. Fewer than half the district's kindergarteners could read in 2003; by 2011, more than 90% could read, and students in the red zone were doing nearly as well as those in the green zone. In 2011, 62% of Montgomery County eighth graders passed algebra, one of the benchmarks on what Weast called the "roadmap to college," and enrollment in Advanced Placement classes, another benchmark, had doubled. (Deputy Superintendent Frieda Lacey became famous for "appearing in principals' offices with a list of names of qualified African American students in their buildings who were not in AP courses, and talking with students themselves about why they were not enrolling."[6]) For each benchmark there is solid progress to report, and the bottom line is much the same—overall the students are doing better and the improvement is greatest in the red zone schools.

Montgomery County is hardly standing pat, congratulating itself on its accomplishments. In recent years, as complaints about the narrowness of the district's curriculum mounted, the district junked its narrow three R's emphasis, opting to include more science, history, phys ed, and art. And direct instruction has been banished, replaced by a more hands-on pedagogy that resembles Union City's approach.[7]

Problems in the high schools have also evoked rethinking. The district's concentration on the top half of its high school students, which led many more of these high-flyers to take AP classes and the SAT, essentially ignored the rest of the students. While enrollments in four-year colleges are up, among the one-third of the graduates who go to the local community college, most have to take remedial courses, dramatically increasing the odds that they'll drop out. What's more, the all-important graduation gap hasn't gone away. In 2010, 95% of whites and Asians, but just 85% of blacks and 79% of Latinos, earned their diplomas. Compared to national figures, that's impressive, but it falls short of what Union City has accomplished, and no one in the Montgomery County administration is satisfied by those figures.

It would be a mistake, though, to conclude from this recital that the district has failed. A fairer assessment is that in Montgomery County, as in Union City and other solid school systems, the hard work—the "plan, do, review" process of continuous improvement—is neverending.

Like Montgomery County, Aldine, Texas dwarfs Union City in size, and its population is considerably more diverse. But the well-off and well-educated families that congregate at the edge of the nation's capital are nowhere to be seen in this pancake-flat part of the country. Aldine's population isn't divided between rich and poor, but between poor Latino and poor black. This is Houston's poor cousin—the per capita income, $12,858 in 2010, is barely half the statewide average—an unincorporated, census-designated territory without a hub, all strip malls and tract homes.[8]

The Aldine school district sprawls over 111 square miles, and though you probably never heard of it unless you're a Texan, it enrolls more students, 64,000, than Boston or Washington, D.C.[9] Two-thirds are Latino, including many new immigrants (a quarter of the students are learning English), and almost all the other youngsters are black. Whether because they're poor, are having a hard time coping emotionally or mastering schoolwork, or don't speak the language, 70% of the students are identified as "at risk," about the same as in Union City, a label that makes them prime candidates for failure. But Aldine, like Union City, has thumbed its nose at the odds.

There is no embracing culture in Aldine to buoy these students, as there is in Union City. And because of its size, cementing good relations between far-flung schools and an administration bent on improving student outcomes is harder to accomplish. Yet despite these disadvantages, Aldine has become a poster-child for boosting achievement and narrowing the achievement gap.

In the mid-1990s Aldine's schools were a disaster area. State achievement tests showed that many high school students could barely read or write, and local employers complained that the graduates lacked the skills needed for skilled jobs. Aldine's school leaders settled on a course of action broadly similar to the approach taken by Montgomery County and Union City. In Aldine, as other poor communities, families may move as often as three or four times in a single year; to make sure that these transient students don't become hopelessly confused, every school needs to teach essentially the same material at the same time. While a common curriculum had long existed on paper, no one in authority had ever gotten specific—demanding, for instance, that place value be taught during the first six weeks of second grade. "We made sure that everyone taught what was supposed to be taught," Wanda Bamberg, Aldine's superintendent, tells me.

In order to win over the teachers and principals persuading them to change their practices, Bamberg made good use of the unity the district did have. "Homegrown" is the watchword—while families come and go, many teachers and administrators have spent their entire career here; and as in Union City, these deep ties have generated a great deal of local pride. "We're tired of this," Bamberg recalls her colleagues' common sentiment when confronted with the fact of the students' abysmal performance. "Our kids can do as well as anyone else's."

In shaping its curriculum, the district didn't turn to an outside specialist. Just as Union City did, it relied on its own, bringing its best teachers together. They laid out what, for example, every second grader should be expected to know in math, and to assure continuity those expectations were shared with the first- and third-grade teams as well. Hundreds of teachers, working over a single feverish summer, produced a K–12 week-by-week blueprint that faithfully tracked the state standards. Some teachers initially disliked the new approach, the superintendent acknowledges, regarding it as too constricting. "But after the first year, they saw that all children truly had access to the complete curriculum, and our test scores reflected that. We became a Recognized School District in one year. Recognized—that is an honor in the state of Texas. What happened then is teachers were willing to do even more."[10]

Achievement scores have been steadily climbing ever since and now exceed the state average. Even without Union City's advantages, Aldine has been able to pursue a similar course, consistently striving to boost the skills of its teachers, closely monitoring its students' progress, keeping expectations high and goals in focus. In 2010, 91% of the students were judged proficient in reading on the state's exam, up from 61% in 2003, and during this period the percentage of students who passed the math test for their grade level doubled to 81%. Aldine currently ranks second-best in the state for black students and third-best for Latinos in terms of achievement—amazing results for a place without much of an identity.

As the test scores in Aldine went up so did the graduation rate. Seventy-one percent of the class of 2009 graduated in four years and 10% more stayed in school an extra year in hopes of finishing. That's a bit better than the national average. But in 2012, the dropout rate among Latino students rose significantly, and this has the superintendent worried. "More and more we have kids coming from Mexico with spotty schooling," she says. "Their families are into survival—they don't see much value in education." At the other end of the academic spectrum, little energy has been devoted to the Advanced Placement classes—the district has focused on helping students at the bottom—and AP test scores have remained stagnant. While more than half of the graduates start college, an abysmally low 17% of them earn a degree.

These items are on Wanda Bamberg's to-do list—she knows that although the district has come a long way, a lot still needs to be done.

Money Matters

Some economists claim that money doesn't affect educational outcomes, but try telling that to any educator and you'll elicit head-shaking disbelief.[11] Of course money doesn't assure good outcomes, just as money doesn't guarantee happiness, but it still can make a considerable difference.

With nearly $18,000 to spend on each of its students, Union City can afford to offer universal preschool, slash class sizes, provide custom-tailored bilingual education, hire coaches and community outreach workers, offer classes in Mandarin Chinese, and pay for user-friendly technology. In Montgomery County, Superintendent Jerry Weast could persuade the board of education to commit an additional $60 million to the red zone schools, because of the county's enviable tax base and its tradition of generously underwriting its public schools. Now those schools spend about as much for each student as Union City. Aldine, which has neither a generous state nor well-off citizens to rely on, spends less than $8,000 per pupil. Those facts of life have forced the district to move much more slowly on key initiatives.

What's happening in early education shows how money really matters. Like all the other successful school systems, Aldine shares Union City's commitment to preschool—even when its budget was being cut it preserved full-day prekindergarten for four-year-olds because of its proven long-term benefits. But Union City delivers full-day prekindergarten for all three- and four-year-olds, while Aldine can only afford to help its poorest families, sparking tensions in the community. "Why them and not us?" complain parents whose children are denied this opportunity. Moreover, well-off districts don't have to make hard choices among priorities—rather than either-or they can do both-and. Montgomery County had the resources to invest on several fronts at the same time, reducing class sizes in the red zone elementary schools and simultaneously raising the profile of Advanced Placement classes. Aldine, obliged to triage, opted to focus on its most vulnerable students at the expense of the brightest.

But despite the skeptics' murmurs, money is not a deal-breaker.

Consider what's happening in Sanger, a small rural district in California's Central Valley. It's a medium-sized town, population 45,000, and close-knit. You can think of those factors as advantages, but Sanger, clobbered by the recession, suffers the same grinding poverty as Aldine.[12]

The average wage-earner makes less than 40% of the state average and the,unemployment rate is twice the state average. The child poverty rate is three times higher than the national average and three-quarters of the youngsters receive government-subsidized meals at school. In this predominantly Mexican American district nearly a quarter of the students are immigrants who have yet to master English. School budgets in California have been decimated, and so this district, like Aldine, is making do with about $8,000 per pupil.

In 2003 Sanger was labeled a "failing" school system and put on the state's watch list, but what a difference a decade can make. Sanger now ranks among the top half of California districts in reading and math, much higher when compared to school systems with a similar profile. In 2011 78% of the Latino students graduated, placing Sanger among the top 10% of districts nationwide.[13]

As in the other high-performing districts, nothing flashy is happening— just a vigilant focus on student learning. Visit these schools, say researchers Jane David and Joan Talbert, who have spent several years studying Sanger, and you'll see teachers and principals working together, not operating as independent contractors; principals trained to "lead the learning," rather than to manage the building; a coherent and uniform curriculum; teachers picking up new skills from coaches and from one another; decisions about what initiatives to introduce based on information that specifies, student by student, what's needed; and "principal summits," the equivalent of Union City's face-to-face meetings, which are designed to set common standards for the schools, gauge each school's progress, and determine what improvements are needed.

"None of these elements is unique," as Talbert and David point out, "but rarely are they found working synergistically in one district over many years." That's what's happening in Sanger—and for Sanger, you can substitute Union City or Montgomery County or Aldine.

If you contrast Sanger with Union City, however, you'll see what money can buy. Despite Sanger's skill at extracting money from foundations, there are more students and fewer supports for teachers; and while some four-year-olds attend preschool, it's impossible to offer prekindergarten to all three- and four-year-olds.[14]

Do those differences matter? It's impossible to draw a straight line between money and student achievement, but you can make a reasonably informed guess. While many more youngsters in Sanger are passing the state's language and math exams now than a decade ago and the achievement gap is narrowing, 40% of the students, and a considerably higher percentage of the immigrant kids, still fail those high-stakes tests. Enrollment in Advanced Placement classes remains relatively low and for many students college seems a remote aspiration. Give Sanger the kind of resources that Union City is blessed with and you'd likely see similarly remarkable outcomes.

POLITICAL CLOUT, QUIESCENT UNIONS, AND RESPECTFUL STUDENTS

Brian Stack, Union City's peripatetic mayor, towers over the local political scene. His clout in statewide affairs explains why his hometown boasts a $180 million state-of-the-art high school and a spare-no-expenses early education center. There are precious few school systems that can lay claim to such a benefactor, but a district doesn't require a friend in high places to do well.

What *is* essential is a solid working relationship between the politicians and the administrators, and that's often a stumbling block. When Jerry Weast became Montgomery County's superintendent, he landed in a fraught and noisome political environment. An impatient school board was accustomed to behaving like its counterparts in other large school systems, chewing up and spitting out superintendents in quick succession. This kind of churn is the enemy of success, for with revolving-door superintendents there's no chance for new ideas to stick. In such places the teachers may well adopt a wait-out-the-new-guy attitude—understandably enough, since the incumbent school chief will be gone before having a chance to implement those bright new ideas.[15]

"When I took the job, I looked at the wall of photos of my predecessors," Weast tells me. "They had lasted an average of less than four years. I had to succeed in a tough environment." The superintendent needed to win over the county council as well: while the Montgomery County school board controls education policy, the council determines how much money the district has to spend. This bifurcated process invites disputes, with the school board naturally wanting more money and the council just as naturally wanting to make sure that the taxpayers' dollars are well spent. The proliferation of interest groups, ranging from business leaders to community-based organizations that represent myriad ethic groups, adds pungency to the political stew. In the diplomatic phraseology of the superintendent's chief of staff, Brian Edwards, "there is a spirited and ongoing debate about education spending." It takes a skillful politician to survive in such an environment, and Weast, with his low-key manner and his "we," not "I" approach, proved a master convincer.

In running a school system, as in most ventures, nothing succeeds like success. "Judge me by the results," Weast declared to the politicians when he took the post, and as the district kept doing better and better, shrinking the achievement gap and raising the bar for all students, these officials became prouder and prouder. In this virtuous circle, the political vote of confidence gave the superintendent the breathing space necessary to make his agenda stick. That led in turn to still-better outcomes and greater political enthusiasm for the district's mission.[16]

Is a docile union essential for the kind of education reform these districts are practicing? Some would lay the blame for every conceivable kind of school failure at the feet of the unions, and certainly if a union goes to war against an administration's reform efforts everyone feels the pain.[17] But experience in these districts shows that quiescent labor relations aren't a necessity. Indeed, the teachers union in Union City is no patsy—as we've seen, among the more serious roadblocks that principals and administrators have to face are contract provisions that make it almost impossible to dismiss bad teachers.

Successful school districts have found ways of working with the local union, often by bringing them to the table, and not just when it's time to negotiate the contract. In Montgomery County, Jerry Weast won over union leaders by inviting them to participate in shaping policy. "I've learned the value of shared governance," he says. "Sometimes it takes a little more time to learn to play team ball, but it *is* team ball."[18]

Labor-management cooperation doesn't come easily or naturally, for these two parties have a history of antagonisms. It requires an arduous process of building mutual understanding and, eventually, trust. Consider the roller-coaster relationship between the school administration and the union in Sanger. In 1999, would-be teachers were confronted by a union-sponsored billboard on the highway into town: "Welcome to the Home of 400 Unhappy Teachers." A decade later, though, things had turned around. "There is not one principal in this town I would not work for," says a union activist.[19] Instead of treating the union as the foe in an I-win-you-lose contest of wills, Superintendent Marc Johnson, like Jerry Weast in Montgomery County, made collaboration a priority. He brought the leadership into the policy conversation, looking for common ground by focusing squarely on students' needs.

There have been hiccups along the way. A few years ago, Sanger High School teachers complained to the union that they had been reprimanded by school administrators for not faithfully following the protocol of direct instruction, the teacher-centered pedagogy that the system uses in all its schools. The approach was ill-suited to getting adolescents to think critically, the teachers complained, and the union president took their concerns to the school board. Meanwhile, the superintendent, alerted to the brewing crisis, worked with key teachers to adapt the pedagogy and make the evaluations less formalistic. That solved the problem in the short term, but it took some time to reassure alienated teachers that the dread "gotcha" style of supervision, with its reliance on intimidation rather than assistance, hadn't become the new norm.[20]

Still, in every one of these exemplary districts, trust has been achieved even as teachers are both evaluated and supported far more intensively than in a typical school system. It isn't the union that makes or breaks a district's efforts to change outcomes for poor and minority students—it's the district's commitment to turning the personnel they have into the professionals they need.[21]

What about the kids themselves—are they Union City's secret sauce? Some educators will contend, sotto voce, that achievement gains can be realized so much more easily with poor Latino kids rather than poor African American youngsters, and with young immigrants, strivers imbued with the culture of *respeto*, instead of American-born youth who have grown suspicious of authority.

This hoary notion of the "model" student, with Latinos filling in for Asians in the equation, gives the skeptics one more reason to dismiss the lessons of Union City, one more way to say "*this* difference makes all the difference."[22] But it won't wash—Montgomery County and Aldine enroll large numbers of African Americans, and they are doing as well as the Latino youngsters who go to those schools.[23]

In sum, small size, money, a union that doesn't obstruct reform, a powerful political ally, a community that is habitually respectful of teachers—these would be pluses in any change-minded school district. But their absence doesn't doom real reform.[24]

No Blueprint, but Bedrock Principles

At the other end of the spectrum from the skeptics—the educators who believe their own circumstances are so idiosyncratic that no lessons can be gleaned from anywhere else—are the copycats who want to xerox the blueprint. I don't need to know the details, they say, just tell me the four or eight or twelve steps we have to take to get the same results. The Sanger school district regularly fields inquiries about how to run a "principal summit," as if that's the way to banish failure, and for the same reason Aldine is asked to share its minutely specified curriculum and Union City shows off its model prekindergarten.

The emissaries are on a fool's errand. These districts didn't change by behaving like magpies, taking shiny bits and pieces and gluing them together. Instead, each of them strove to develop a coherent system reaching from preschool to high school, based on evidence of what works in their own district, and they have kept tinkering with it, learning as they go.

Would-be reformers cannot act like copycats because there's no blueprint they can copy, no off-the-shelf model they can take home and plug in. You'd never confuse Aldine, Texas, land of the endless strip mall, with cosmopolitan Montgomery County, or gritty Union City with rural Sanger, and so it shouldn't come as a revelation that each place will do some things in its own idiosyncratic way. Sanger relies on a teacher-centered approach while Union City students have a hands-on experience; Montgomery County concentrated on the most promising high school students, while Aldine made the weakest and most vulnerable youngsters its top priority.

What do these effective school systems have in common? Core principles.

They put the needs of students, not the preferences of the staff, at the center of decision making.

They start early by investing in quality preschool.

They rely on a rigorous, consistent, and integrated curriculum.

They make extensive use of data to diagnose problems and pinpoint what's required to solve them.

They build a culture that combines high expectations with respect and a "we can do it" emphasis on the positive.

They value stability and avoid political drama.

They are continuously improving—planning, doing, reviewing—turning a system comprised of schools into a school system.

WHAT *DOESN'T* WORK—LEADING BY INTIMIDATION AND EXALTING CHOICE

The skeptics can be won over by facts and the copycats can be convinced that they have to figure out the needs of their own community. But the transformers detest mainstream school systems as deadwood bureaucracies that habitually shortchange our children, and evidence to the contrary won't budge them. They won't find much to like in Union City's approach because they're sure that they have a better idea. A couple of ideas, actually—tighten the screws on the public schools and rely on the market. Neither one works.

Rather than cultivating a sense of esprit and a culture of high expectations, as a place like Union City does, the transformers embrace a boot camp approach. *No excuses*—teachers' and principals' heads must roll if test scores don't pick up. "As a teacher in this system," asserted Michelle Rhee, the former chancellor of schools in Washington, D.C., and a star in this galaxy, "you have to be willing to take personal responsibility for ensuring your children are successful despite obstacles. You can't say, 'My students didn't get any breakfast today,' or 'No one put them to bed last night,' or 'Their electricity got cut off in the house, so they couldn't do their homework.'"[25] It's an article of faith that instilling fear among teachers and principals will prod them into doing better, and they cite the supposed successes of celebrities such as Joel Klein in New York City and Michelle Rhee in Washington to prove their point. But the facts at hand do not square with the faith.[26]

Thirty years ago, when Joe Clark became the principal of Eastside High in Paterson, New Jersey, he inherited one of the roughest inner-city schools in the state. Determined to restore order at all costs, Clark became the educator's equivalent of a drill sergeant. He took to roaming the corridors, carrying a baseball bat and bullhorn, convinced that he could terrorize students into learning.

Clark made for great copy. His photo, with his trademark Louisville Slugger in hand, graced the cover of *Time* magazine. *60 Minutes* profiled him twice. A bio-pic, *Stand by Me*, starring Morgan Freeman, topped the box-office charts. New Jersey governor Thomas Kean proclaimed Eastside a "model school" and President Reagan was so impressed that he offered Clark a job as his White House education adviser. In 1990, Clark quit his post to become a motivational speaker. His website lists the top-dollar appearances he made at universities across the country.[27]

But Clark proved to be more of a self-promoter than an educator. Even after he expelled hordes of adolescents—he once tossed out 300 students in a single day, leaving them to acquire their education on the streets—Eastside High remained a disaster area. Indeed, so appalling was its academic record that, the year after Clark departed, New Jersey declared Eastside a failing school and took it over.

Joe Clark has long since faded into history. But is Michelle Rhee, the chancellor of the Washington, D.C., schools from 2007 to 2010 and still a commanding presence in education circles, déjà vu all over again?

In her unwavering commitment to the discipline-and-punish approach, Rhee can fairly be characterized as Clark's spiritual heir. Clark aimed his fire at miscreant students. Rhee made herself the scourge of teachers and principals who in her estimation weren't up to the job. (Among the hundreds who Rhee fired was the principal of the high-performing school that her own children attended.) "I got rid of teachers who had hit children, who had had sex with children. Why wouldn't we take those things into consideration?" she told a *Washington Post* reporter, without proffering any evidence to back up her charges. She relied on fear as a motivator. "We want educators to feel the pressure."[28]

Like Clark, Rhee figured out how to use the outsized gesture to keep herself in the headlines. Clark had his baseball bat. Rhee's weapon of choice was a broom, meant to represent her iron determination to make a clean sweep, and she posed, broom in hand, for a *Time* magazine cover story. "I'm going to fire [a principal] in a little while," she told a PBS crew. "Do you want to see that?" No reporter could turn down such an offer, and the principal was humiliated on the air. Message sent.

To this day, Michelle Rhee's reputation rests on the remarkable gains in achievement scores recorded in Washington, D.C., during her tenure. "People say, 'Well, you know, test scores don't take into account creativity and the love of learning,' . . . I'm like, 'You know what? I don't give a crap.'"[29] After resigning as chancellor, she was rewarded for her accomplishments with more than half a billion dollars in grants to launch Students First, an organization that promotes state legislation that ends teachers' collective bargaining rights and favors vouchers.

But policy analyst Matthew Di Carlo, senior fellow at the Albert Shanker Institute, takes issue with Rhee's claim that her patented approach—mass dismissals, coupled with higher salaries for teachers whose students showed rapid progress—affected students' performance. "Her performance bonus program has not worked," Di Carlo writes, "there was little meaningful change in [District of Columbia] testing performance. . . . Moreover, the graduation rate was also essentially unchanged—moving from 72% in 2009 to 73% in 2010."[30]

What's worse, those purported gains on the achievement tests may well be bogus. A team of USA Today reporters that spent months digging into the data identified an unusually high rate of erasures on tests as well as suspiciously large gains at one-third of Washington's elementary and middle schools.[31]

Was cheating by adults, not better performance by students, the true explanation of the D.C. miracle? Did Rhee's style of leading through fear, which earned her such renown, prompt fretful subordinates to cheat in order to keep their jobs? Was the broom-wielding approach as much of a failure as Joe Clark's bat-brandishing? The year after Rhee departed, the district's test scores didn't improve, as they had in previous years, and sharp declines were recorded in several schools where cheating was alleged to have occurred. So much for the D.C. miracle.[32]

A few months after the USA Today expose appeared, the Atlanta Constitution uncovered cheating in fully half of Atlanta's elementary and middle schools, the biggest such scandal ever recorded. An investigation conducted by state officials found that nearly 200 administrators, principals, and teachers had changed children's test scores for at least a decade.[33]

The parallels with Washington are striking. Atlanta Superintendent Beverly Hall, who had been chosen national Superintendent of the Year in 2009 on the basis of similarly dramatic test-score gains, was as hard-hearted as Rhee, warning principals that they'd lose their jobs if test scores didn't improve enough in three years.

No one has proven that Michelle Rhee or Beverly Hall orchestrated, or even knew about, the cheating. These superintendents may well have clean hands, but that's really beside the point. If you're a teacher or a principal whose job is on the line and you're ordered to accomplish what seems unattainable, cheating is a predictable response. Meanwhile, real gains in test scores as impressive as the phony gains reported in Atlanta and Washington continue to be chalked up in Union City, as well as in Montgomery County, Aldine, and Sanger.

What's the difference? As the old proverb goes, you can catch more flies—or gain the allegiance of more teachers—with honey than vinegar. The superintendents in the true success-story school districts lead by encouragement, not fear. Their enthusiasm helps teachers to do a better job, and it's the students who ultimately benefit.

The transformers also pin their faith on the market. Students who are now dropping out in droves would make great strides, they insist, if only they could escape the deadening hand of public schools.[34] That's why they favor voucher plans, which let parents choose a school for their kids, as well as charter schools, publicly funded but largely free from state strictures.

The jury is still out when it comes to vouchers. Several studies, including a 2002 analysis by the Government Accountability Office, Congress's watchdog, find that, while parents like having a say in where their youngsters go to school, the youngsters who use vouchers to attend private schools generally fare no differently than those, also eligible for vouchers, who go to public schools.[35]

The best-designed study, a 2012 evaluation of Milwaukee's voucher plan, reaches the same nonconclusion. The Brew City has operated a voucher system for more than a generation; currently, 23,000 children from poor families, more than a quarter of the students in the district, attend 106 private schools. To what end? While reading and science test scores are higher for the voucher students in high school than for those who remain in the public schools, their math scores are worse for all grades. And the fourth graders in the public schools outperform voucher students in science and

English as well as math. None of these effects is especially large. The bottom line: "no clear positive impact."[36]

Neither Milwaukee's private academies nor its public schools are doing well by the kids. Students' test scores remain among the worst of any big city, rivaling Detroit and Cleveland, on a par with the performance of black students in the rural Deep South. The city-run schools contain a hodgepodge of options, and this scattershot approach may be contributing to the problem. Consistency would make much better sense.

What's happening in Louisiana, which has embarked on the nation's biggest voucher experiment, is unambiguously scary. The scheme, adopted in 2012 and open to half of the state's students, lets anyone who can breathe set up shop as a voucher-eligible school. That makes perfect sense to the state's education commissioner, John White, who contends that "it's a moral outrage that the government would say, 'We know what's best for your child.' Who are we to tell parents we know better?"[37]

You might wonder whether the state's chief school officer should be admitting that he doesn't know what children and schools should be doing, but a look at the academies he has approved for vouchers shows how right he is. What they teach makes a mockery of the constitutional separation of church and state—a mockery of good educational practice as well. At New Living Word, the state's biggest voucher school, students learn by watching DVDs that mix Biblical verses with subjects like chemistry or composition. (The school has a high-scoring football team but no library.) First- through eighth-grade students at Eternity Christian Academy sit in cubicles, learning from Christian workbooks, like the science text that explains "what God made" on each of the six days of creation. Other voucher schools use social studies texts warning that liberals threaten global prosperity and biology texts saying the Loch Ness Monster proves that evolution never happened.[38]

This is shooting-fish-in-a-barrel fodder for a Jon Stewart monologue, but nobody has to wait for the researchers to conclude that it's disastrous for the kids. What's happening in Louisiana, and may well happen in other states, is the ideology of "market knows best" carried to its logical extreme.

Charter schools, the kinder and gentler face of privatization, have proliferated in recent years. More than two million students attend charters, prompting *Wall Street Journal* editorial-writers to hail 2011, when thirteen states passed legislation liberalizing voucher and charter regulation, as "the year of school choice."[39]

Like their cousins in the voucher movement, charter advocates contend that the public schools have hit the skids and that charters are the only way to rescue education. But this rhetoric can't be squared with the data.[40]

The most rigorous evaluation, *Multiple Choice: Charter School Performance in 16 States*, conducted by the Stanford Center for Research on Educational Outcomes, concludes that charter students do slightly worse overall than youngsters in the regular public schools on state achievement tests. *The Evaluation of Charter School Impacts*, a 2010 study prepared by the U.S. Department of Education, reaches a similar conclusion—"no significant difference" in academic outcomes.[41]

Charter schools were originally conceived of as sites for innovation, launched by creative educators eager to test out new approaches to teaching and learning, but that romantic vision doesn't depict contemporary reality. Now many charters belong to chains, and rather than feeding ideas into the public schools, they often behave so antagonistically that for all intents and purposes they have become private schools.

The best charter school systems, such as KIPP and Green Dot, do a fine job of educating poor and minority kids, but they are rarities.[42] The fastest-growing segment of the charter market, online schools, do a wretched job. A study of students enrolled in virtual charters in Pennsylvania concluded that, although they were academically stronger than their counterparts when they enrolled, they ended up with gains "significantly worse" than youngsters who attended brick-and-mortar schools.[43]

Charters can claim a place in the education galaxy, but that place ought to be at the margin. They are not the panacea the transformers imagine them to be; what's more, they don't have the bandwidth to educate fifty-five million children. This is why Union City's accomplishments are so heartening and so instructive: that record shows that a system of outstanding common schools is within the grasp of *any* district that's willing to do the work.

The Secret Shared by America's Prize-Winning Urban Districts

Billionaire Eli Broad is a rarity in education reform circles, a man of great influence who has placed big bets on both charters and public schools. Since 2002, his foundation's eponymous prize, a $550,000 scholarship fund, has been awarded each year to the urban school system that has shown the greatest improvement in student achievement while narrowing the achievement gap for poor and minority students.[44]

Over the course of the past decade, the foundation has assiduously canvassed the efforts of big-city school systems. "This is exceptionally well organized," says the Urban Institute's Jane Hannaway. "A real effort is made to get as much hard data as possible on the table." And the researchers don't just crunch the numbers. They spend weeks in the field, looking for what the foundation regards as essential elements of success—the clarity of the district's academic goals, the effectiveness of teachers' and administrators' training, the implementation of the curriculum strategy, the use of evidence to inform decisions, and the support that teachers receive. They're looking for sustained improvement, not too-good-to-be-true, instant turnarounds. And they investigate whether the district learns from its mistakes.

Sound familiar? Aldine won this coveted award in 2009 and Montgomery County was a finalist in 2011. You'd nod off if I detailed what each prize-winner, from Houston to Long Beach, Brownsville to Charlotte, did to earn the award. You've heard it all before.[45]

What's more, a number of studies pinpoint common characteristics of high-performing school systems. The measure of "success" differs in those studies—one focuses on why some places do an especially good job of implementing a new math curriculum, for instance, while another asks why some high-poverty districts fare better than expected on the state's achievement test—but the findings are remarkably similar. "The main themes [are] *continuity* of focus on core instruction . . . *heavy investments* in highly targeted professional development . . . *strong and explicit accountability* by principals and teachers . . . and *a normative climate in which adults take responsibility for their own, their colleagues' and their students' learning.*"[46]

No surprises here—the researchers could be describing Union City or any of our high-performing districts.

Among the Broad Prize winners, New York City stands out as the conspicuous exception to the high expectations–high support approach. Chancellor Joel Klein, a onetime prosecutor recruited by Mayor Michael Bloomberg to run the schools, seemed to savor the chance to pick fights, priding himself on confrontation and sneering at collaboration with the union or community groups as "the elixir of the status quo." In a 2011 *Atlantic* diatribe, "The Failure of the Schools," Klein assailed the unions ("recalcitrant"), the teachers (often "mediocre"), and the politicians ("feckless," if not corrupt). The only actors who escaped his withering gaze were the mayor and the chancellor himself.[47]

By the time Klein wrote the *Atlantic* piece he was out of a job, having been canned by the mayor who appointed him. Live by the tests, die by the tests—the chancellor had put principals under excruciating pressure to improve reading and math scores, tying those results to bonuses for teachers and principals, as well as to the city's controversial A-through-F grading system for schools. During Klein's first years on the job, test scores did rise rapidly. The chancellor looked like a wizard, and those results weighed heavily in the 2007 decision to award the Broad Prize to New York.

But soon afterward came the reckoning. In 2009, the National Assessment of Education Progress, or NAEP, the country's most reliable index of student achievement, showed that reading and math scores for New York City's fourth and eighth graders were essentially stagnant during the Klein era. The city fared no better than school systems led by superintendents Klein derided as "apologists for the status quo." The achievement gap didn't shrink. Some principals, faced with enormous pressure to increase graduation rates or jeopardize their posts, boosted their numbers by granting degrees to unqualified students. And when state education officials announced in 2010 that the reading and math test scores had been inflated in Klein's early years, because the exams had grown too easy to pass, the "narrative of historic gains" didn't hold up.[48]

Mayor Bloomberg had basked in the schools' success, and these statistical reversals of fortune became an embarrassment. Not long afterward, Klein was gone, though he was hardly humbled by his demise. In 2012 he resurfaced as a moving force behind the incendiary report, *U.S. Education Reform and National Security*, with its rhetorical call to rearm the nation by disarming public schools.[49]

In the other Broad Prize–winning cities, the school chiefs who spearheaded major reforms were lionized while on the job and eulogized after they departed. But Klein remained a polarizing figure even after departing the scene. Some praised him for having given the school system a much-needed kick in the pants, while others remained bitter. "He is leaving us with a legacy of classroom overcrowding, communities fighting over co-located schools, kindergarten waiting lists, unreliable school grades based on bad data, substandard credit recovery programs and our children starved of art, music and science—all replaced with test prep," Leonie Haimson, the executive director of Class Size Matters, an advocacy group, told a *New York Times* reporter.[50]

"[Klein] and like-minded school leaders such as Michelle Rhee use these claims that the status quo is a failure and that incremental change won't work] as a license to do just about anything that strikes their fancy, without regard to the time it takes to build the structures and cultures that can support reform," writes Columbia Teachers College professor Aaron Pallas. "The consequence is an unstable system that threatens to collapse at any moment. Substituting a sense of urgency for a deliberate and well-planned approach to incremental change may feel good, but it's bad public policy."[51]

By now, this summing up of what's wrong with how Klein and Rhee conduct business should sound like boilerplate.

Successful rewrites of venerable organizational scripts take effect slowly and encounter resistance. Politics sometimes intrudes, upsetting best-laid plans. And sometimes the teachers union goes to war with the school system.

Meaningful reforms are hard to secure and still harder to maintain. So far, Union City and the other high-performing districts that we've been looking at have managed to accomplish this feat, and they have a lot to teach the rest of the nation. But even in those places, determining what it takes to do even better is an endless task.

To the sharpshooter critics, like the éminences grises who penned the 2011 jeremiad, *Education Reform and National Security*, this rendering of the tortoise-and-hare fable—"slow and steady wins the race"—is intolerable. We don't have time to "plan, do, review," they say. With "the very security of the nation" at risk, anything less than transformation means waving the white flag of surrender.

But those naysayers haven't witnessed Alina Bossbaly working her magic with third graders who are beginning to read and write in English, or sat in on classes stage-managed by a host of teachers who can excite their students by bringing lessons to life. They haven't seen how John Bennetti is transforming the culture of a high school from an acceptance of "good enough" to an insistence on "good." They haven't observed Superintendent Sandy Sanger and Assistant Superintendent Silvia Abbato doing the quotidian work that's required to keep a good school system moving forward, perpetually retooling to meet ever-tougher challenges. In short, they haven't seen what extraordinary feats can be accomplished in a deceptively ordinary school district such as Union City, New Jersey.

ACKNOWLEDGMENTS

If you've made it this far, you might want to know how this book came into being. Most of what I've written over the years, whether about market forces in higher education or gender justice, has been sparked by serendipity. So too here.

The story starts with my abiding interest in preschool. In the spring of 2009, while doing the research for *Kids First: Five Big Ideas for Transforming Children's Lives and America's Future*, I set out to identify communities with great prekindergartens—places to which you'd be happy to send your own child. In an earlier book, *The Sandbox Investment*, I described a number of such schools and I didn't want to repeat myself. When I turned to Steve Barnett and Ellen Frede, codirectors of the National Institute for Early Education Research, who know this field as well as anyone, they pointed me to Union City. Off I went, accompanied by Gordon MacInnes, who as Assistant Commissioner in the New Jersey Department of Education had spent a great deal of time there.

That initial visit went well—so well, in fact, that I extended my stay, dropping in on a number of elementary and middle school classes. I knew that Union City's students were doing well on the state's high-stakes exams, and I wondered why. The teaching that I observed was animated—no one was relying on drill-and-kill pedagogy to drum knowledge into the students' heads—and the youngsters were engaged.

Over the following months I kept wondering why Union City was doing so much better than many other ostensibly similar districts. To do a decent job of answering that question required that I spend time in a host of settings, from preschool to high school, from the classrooms to the offices of top-echelon administrators. Superintendent Sandy Sanger immediately embraced the idea and so did the school board.

The arrangement we struck was both straightforward and unusual—I had free rein, a license to go anywhere at any time, sit in on any meeting, observe any class and talk with anyone I wished to, all on the record. I especially wanted to be connected to a third grade class, because that's the first year of high-stakes testing; what's more, that class should include students who were learning English, since exemplary bilingual education is one of Union City's calling cards. I wasn't interested in spending time in a "model" classroom or an exemplary school, but rather in a typical setting. That's how I found myself in Room 210, Alina Bossbaly's world-of-wonders classroom, in George Washington Elementary School, whose students are among the poorest in a poor city. "They must really be confident if they're sending you there!" marveled Fred Carrigg, who years earlier had launched Union City's turnaround.

At Washington, Principal Les Hanna made me feel immediately at home; her effervescence shapes the culture of the school. On the very first day of school I became "Mr. David" in Alina's classroom. Only months later did I learn that Les and Alina—indeed, every teacher and school administrator whom I got to know during my stay—had been fretful about having a Berkeley professor in their midst. By then, however, I'd become a fixture. The willingness of many teachers and administrators to discuss their approaches to teaching, candidly reflecting on their experience in long conversations and written responses, brings this account to life.

I spent many days in Alina's classroom, and she poured out her thoughts about the kids, about the school, about teaching, and about her life as well. Everyone should be so lucky as to have a teacher who can stir up such excitement about writing. I also visited the classrooms of the other third grade teachers: the "Dream Team" of Irene Stamatopolous, Marilyn Corral, Mary Ann Rick (Mary Ann has subsequently married and changed her name to Hart), and Jen Schuck, as well as resource co-teacher Lourdes Garcia. Other teachers at Washington School, especially Maria Casanovas, Sue Emmerling, and Barbara Tellechea, were an inspiration, for they remain as alive to the possibilities of good teaching as they were decades ago, at the outset of their careers. Martha Jones, who is responsible for the welfare of bilingual youngsters and so much more at the school, made Washington an especially inviting place. I benefited as well from discussions with Jennifer Rodriguez, Candace Capuano, Marilyn Hildebrandt, Veronica Pardo, Jennifer Mondelli, Libby Gonzalez, parent liaison Maria

Kanik, former assistant principal John Coccioli and his successor Mike Cirone.

The kids in Room 210—rambunctious, creative, infuriating, loving, capable of constant surprises—stole my heart. I hope that they aim high and that they get what they want from life, whether it's becoming a policeman, a parent, a pediatrician, or a politician. In the Union City public schools they're surrounded by adults who care about them and support their aspirations.

At the Hostos Center for Early Childhood Education, Suzy Rojas demonstrated what great teaching looks like—she could instruct teachers at any grade level, from kindergarten to college. Marnie Lupo made the link between preschool and elementary school come alive. The effervescent Adriana Birne, head of the early childhood program, enabled me to see how a highly effective early education system could be fashioned from a motley confederation of preschools.

Principal Vicki Dickson became my informative guide to Union Hill Middle School, where April Sinise had her seventh graders writing sophisticated short stories. Chris Campbell and Rino Poli showed me that, in the right hands, special education can truly be special. Walking into their high-energy classrooms, you'd never know that this is special ed, and that's precisely the point. Gian Paul Gonzalez at Jose Marti Ninth Grade Academy, who turned his back on a pro basketball career to return to his hometown, made the Peloponnesian Wars compelling to a bunch of fifteen-year-olds—no mean feat. He has also done a fine job of linking coaching and character building.

At the high school I had the pleasure of watching Desiree Hernandez, Nadia Makar, Scott Emmerling, and Mark Fusco set loose in their classrooms and of talking at length with each of them. Michelle Cowan is the model of a coach who knows how to bring out the best in teachers. Chris Abbato has worked wonders with the English-Language Learner program, which has deservedly garnered national awards. Dave Wilcomes, the former principal, gave me a solid grounding in the history of secondary education in Union City. Special thanks to Principal John Bennetti, who has infused the school with warmth and academic rigor. John's efforts are plainly paying off. In *Best High School Rankings*, a 2012 study of 22,000 secondary schools prepared by the American Institutes for Research, the school was ranked in the top 13% nationwide.

At the central administration offices, I was tutored in district-wide initiatives by Lucy Soovajian, Diane Capizzi, Edernis Garcia, Delia Menendez, and Anthony Dragona. Former superintendent Tom Highton filled me in on school politics in the 1980s, a tumultuous period in the school system's history. I'm particularly grateful to Superintendent Sandy Sanger and Assistant Superintendent Silvia Abbato. These two exemplary administrators devoted many hours to educating me on everything from the details of the curriculum and the minutiae of management to the delights of the local cuisine.

My instruction in Union City politics came from spending time with a master at the craft, Brian Stack, the peripatetic 24-hour-a-day mayor and state senator; Mark Albiez, his assistant, who almost manages to keep up with him; and political consultant Kay LiCausi. Gerald Karabin's brief history of the city was a helpful source.

Margaret Honey, president and CEO of the New York Hall of Science, and Andres Henriquez, a program director at the National Science Foundation (formerly at the Carnegie Corporation), introduced me to the school district's pioneering technology initiatives in the 1990s.

I've surely omitted some people who were helpful during my stint in Union City. To them, my apologies—chalk up the omissions to lapses of memory and not intent.

Foundation grants made it possible for me to conduct the fieldwork, hire research assistants, and turn my voluminous field-notes into a book. A shout-out to Mark Steinmeyer at the Smith Richardson Foundation, whose reasoned criticisms made for a stronger research design. The foundation's continuing support has enabled me to complete not only this project but also my two prior books, *Kids First* and *Sandbox Investment*. Shout-outs as well to Andres Henriquez, then at the Carnegie Corporation, who quickly grasped the potential importance of a book about a community where Latino immigrant kids were being transported into the education mainstream; Ruby Takanishi, the former president of the Foundation for Child Development, who urged me to look into the linkages between preschool and elementary school; Eric Wanner, president of the Russell Sage Foundation, who pointed out the connection between my work and the foundation's priorities; and Annie Brinkman at the Spencer Foundation, who walked me through that foundation's grant-making process.

I was fortunate to find able research assistants to work with me during the course of the project. David Braslow and Abran Maldonado did close-grained fieldwork in Union City; David also explored the economics of the community. Mark Beasley-Murray examined what was happening in other New Jersey school districts. Erika Maldonado conducted in-depth interviews with several Washington School families. At the Goldman School of Public Policy at Berkeley, where I teach, Shannon Hovis and Lindsey Jenkins-Stark pulled together the research on pedagogy and school leadership. Will Chen, Sachi Takahashi, and Dat Phan analyzed the strategies used by other school districts that have succeeded in narrowing the achievement gap; and Paul Perry reviewed education policy at the state level. Jane David, education researcher par excellence, shared her ongoing study of the Sanger, California school system that she coauthored with Joan Talbert. Wanda Bamberg, Aldine, Texas school district superintendent, former superintendent Jerry Weast, and Brian Edwards, chief of staff for the Montgomery County, Maryland school district, provided helpful descriptions and candid appraisals of the progress their districts have made and the challenges they continue to confront.

As ever, my level-headed assistant, Rebecca Boles, kept me organized, and Louise Clark at the Institute for Education Leadership made managing five separate grants appear effortless.

Gordon MacInnes introduced me to Union City; time and again he offered a dispassionate view of what was happening there and elsewhere in the state. Gordon combines a keen understanding of strategies for reforming urban education with a politician's grasp of the machinery of state government. Fred Carrigg was a rich and vital source of information about the overhaul of the district's schools, much of which was his doing.

While I was doing research in Union City, I hung my hat at the Center for Population Studies at Columbia's School of Social Work. During those critical initial stages of the project, Irwin Garfinkel, the center's director, brought me into the vibrant life of the center, and Jane Waldfogel was an invaluable sounding board and fount of ideas. I benefited from the wise counsel of colleagues and friends, including Jennifer Hochschild, Hank Levin, Jeff Henig, Pedro Noguera, and Carola and Marcelo Suarez-Orozco. The faculty and students at the Goldman School of Public Policy, University of California at Berkeley, were, as ever, good critical friends. I know of no academic community that's more supportive or more lively intellectually.

Despite a difficult climate for book publishing, my longtime agent, Carol Mann, found the ideal home for the book. My editor at Oxford, James Cook, has been an enthusiast from the get-go. In an era when editors rarely have time to do more than acquire books, his old-fashioned pencil-editing considerably improved the manuscript and he shepherded it through to publication. Ryan Sarver did a fine job of steering the manuscript through the Scylla and Charybdis of production. The publicity and marketing teams at Oxford have been a pleasure to work with, and publicists Meg Walker and Gretchen Koss at Tandem Literary worked overtime to engage the interest of policymakers, educators, and general readers.

For nearly three decades, Rhea Wilson has been a great friend and a wise editor. For more than a year, we worked together to mold the book's overall structure, giving coherence to hundreds of pages of notes as well as shaping the trajectory of each chapter. Then, as the book took form, she dug deeply into the prose. In this project, as in several of my earlier books, Rhea has been an indispensable helpmate.

My partner, Remmert Dekker, is also my best friend—smart, supportive, and understanding. During the months that I spent in Union City, he listened patiently as I detailed my disappointments ("Did you know that some teachers actually hate kids?") as well as the "aha!" moments. His comments on the manuscript, sections of which he read several times, were invariably on target. And he cheerfully persevered during my sixty-hour-a-week writing regimen that extended for many months.

NOTES

INTRODUCTION

1. *U.S. Education Reform and National Security: Report of a CFR-Sponsored Independent Task Force* (2012), http://www.cfr.org/united-states/us-education-reform-national-security/p27618. This is not the first time that militaristic rhetoric has prominently figured in an attack on public education. *A Nation at Risk*, a 1982 presidential commission report, declared that "if an unfriendly foreign power had attempted to impose on America the mediocre educational performance that exists today, we might well have viewed it as an act of war." That report was highly influential, and the authors of the 2012 report may have hoped that the imagery would have a similar impact.

2. Wendy Kopp, the founder of Teach for America, served on the task force.

3. U.S. Department of Education, *Race to the Top Program: Executive Summary* (November 2009), http://www2.ed.gov/programs/racetothetop/executive-summary.pdf.

4. Diane Ravitch, "Waiting for a School Miracle," *New York Times*, May 31, 2011 ("turnaround" schools); Sam Dillon, "'No Child' Law Isn't Closing Achievement Gaps," *New York Times*, April 29, 2009 (achievement gap) www.nytimes.com/2009/04/29/education/29scores.html; Diane Ravitch, "Waiting for a School Miracle," www.nytimes.com/2011/06/01/opinion/01ravitch.html; Jaekyung Lee, "Tracking Achievement Gaps and Assessing the Impact of NCLB on the Gaps" (Los Angeles: UCLA Civil Rights Project, 2006), http://citeseerx.ist.psu.edu/viewdoc/summary?doi=10.1.1.184.8931. See generally Richard Rothstein, *Class and Schools: Using Social, Economic, and Educational Reform to Close the Achievement Gap* (Washington, DC: EPI, 2004). The same "no benefit" conclusion applies to voucher schemes. See chapter 9.

5. www.ncsl.org/issues-research/educ/charter-schools-overview.aspx. On KIPP Schools, see Jay Matthews, *Work Hard. Be Nice: How Two Inspired Teachers Created the Most Promising Schools in America* (New York: Algonquin, 2009); on Green Dot Public Schools, see Alexander Russo, *Stray Dogs, Saints, and Saviors: Fighting for the Soul of America's Toughest High School* (San Francisco: Jossey Bass, 2011).

6. *Racial/Ethnic Enrollment in Public Schools* (Washington, DC: NCES, 2012). http://nces.ed.gov/programs/coe/indicator_1er.asp.

7. See generally Peter Schrag, *California: America's High-Stakes Experiment* (Berkeley and Los Angeles: University of California Press, 2006).

8. On the miseducation of minority and Latino students, see Carola Suarez-Orozco, Marcelo Suarez-Orozco, and Irina Todorava, *Learning a New Land: Immigrant Students in American Society* (Cambridge, MA: Harvard University Press, 2010); and Patricia Gandara and Frances Contreras, *The Latino Education Crisis: The Consequences of Failed Social Policies* (Cambridge, MA: Harvard University Press, 2010). See generally Peter Schrag, *Not Fit for Our Society: Immigration and Nativism in America* (Berkeley and Los Angeles: University of California Press, 2010).

   On student achievement in charter schools versus public schools, see *Multiple Choice: Charter School Performance in 16 States* (Center for Research on Education Outcomes (CREDO), 2009) credo.stanford.edu/reports/MULTIPLE_CHOICE_CREDO.pdf. Chapter 9 discusses the place of charter schools in American education.

9. Andrew Sum et al., *The Consequences of Dropping Out of High School* (Boston: Center for Labor Market Studies, Northeastern University, 2009), http://iris.lib.neu.edu/clms_pub/23/; Dan Bloom and Ron Haskins, "Policy Brief: Helping High School Dropouts Improve Their Prospects," *The Future of Children* (Spring 2010), www.brookings.edu/~/media/centers/ccf/0427_helping_dropouts_haskins. See also *The Dropout Problem* (Washington, DC: Communities in Schools, 2012), www.communitiesinschools.org/media/uploads/attachments/The_Dropout_Problem_2012.pdf; Alliance for Excellence Education, America's Promise Alliance, Civic Enterprises and Everyone Graduates Center at Johns Hopkins University, "Building a Grad Nation: Progress and Challenge in Ending the High School Dropout Epidemic" (2012), www.americaspromise.org/Our-Work/Grad Nation/~/media/Files/Our%20Work/Grad%20Nation/Building%20a%20Grad%20Nation/BuildingAGradNation2012.ashx.

10. Claudia Goldin and Lawrence Katz, *The Race between Education and Technology* (Cambridge, MA: Harvard University Press, 2008); Martin Trow, *Twentieth-Century Higher Education: Elite to Mass to Universal* (Baltimore: Johns Hopkins University Press, 2010).

11. Richard Perez-Pena, "Waivers for 8 More States from 'No Child Left Behind,'" *New York Times*, May 29, 2011, www.nytimes.com/2012/05/30/education/eight-more-states-get-waiver-from-no-child-law.html. The Department of Education has not defined this amorphous requirement. See chapter 7 for a discussion of the federal role in education.

12. Mary Walton, *The Deming Management Method* (New York: Dodd Mead, 1986).

13. For a discussion of other school districts that have improved achievement scores for poor and minority students and also reduced the achievement gap, see chapter 9.

14. As you might well imagine, Swiss watches are quite complex: "The most complicated automatic winding wristwatch to be produced as a series (limited to 30 pieces) is the Blancpain 1735, which contains 740 components, each one individually adjusted, hand-finished and hand-decorated. Some components are no thicker than a human hair, and their intricacy is such that very few watchmakers have the

skills required to make all of the complications." www.swissworld.org/en/switzer-
land/swiss_specials/swiss_watches/the_parts_of_a_watch/.

CHAPTER 1

1. For a history of this migration, see Yolana Prieto, *The Cubans of Union City: Immigrants and Exiles in a New Jersey Community* (Philadelphia: Temple University Press, 2009).

2. http://americasvoiceonline.org/research/entry/the_ugly_face_of_the_dream_act_debate.

3. Carola Suarez-Orozco, Marcelo Suarez-Orozco, and Irina Todorova, *Learning a New Land: Immigrant Students in American Society* (Cambridge, MA: Harvard University Press, 2008); Patricia Gandara and Frances Contreras, *The Latino Education Crisis: The Consequences of Failed Social Policies* (Cambridge, MA: Harvard University Press, 2009); Randy Capps, Michael Fix, and Julie Murray, *The New Demography of America's Schools: Immigration and the No Child Left Behind Act* (Washington, DC: Urban Institute, 2005), http://americasvoiceonline.org/research/entry/the_ugly_face_of_the_dream_act_debate.

4. Richard Elmore, *School Reform from the Inside Out* (Cambridge, MA: Harvard Education Press, 2004).

5. The debate between the "no excuses" camp and the "social context" reformers has been vitriolic. On the "no excuses" side, see Michelle Rhee, *Dare to Dream: My Fight for Better Schools and a Brighter Future* (New York: Harper, 2013); Joel Klein, "The Failure of American Schools," *Atlantic*, June 2011. http://www.theatlantic.com/magazine/archive/2011/06/the-failure-of-american-schools/8497/. On the "social context" side, see Diane Ravitch, *The Birth and Death of the Great American School System* (New York: Basic Books, 2010); Richard Rothstein, *Class and Schools: Using Social, Economic, and Educational Reform to Close the Black-White Achievement Gap* (New York: Teachers College Press, 2004).

6. These aren't merely generalizations: during the course of the year the students talked about these things with me quite matter-of-factly, as if they were normal features of life.

7. For an historical account of the Cuban immigration and its impact on the United States, see Susan Eckstein, *The Immigrant Divide: How Cuban Americans Changed the U.S. and Their Homeland* (New York: Routledge, 2009). Union City's experience is chronicled in Yolanda Prieto, *The Cubans of Union City: Immigrants and Exiles in a New Jersey Community* (Philadelphia: Temple University Press, 2009).

8. Shane Jimerson, "Meta-analysis of Grade Retention Research," *School Psychology Review* 30, no. 3 (2001).

9. On the craft of teaching, see Larry Cuban, *How Teachers Taught: Constancy and Change in American Classrooms* (New York: Longman, 1984); Dan Lortie, *Schoolteacher* (Chicago: University of Chicago Press. 1975); and David Cohen, *Teaching and Its Predicaments* (Cambridge, MA: Harvard University Press, 2011).

   On the efficacy of ability grouping, see Adam Gamoran, "Is Ability Grouping Equitable?" *Educational Leadership* 50, no. 2 (1992); Robert Slavin, "Ability Grouping: A Best-evidence Synthesis," *Review of Educational Research* 57, no. 2 (1987).

10. John Merrow, "The 'Alien Structure' of Education and Other Thoughts," *Taking Note* blog, August 2011, http://takingnote.learningmatters.tv/?p=5221.

11. David Cohen, *Teaching and Its Predicaments* (Cambridge, MA: Harvard University Press, 2011), 42.

12. Howard Gardner, *Multiple Intelligences: The Theory in Practice* (New York: Basic Books, 1993). In *Wisdom, Intelligence, and Creativity Synthesized* (New York: Cambridge University Press, 2007), psychologist Robert Sternberg propounds a similar model of "triarchic intelligences."

13. Joel Michael, "Where's the Evidence That Active Learning Works?" *Advances in Physiology Education* 30, no. 1 (2006). See also Phyllis Blumenfeld, Ronald Marx, Elliot Solloway, and Joseph Krajcik, "Learning with Peers: From Small Group Cooperation to Collaborative Communities," *Educational Researcher* 25, no. 8 (1996).

14. On the overdiagnosis of Attention Deficit Disorder, see Larry Goldman et al., "Diagnosis and Treatment of Attention-Deficit/Hyperactivity Disorder in Children and Adolescents," *JAMA* 279, no. 14 (1998).

15. Gordon MacInnes, *In Plain Sight: Simple, Difficult Lessons from New Jersey's Expensive Effort to Close the Achievement Gap* (New York and Washington, DC: Century Foundation, 2009); Tracy Tully, "Spotlight District: A Remarkable Turnaround," *Scholastic Administrator* (April/May 2003), www.scholastic.com/browse/article.jsp?id=8.

16. James Cummins, "Linguistic Interdependence and the Educational Development of Bilingual Children," *Review of Education Research* 49, no. 2 (1979); Fred Genesee, *Learning through Two Languages* (Cambridge, MA: Newbury House, 1988); Yeong-Won Lee and Diane Lemmonier Shallert, "The Relative Contribution of L2 Language Proficiency and L1 Reading Ability to L2 Reading Performance: A Test of the Threshold Hypothesis in an EFL Context," *TESOL Quarterly* 31, no. 4 (1997); Naomi Schiff-Myers, "Considering Arrested Language Development and Language Loss in the Assessment of Second Language Learners," *Language, Speech, and Hearing Services in Schools* 23, no. 1 (1992). But see Rosalina Pedalino Porter, "The Case against Bilingual Education," *Atlantic*, May 1998, www.theatlantic.com/magazine/archive/1998/05/the-case-against-bilingual-education/5426/?single_page=true.

CHAPTER 2

1. Task Force on the Principalship, *Leadership for Student Learning: Reinventing the Principalship* (Washington, DC: Institute for Educational Leadership, 2000), www.iel.org/programs/21st/reports/principal.pdf; Susan Black, "Finding Time to Lead," *American School Board Journal* 187, no. 1 (2000), www.eric.ed.gov/ERIC-WebPortal/recordDetail?accno=EJ614582; Mildred Blackman and Leslie Fenwick, "The Principalship: Looking for Leaders in a Time of Change," *Education Week*, March 29, 2000, www.edweek.org/ew/articles/2000/03/29/29blackman.h19.html.

There's an immense literature on the characteristics of effective leadership. See, e.g., Joseph Murphy, ed., *The Education Leadership Challenge* (Chicago: University of Chicago Press, 2002); James Spillane, "Educational Leadership," *Educational*

Evaluation and Policy Analysis 25, no. 4 (2003). Linda Tillman, "Mentoring New Teachers: Implications for Leadership Practice in an Urban School," *Educational Administration Quarterly* 41, no. 4 (2005); Thomas Corcoran, "Helping Teachers Teach Well: Transforming Professional Development," *Consortium for Policy Research in Education Policy Briefs* 16 (1995), http://www2.ed.gov/pubs/CPRE/t61/index.html.

2. See generally Seymour Sarason, *Revisiting "The Culture of School and the Problem of Change"* (New York: Teachers College Press, 1996).

3. Anthony Bryk and Barbara Schneider, *Trust in Schools: A Core Resource for Improvement* (New York: Russell Sage, 2005); see also Karen Louis, "Trust and Improvement in Schools," *Journal of Education Change* 8, no. 1 (2007).

4. The school system's tortuous political history is discussed in chapter 3.

5. Winnie Hu, "Anti-Bullying Law Puts New Jersey on the Spot," *New York Times*, August 20, 2011, www.nytimes.com/2011/08/31/nyregion/bullying-law-puts-new-jersey-schools-on-spot.html?pagewanted=all.

6. Charles Clotfelter et al., "Teacher-Student Matching and the Assessment of Teacher Effectiveness," *Journal of Human Resources* 41, no. 4 (2006).

7. Ben Levin, *How to Change 5000 Schools: A Practical and Positive Approach for Leading Change at Every Level* (Cambridge, MA: Harvard Education Press, 2008), 8.

8. Mayor Stack's influence on the schools is discussed in chapter 5.

9. In complementary ways, Maria Kanik and Martha Jones connect the school and the families it serves, and the engagement of the families helps to explain Union City's success. On the difficulties of nurturing such relationships, see James Coleman, "Families and Schools," *Education Researcher* 16, no. 6 (1987), www.jstor.org/stable/pdfplus/1175544.pdf?acceptTC=true.

10. Numerous books describe and appraise the impact of the No Child Left Behind Act. See, e.g., Patrick McGuinn, *No Child Left Behind and the Transformation of Education Policy, 1965–2005* (Lawrence: University Press of Kansas, 2006); Frederick Hess and Michael Petrillli, *No Child Left Behind Primer* (New York: Peter Lang, 2007). For critiques of the law, see Diane Ravitch, *The Birth and Death of the Great American School System* (New York: Basic Books, 2010); Deborah Meier and George Wood, eds., *Many Children Left Behind* (Boston: Beacon, 2004).

11. Tina Trujillo, "The Paradoxical Logic of School Turnarounds: A Catch 22," *Teachers College Record*, June 14, 2012, www.tcrecord.org/Content.asp?ContentId=16797.

12. See generally Martin Krovetz and Gilberto Arriaza, *Collaborative Teachers Leadership: How Teachers Can Foster Equitable Schools* (Thousand Oaks, CA: Corwin, 2006); Joseph Murphy, *Connecting Teacher Leadership and School Improvement* (Thousand Oaks, CA: Corwin, 2005).

13. Dara Barlin, Ellen Moir, Janet Gless, and Jan Miles, *New Teacher Mentoring: Hopes and Promise for Improving Teacher Effectiveness* (Cambridge, MA: Harvard Education Press, 2009); Linda Tillman, "Mentoring New Teachers: Implications for Leadership Practice in an Urban School," *Educational Administration Quarterly* 41, no. 4 (2005).

14. Robert Pianta, *Teaching Children Well: New Evidence-Based Approaches to Teacher Professional Development and Training* (Washington, DC: Center for American Progress, 2011), www.americanprogress.org/wp-content/uploads/issues/2011/11/pdf/piana_report.pdf.

15. On the particular challenges involved in teaching English learners, see Margarita Calderón, Robert Slavin, and Marta Sánchez, "Effective Instruction for English Learners," *Immigrant Children* 21, no. 1 (2011).

16. In 2012, Education Secretary Arne Duncan began waiving the 2014 "100% proficiency" requirement for states, including New Jersey, that pledged that by 2020 every high school student would graduate and would be ready for college or a career. This policy shift in effect rewrites the No Child Left Behind Act.

17. *Teachers' Ability to Use Data to Inform Instruction: Challenges and Supports* (Washington, DC: Department of Education, 2011) (prepared by Barbara Means et al., SRI International).

18. Benjamin Bloom, *Taxonomy of Educational Objectives* (Boston: Allyn & Bacon, 1956).

19. The research is summarized in David Kirp, *The Sandbox Investment* (Cambridge, MA: Harvard University Press, 2008).

20. Steven Brill, "The Rubber Room," *New Yorker*, August 31, 2009, www.newyorker.com/reporting/2009/08/31/090831fa_fact_brill.

21. Steven Rivkin, Eric Hanushek, and John Kain, "Teachers, Schools, and Academic Achievement," *Econometrica* 73, no. 2 (2005); Helen Ladd, "Value-Added Modeling of Teacher Credentials: Policy Implications," (Durham, NC: CALDER, Duke University, 2008), www.caldercenter.com/upload/Sunny_Ladd_presentation.pdf.

22. Wendy Kopp, *One Day, All Children . . .: The Unlikely Triumph of Teach for America and What I Learned Along the Way* (New York: Public Affairs, 2003).

23. Steven Rivkin, Eric Hanushek, and John Kain, "Teachers, Schools, and Academic Achievement," *Econometrica* 73, no. 2 (2005); Charles Clotfelter, Helen Ladd, and Jacob Vigdor, "Teacher Credentials and Student Achievement in High School: A Cross-Subject Analysis with Student Fixed Effects," CALDER Working Paper No. 11 (Washington, DC: National Center for Analysis of Longitudinal Data in Education Research, 2007), www.caldercenter.org/PDF/1001104_Teacher_Credentials_HighSchool.pdf.

24. On veteran teachers' willingness to make significant changes in how and what they teach, see James Spillane, *Standards Deviation* (Cambridge, MA: Harvard University Press, 2004).

25. Mike Schmoker, "Tipping Point: From Feckless Reform to Substantive Instructional Improvement," *Phi Delta Kappan* 85, no. 6 (2004). See generally John Seeley Brown and Paul Duguid, *The Social Life of Information* (Boston: Harvard Business School Press, 2000); Peter Senge et al., *The Dance of Change: The Challenge of Sustaining Momentum in Learning Organizations* (New York: Doubleday, 1999); Ikujiro Nonaka and Hirotaka Takeuchi, *The Knowledge-Creating Company* (New York: Oxford University Press, 1995).

26. On the importance of "chemistry" among teachers, see Donna Sabers, Katherine Cushing, and David Berliner, "Differences among Teachers in a Task Characterized by Simultaneity, Multidimensional, and Immediacy," *American Education Research Journal* 28, no. 1 (1991).

27. Paul T. Decker, Daniel P. Mayer, and Steven Glazerman, *The Effects of Teach for America on Students: Findings from a National Evaluation* (New York: Mathematica, 2004), www.mathematica-mpr.com/publications/pdfs/teach.pdf.

28. Cynthia Coburn and Jennifer Lin Russell, "District Policy and Teachers' Social Networks," *Educational Evaluation and Policy Analysis* 30, no. 3 (2008); Helen Marks and Karen Louis, "Does Teacher Empowerment Affect the Classroom? The Implications of Teacher Empowerment for Instructional Practice and Students' Educational Performance," *Educational Evaluation and Policy Analysis* 19, no. 3 (1997); Helen Marks and Sharon Kruse, "Teachers' Professional Community in Restructuring Schools," *American Educational Research Journal* 33, no. 4 (1996).

29. Irene Stamatopolous readily relates to these youngsters' problems, because in some ways her early life paralleled theirs. When she was an infant, her family emigrated from Greece. As a young child she grew up in a Greek neighborhood in the Bronx, speaking only Greek, and when her family moved to the suburbs she had a hard time adjusting. "I never got any extra help in school because I spoke a different language," she recalls. "And I never quite fit in those first few years."

30. Carol Briscoe and Joseph Peters, "Teacher Collaboration across and within Schools: Supporting Individual Change in Elementary Science Teaching," *Science Education* 81, no. 1 (1997); Mike Schmoker, "Tipping Point: From Feckless Reform to Substantive Instructional Improvement," *Phi Delta Kappan* 85, no. 6 (2004): Roger Stewart and Jonathan Brendefur, "Fusing Lesson Study and Authentic Achievement: A Model for Teacher Collaboration," *Phi Delta Kappan* 66, no. 9 (2005).

31. Richard Anderson and William Nagy, "The Vocabulary Conundrum," *American Educator* 16, no. 1 (1992); George Miller and Patricia Gildea, "How Children Learn Words," *Scientific American* 257, no. 3 (1987).

32. E. D. Hirsch Jr., "How to Stop the Drop in Reading Scores," *New York Times*, September 18, 2011, www.nytimes.com/2011/09/19/opinion/how-to-stop-the-drop-in-verbal-scores.html.

33. Elaine Whitehouse, "Deliver Us from Evil—Teaching Values to Elementary School Children," *International Schools Journal* 15, no. 1 (1995).

34. See Donna Sabers, Katherine Cushing, and David Berliner, "Differences among Teachers in a Task Characterized by Simultaneity, Multidimensional, and Immediacy," *American Education Research Journal* 28, no. 1 (1991).

CHAPTER 3

1. Some superintendents focus on recruiting "star" principals more than system-building. "I believe a strong principal is the key to almost everything," says Newark superintendent Cami Anderson. "Where you have great performance, you have great principals, period, full stop." Winnie Hu and Nate Schweber, "For the Next Chief of Newark Schools, Hard Choices," *New York Times*, May 5, 2011, www.nytimes.com/2011/05/05/nyregion/next-newark-schools-chief-faces-challenges.html?pagewanted=all.

2. Fred Carrigg and Margaret Honey, "Literacy as the Key to Academic Success and Educational Reform," in Dorothy Strickland and Donna Alvermann, eds., *Bridging the Literacy Gap* (New York: Teachers College Press, 2004).

3. Todd Risley, Betty Hart, and Louis Bloom, *Meaningful Differences in the Everyday Experiences of Young American Children* (Baltimore: Brookes, 1995).

4. Patricia Gandara and Alice Contreras, *The Latino Educational Crisis* (Cambridge, MA: Harvard University Press, 2010).

5. See, e.g., Note, "Darwin, Design, and Disestablishment: Teaching the Evolution Controversy in Public Schools," *Vanderbilt Law Review* 56, no. 5 (2003); Pat Griffin and Mathew Ouellett, "From Silence to Safety and Beyond: Historical Trends in Addressing Lesbian, Gay, Bisexual, Transgender Issues in K–12 Schools," *Equity and Excellence in Education* 36, no. 2 (2003).

6. P. David Pearson, "The Reading Wars," *Educational Policy*, 18, no. 1 (2004).

7. Seymour Sarason, *Revisiting "The Culture of the School and the Problem of Change"* (New York: Teachers College Press, 1996).

8. In essence, Union City was adopting the "constructivist," hands-on approach to learning pioneered by John Dewey, America's foremost education theorist, in the early twentieth century. See John Dewey, *Experience in Education* (New York: Collier, 1938). But compare Seymour Engelmann, *Teaching Needy Kids in Our Backward System* (Eugene, OR: ADI Press, 2007) (arguing that "direct instruction," the explicit teaching of a skill using lectures or demonstrations, rather than students' participation, works best for "needy" students).

9. Margaret Honey and Andres Henriquez, *The Union City Story: Education, Reform and Technology, Students' Performance on Standardized Tests* (New York: Center for Children and Technology, 1996), http://cct.edc.org/admin/publications/report/uc_story98.pdf.

10. John Welfing, "New Jersey Supreme Court 1948–1998: Fifty Years of Independence and Activism," *Rutgers Law Review* 29, no. 4 (1997–1998). David Kirp, John Dwyer, and Larry Rosenthal, *Our Town: Race, Housing, and the Soul of Suburbia* (New Brunswick NJ: Rutgers University Press, 1993), focuses on the affordable housing litigation.

11. Deborah Jaffe, *Other People's Children* (New Brunswick, NJ: Rutgers University Press, 2007), describes in detail the courtroom battles in *Abbott*, the judicial opinions, and the key figures in the case. The Education Law Center, which for more than thirty years has represented the plaintiffs in *Abbott*, has posted a voluminous amount of material about the case at its website, www.edlawcenter.org/cases/abbott-v-burke/abbott-history.html.

12. *San Antonio Independent School District et al. v. Rodriguez*, 411 U.S. 1 (1973).

13. *Abbott v. Burke*, 119 N.J. 287 (1990); Paul Minorini and Steven Sugarman, "School Finance Litigation in the Name of Educational Equity: Its Evolution, Impact and Future," in Helen Ladd, Rosemary Chalk, and Janet Hansen, eds., *Equity and Adequacy in Education Finance* (Washington, DC: National Academy Press, 1999).

The New Jersey court was well aware of the legal pitfalls, and for that reason it did not rush to judgment. *Abbott* was initially filed in 1981, and several times the case went up and down the judicial ladder before the justices issued their first substantive opinion. By then the record was voluminous—ninety-nine witnesses testified at an eight-month-long administrative hearing that the court insisted upon, generating a transcript that ran 16,000 pages and a 607-page ruling by the administrative law judge that accepted almost all of the plaintiffs' contentions.

As the case chugged along, the state's education commissioner, Saul Cooperman, spent a considerable amount of time in the blighted cities that he had known only by reputation. The self-confessed naïf got an education in the realpolitik of city schools, the kickbacks and cronyism and no-show jobs, and concluded that some districts were simply beyond help. That revelation eventually led to the passage of legislation that enabled the state to seize control of these seemingly hopeless districts—the category in which, in 1989, Union City almost found itself.

14. In an interview with Deborah Jaffe, Justice Gary Stein assailed one piece of legislative handiwork as "almost a paradigm of a statute that violated the intent and spirit of *Abbott*." Some Republican lawmakers proposed to make the problem go away by simply removing the "thorough and efficient" language from the state constitution. Deborah Jaffe, *Other People's Children* (New Brunswick, NJ: Rutgers University Press, 2007).

15. *Abbott v. Burke*, 153 N.J. 480 (1998). An *Abbott* district could also secure additional funds from the state to finance summer school, computers, health clinics, and the like by demonstrating that such supports were needed to overcome students' educational disadvantage. Several cities availed themselves of this option, but Union City chose not to do so.

16. *Abbott v. Burke*, 163 N.J. 95 (2000).

17. Margaret Goertz and Michael Weiss, "Assessing Success in School Finance Litigation: The Case of New Jersey," *Education, Equity and the Law* 1 (2009), www.equitycampaign. org/i/a/document/11775_EdEquityLawNo1.pdf. State-to-state comparisons are fraught with problems. "Fact-Checking Linda Darling-Hammond," *New Jersey Left Behind* (blog), April 30, 2010, http://njleftbehind.blogspot.com/2010/04/fact-checking-linda-darling-hammond.html.

18. On early education, see chapter 4.

19. Gordon MacInnes, *In Plain Sight: Simple, Difficult Lessons from New Jersey's Expensive Effort to Close the Achievement Gap* (New York: Century Foundation Press, 2009).

20. The importance of stability in a school district and the consequences of "churn" are discussed in chapter 9. See Frederick Hess, *Spinning Wheels: The Politics of Urban School Reform* (Washington, DC: Brookings Institution Press, 1999).

21. Malcolm Gladwell, "The Talent Myth," *New Yorker*, July 22, 2002, http://www.gladwell.com/2002/2002_07_22_a_talent.htm.

22. William Scherkenbach, *Deming's Road to Continual Improvement* (Knoxville, TN: SPC Press, 1991).

23. See chapter 9 for a critique of the "no excuses" critics.

24. Gordon MacInnes, *In Plain Sight: Simple, Difficult Lessons from New Jersey's Expensive Effort to Close the Achievement Gap* (New York Century Foundation Press, 2009); Tracy Tully, "Spotlight District: A Remarkable Turnaround," *Scholastic Administrator* (April/May 2003), www.scholastic.com/browse/article. jsp?id=8.

25. Compare Jerome Murphy, "Title 1 of ESEA: The Politics of Implementing Federal Education Reform," in Allan Odden, ed., *Education Policy Implementation* (Albany: SUNY

234 • NOTES TO PAGES 97–104

Press, 1991), at 34, with Paul Peterson and Martin West, eds., *No Child Left Behind? The Politics and Practice of School Accountability* (Washington, DC: Brookings, 2003).

26. For New Jersey graduation rates, see www.state.nj.us/education/data/grate/rates. pdf. For an account of a perpetually failing district, see "How We Fail the Kids in Camden," *NJ Left Behind* (blog), April 27, 2010, http://njleftbehind.blogspot. com/2010/04/how-we-fail-kids-in-camden.html. See also David Kirp, John Dwyer, and Larry Rosenthal, *Our Town: Race, Housing and the Soul of Community* (New Brunswick, NJ: Rutgers University Press, 1993).

CHAPTER 4

1. Karl Weick, "Educational Organizations as Loosely Coupled Systems," *Administrative Science Quarterly* 21, no. 1 (1976). This landmark article has been cited more than 5,000 times.
2. Luis Laosa and Pat Ainsworth, "Is Public Pre-K Preparing Hispanic Children to Succeed in School?" (New Brunswick, NJ: NIEER, Rutgers University, Preschool Policy Brief # 7, 2007), http://nieer.org/resources/policybriefs/13.pdf. Union City families living below the poverty line are also eligible for free childcare before and after preschool.
3. Paul Munshine, "Steve Lonegan Winning Ideological Debate in NJ's Republican Race," *Newark Star-Ledger*, May 14, 2009, http://blog.nj.com/njv_paul_mulshine/ 2009/05/steve_lonegan_winning_ideologi. html.
4. Jack Shonkoff and Deborah Phillips, eds., *From Neurons to Neighborhoods: The Science of Early Childhood Development* (Washington, DC: National Research Council: Institute of Medicine, 2000), 90. See David L. Kirp, *The Sandbox Investment: The Preschool Movement and Kids-First Politics* (Cambridge, MA: Harvard University Press, 2007), for a thorough discussion of this research.
5. Lawrence Schweinhart et al., *Lifetime Effects: The HighScope Perry Preschool Study through Age 40* (Ypsilanti, MI: HighScope Press, 2005).
6. W. Steven Barnett, Cynthia Lamy, and Kwanghee Jung, "The Effects of State Prekindergarten Programs on Young Children's School Readiness in Five States" (New Brunswick, NJ: National Institute for Early Education Research, Rutgers University, 2005); William Gormley et al., "The Effects of Universal Pre-K on Cognitive Development," *Developmental Psychology* 41, no. 6 (2005).
7. Flavio Cunha, James Heckman, Lance Lochner, and Dimitry Masterov, "Interpreting the Evidence on Life Cycle Skill Formation" (Cambridge, MA: National Bureau of Economic Research, 2005), www.nber.org/papers/w11331 (skill begets skill); Clive Belfield, Steven Barnett, and Lawrence Schweinhart, "The Perry Pre-School 40-Year Follow-up Cost-Benefit Analysis," *Journal of Human Resources* 42, no. 2 (2006); Clive Belfield, *Early Childhood Education: How Important Are the Cost-Savings to the School System?* (New York: Center for Early Care and Education, Columbia University, 2004). See also Arthur Reynolds et al., "Age 21 Cost-Benefit Analysis of the Title I Chicago Child-Parent Centers," *Educational Evaluation and Policy Analysis* 24, no. 2 (2005).
8. Gordon MacInnes, *In Plain Sight: Simple, Difficult Lessons from New Jersey's Expensive Effort to Close the Achievement Gap* (New York: Century Foundation, 2009)

9. For descriptions of exemplary preschools, see David L. Kirp, *The Sandbox Investment: The Preschool Movement and Kids-First Politics* (Cambridge, MA: Harvard University Press, 2007); and David L. Kirp, *Kids First: Five Big Ideas for Transforming Children's Lives and America's Future* (New York: Public Affairs, 2011).

10. Here's a telling anecdote. On the first day of the 2010–2011 school year, three parents showed up at Hostos, their children in tow, brandishing letters that stated that their offspring were supposed to be enrolled there. Adriana Birne had the unhappy task of informing them that the letters were bogus and that there was a waiting list. She never solve the mystery of who sent those letters, though she wondered whether the parents themselves might have written them. If that was the case, it's easy enough to understand why—parents want the best for their kids and Hostos is Union City's premier pre-k.

11. Alison Gopnik, *The Philosophical Baby* (New York: Picador, 2010).

12. The *Abbott* case is discussed in chapter 3.

13. The contention that the gains of early education "fade out" was first made in Westinghouse Learning Corporation, Impact of Head Start (Washington, DC: Clearinghouse for Federal, Scientific and Technical Information, 1969), www.eric.ed.gov/PDFS/ED036321.pdf. Later evaluations rebut that contention. Eliana Garces, Duncan Thomas, and Janet Currie, "Longer Term Effects of Head Start," NBER Working Paper No. 8054 (2000), www.nber.org/papers/w8054; David Deming, "Early Childhood Intervention and Life-Cycle Skill Development: Evidence from *Head Start," American Economic Journal: Applied Economics* 1, no. 3 (2009). On the interaction between early education and K–12, see Rucker Johnson, "School Quality and the Long-Term Effects of Head Start," Goldman School of Public Policy Working Paper, Berkeley, CA, n.d., http://socrates.berkeley.edu/~ruckerj/RJabstract_LRHeadStartSchoolQuality.pdf.

14. "The New First Grade: Much Too Soon," *Newsweek*, September 6, 2006.

15. The Foundation for Child Development has assiduously promoted the pre-k-to-grade-3 strategy. See http://fcd-us.org/sites/default/files/PreK-3rd%20Resources%20-%20USE%20AS%20Template.pdf. At the Annie E. Casey Foundation, Ralph Smith has led a national campaign to assure that all children are able to read by third grade, an effort closely tied to the pre-k-to-grade-3 initiatives. *Early Warning: Why Reading by the End of Third Grade Matters* (Baltimore: Annie E. Casey Foundation, 2010), http://datacenter.kidscount.org/reports/readingmatters.aspx.

CHAPTER 5

1. For a primer on school politics, see Michael Kirst and Frederick Wirt, *The Political Dynamics of American Education* (Richmond, CA: McCutchan, 2009).

2. On mayoral control, see Joseph Veritti, ed., *When Mayors Take Charge* (Washington, DC: Brookings, 2009); Kenneth Wong et al., *The Education Mayor* (Washington, DC: Georgetown University Press, 2007).

3. Bob Ingle and Sandy McClure, *The Soprano State: New Jersey's Culture of Corruption* (New York: St. Martin's, 2009). On Boss Hague, see Richard Connors, *A Cycle of Power: The Career of Jersey City Mayor Frank Hague* (Metuchen, NJ: Scarecrow Press, 1971); Charles Van Devander, *The Big Bosses* (New York: Arno Press, 1974).

4. "Anything in Union City Gotta Go by Bill Musto First," *Hudson County Facts* (December 30, 2009), http://hudsoncountyfacts.getnj.com/hudsoncounty/?cat=77. See also Jessica Rosero, "The Last Boss: Former Mayor, State Senator and Assemblyman William Musto Dies at 88," *Union City Reporter*, March 4, 2006.

5. Jeffrey Gettleman, "Robert Menendez, a Politician Even at 20," *New York Times*, December 10, 2005, http://www.nytimes.com/2005/12/10/nyregion/10menendez.html.

6. The living-room window in Brian Stack's own apartment remained boarded up for months after a fire in the adjacent building blew it out, since the mayor didn't take the time to have it fixed.

7. Agustin Torres, "Sen. Stack Racks Up Monster Numbers," *Jersey Journal*, June 8, 2011, www.nj.com/hudson/voices/index.ssf/2011/06/hcdo_candidates_enjoy_victorie.html.

8. Max Pizarro, "Vega Calls for Investigation of 'Lenin-Like Stack,'" *PolitickerNJ*, May 10, 2007, www.politickernj.com/vega-calls-criminal-investigation-lenin-stack-8212.

9. Tom Moran, "Sweeney Unleashes His Fury as Budget Battle Turns Personal," *Star-Ledger*, July 3, 2011, http://blog.nj.com/njv_tom_moran/2011/07/democrats_cry_foul_at_gov_chri.html

10. Editorial, "Union City Mayor Brian Stack Needs to Play by the Rules," *Star-Ledger*, March 19, 2012, http://blog.nj.com/njv_editorial_page/2012/03/union_city_mayor_brian_stack_n.html.

11. Ibid.

12. The names of the Union City residents meeting with the mayor have been changed.

13. The classics in the field are Edward C. Banfield and James Q. Wilson, *City Politics* (Cambridge, MA: Harvard University Press, 1963) and Samuel Lubell, *The Future of American Politics* (New York: Harper & Row, 1965).

14. Camden is the paradigm of the ungovernable city. See Staff, "Camden's Crisis—Ungovernable?—The State May Have Failed the City It Took Over," *Economist*, November 26, 2009, www.economist.com/node/14974307; David Kirp, John Dwyer, and Larry Rosenthal, *Our Town: Race, Housing, and the Soul of Suburbia* (New Brunswick, NJ: Rutgers University Press, 1997). On Detroit, see Alan Digaetano and Paul Lawless, "Urban Governance and Industrial Decline: Governing Structures and Policy Agendas in Birmingham and Sheffield, England, and Detroit, Michigan, 1980–1997," *Urban Affairs Review* 34, no. 4 (1999).

15. In other contexts, diversity may undermine the sense of community. Robert Putnam, "*E Pluribus Unum:* Diversity and Community in the Twenty-First Century," *Scandinavian Political Studies* 30, no. 2 (2007).

16. Anthony Bryk, *Organizing Schools for Improvement: Lessons from Chicago* (Chicago: University of Chicago Press, 2010), 211.

17. Robert Putnam, *Bowling Alone: The Collapse and Revival of American Community* (New York: Simon & Schuster, 2000), 290.

18. James Coleman, "Social Capital in the Creation of Human Capital," *American Journal of Sociology* 94, supp. (1988).

19. Partha Dasgupta and Ismail Serageldin, eds., *Social Capital: A Multifaceted Perspective* (Washington, DC: World Bank, 2000).

20. Steven Strunsky, "For 125 Years, a Big Industry That Produces Delicate Lace," *New York Times*, August 31, 1997, www.nytimes.com/1997/08/31/nyregion/for-125-years-a-big-industry-that-produces-delicate-lace.html.

21. Antoinette Martin, "Hoboken Comes to Union City," *New York Times*, March 9, 2008, www.nytimes.com/2008/03/09/realestate/09njzo.html?_r=1&pagewanted=print.

22. Antoinette Martin, "Residential Up-and-Comer: Union City," *New York Times*, October 2, 2005, www.nytimes.com/2005/10/02/realestate/02njzo.html.

23. John Chubb and Terry Moe, *Politics, Markets, and America's Schools* (Washington, DC: Brookings, 1990); Clarence Stone et al., *Building Civic Capacity: The Politics of Reforming Urban Schools* (Lawrence: University Press of Kansas, 2001), 1. See also John Portz, Lana Stein, and Robin Jones, *City Schools and City Politics* (Lawrence: University Press of Kansas, 1999).

24. Dylan Archilla, "Changing of the Guard: UC Gets a New School Superintendent: Some Charge Nepotism," *Hudson Reporter*, June 8, 2003, www.hudsonreporter.com/view/full_stories_home/2390667/article-Changing-of-the-guard-UC-gets-new-schools-superintendent--some-charge-nepotism.

25. On "churn," see Frederick Hess, *Spinning Wheels: The Politics of Urban School Reform* (Washington, DC: Brookings Institution, 1999). On the politics of city school systems, see Jeffrey Henig et al., *The Color of School Reform: Race, Politics and the Challenge of Urban Education* (Princeton, NJ: Princeton University Press, 2000) and Charles Payne, *So Much Reform, So Little Change: The Persistence of Failure in Urban Schools* (Cambridge MA: Harvard Education Press, 2009).

26. Kenneth Wong et al., *The Education Mayor: Improving America's Schools* (Washington, DC: Georgetown University Press, 2007), 188. This interaction between politics and schools also changes the role of the superintendent. "Leadership . . . extends beyond the immediate school community, embracing the many actors on the wider leadership stage (i.e., governments, unions). It is a network of relationships among people, structures, and cultures." Kathryn A. Riley and Karen Seashore Louis, eds., *Leadership for Change and School Reform* (London: Routledge, 2000).

27. Gerald Grant, *Hope and Despair in the American City: Why There Are No Bad Schools in Raleigh* (Cambridge, MA: Harvard University Press, 2009) (contrasting the public schools of Raleigh and Syracuse); Stacey Childress et al., *Leading for Equity: The Pursuit of Excellence in Montgomery County Public Schools* (Cambridge, MA: Harvard Education Press, 2009). The experience of school districts including Montgomery County that have raised achievement levels and narrowed the achievement gap is analyzed in chapter 9.

28. Joseph Veritti, ed., *When Mayors Take Charge* (Washington, DC: Brookings, 2009).

29. Linda Shear et al., "Contrasting Paths to Small School Reform: Results of a 5-Year Evaluation of the Bill & Melinda Gates Foundation's National High Schools Initiative," *Teachers College Record* 110, no. 9 (2008). See also Catherine Wallach, "The Complexities of Operating Multiple Small Schools in a High School Conversion," *Peabody Journal of Education* 85, no. 3 (2010); Sam Dillon, "4100 Massachusetts Students Prove 'Small Is Better' Rule Wrong," *New York Times*, September 20, 2010, www.nytimes.com/2010/09/28/education/28school.html?pagewanted=all.

30. Max Pizarro, "Stack Honors McGreevey at New High School Opening," *PolitickerNJ* October 3, 2009, www.politickernj.com/max/33736/stack-honors-mcgreevey-new-high-school-opening.

CHAPTER 6

1. See chapter 3 for a discussion of Fred Carrigg's role in rebuilding the school system.
2. See, e.g., Pauline Lipman, *High Stakes Education: Inequality, Globalization, and Urban School Reform* (New York: Routledge, 2003); Arthur Powell, Eleanor Farrar, and David Cohen, *The Shopping Mall High School: Winners and Losers in the Educational Marketplace* (New York: Houghton Mifflin, 1984); Patrick McQuillan, "Humanizing the Comprehensive High School," *Educational Administration Quarterly* 33, no. 1 (1997).
3. On the characteristics of effective leadership see James Spillane, *Distributed Leadership* (San Francisco: Jossey Bass, 2006); Joseph Murphy, ed., *The Education Leadership Challenge* (Chicago: University of Chicago Press, 2002); James Spillane, "Educational Leadership," *Educational Evaluation and Policy Analysis* 25, no. 4 (2003).
4. Larry Cuban, "Why Has Frequent High School Reform since World War II Produced Disappointing Results, Again and Again?" in *Using Rigorous Evidence to Improve Policy and Practice: Colloquium Report* (New York: MDRC, 2004). See generally Seymour Sarason, *Revisiting "The Culture of School and the Problem of Change"* (New York: Teachers College Press, 1996).
5. Achieve Inc., *Do Graduation Tests Measure Up? A Closer Look at State High School Exit Exams* (2004), www.achieve.org/files/TestGraduation-FinalReport.pdf.
6. Alice Sullivan, "Cultural Capital and Educational Attainment," *Sociology* 35, no. 4 (2001).
7. John Mooney, "State Decides Not to Expel Alternative Graduation Test," *Star Ledger*, January 9, 2008, www.nje3.org/?p=811.
8. On the value of using data on student achievement to reform high schools, see Mary Ann Lachat and Stephen Smith, "Practices That Support Data Use in Urban High Schools," *Journal of Education for Students Placed at Risk* 10, no. 3 (2005).
9. Linda Tillman, "Mentoring New Teachers: Implications for Leadership Practice in an Urban School," *Educational Administration Quarterly* 41, no. 4 (2005); Thomas Corcoran, "Helping Teachers Teach Well: Transforming Professional Development," *Consortium for Policy Research in Education Policy Briefs* 16 (1995), www2.ed.gov/pubs/CPRE/t61/index.html; Judith Warren Little, "The Mentor Phenomenon and the Social Organization of Teaching," *Review of Research in Education* 16, no. 3 (1990).
10. On the positive relationship between athletics and success in school, see Ralph McNeal, "Extracurricular Activities and High School Dropouts," *Sociology of Education* 68, no. 1 (1995).
11. I have been unable to locate a scholarly literature on the phenomenon of teachers who hate students—it's as if no such individuals existed. But that's a professional blind spot. The web is redolent with teachers posting hateful blogs about their students as well as plaints from students about hateful teachers. Ask any teacher and she'll point out an example or two.

12. Carola Suárez-Orozco, Marcelo M. Suárez-Orozco, and Irina Todorov, *Learning a New Land: Immigrant Students in American Society* (Cambridge, MA: Harvard University Press, 2010); Patricia Gándara and Frances Contreras, *The Latino Education Crisis: The Consequences of Failed Social Policies* (Cambridge, MA: Harvard University Press, 2010); Laurie Olson, *Made in America: Immigrant Students in Our Public Schools* (New York: New Press, 2008).

13. In 2012 the Obama administration issued an administrative order specifying that immigrant youngsters would not face deportation. Nonetheless their fearfulness persists, because their parents and other relatives still risk deportation. Julia Preston and John H. Cushman, "Obama to Permit Young Migrants to Remain in U.S.," *New York Times*, June 15, 2012, www.nytimes.com/2012/06/16/us/us-to-stop-deporting-some-illegal-immigrants.html?pagewanted=all&_r=0.

14. Deborah Short and Shannon Fitzsimmons, *Double the Work: Challenges and Solutions to Acquiring Language and Academic Literacy for Adolescent English Language Learners* (New York: Carnegie Corporation, 2007), www.all4ed.org/files/DoubleWork.pdf.

15. Gennarose Pope, "Speaking No English: UC Immigrant High Schoolers Thrive in National Program," *Hudson Reporter*, March 11, 2012.

16. Special needs teachers at Union City High School find themselves in the same situation as those who instruct native Spanish-speakers—10% more of their students must demonstrate that they're proficient in English and math if the school is no longer to be treated as "in need of improvement." Among all the juniors in the school, only eight youngsters, those with IQs below 65, aren't required to take the test. (Their progress gets measured in other ways.) The rest of these 289 students, those who cannot keep up with their classmates as well as those who are battling their emotional demons, will join in the March testing madness.

    Each special needs student has a schedule calibrated to match his or her particular abilities. For instance, a youngster who's out of her depth in English may be placed in a class with others in the same boat; if she is barely managing in history she'll be attending a regular class with an instructor by her side for in-the-moment tutoring; and if she's a solid math student she'll get no extra help there.

    "This strategy is where our success comes from," says Delia Menendez, the district's special needs director, who helped to set up the model. But it poses a logistical nightmare because it must be coordinated with the schedules of the rest of the student body, and that may explain why few high schools follow suit. "Unlike any school I know, we schedule special needs students first," says Delia. "Here it's the priority."

17. When I tell this story to Superintendent Sandy Sanger he responds with a similar tale of his own. "When I was a principal we paired with a suburban elementary school on a project. The culmination was a field trip to Ellis Island. The suburban parents, worried about what our kids might do, insisted on riding on the bus. 'Your kids were great,' they told Sandy after the outing, 'much better than ours. Our kids were making a racket and we had to kick two of them off the bus because they were kissing.'"

18. In 2012 New Jersey adopted a new methodology for calculating graduation rates, requiring districts to report the percentage of students who graduate in four years.

Union City had a graduation rate of 89.41%, considerably higher than the state average, 83.1%. www.state.nj.us/education/data/grate/rates.pdf. A 4% increase in Latino students' graduation rates helped to boost the national rate by 1.7%, to 73%, between 2008 and 2009, the most recent years for which national data is available. "Diplomas Count 2012," *Education Week*, June 7, 2012, www.edweek.org/ew/toc/2012/06/07/index.html.

CHAPTER 7

1. For methodological criticisms of the use of "value-added" calculations of teachers' skills, see Jesse Rothstein, "Student Sorting and Bias in Value-Added Estimation: Selection on Observables and Unobservables," *Education Finance and Policy* 4, no. 4 (2009); Audrey Amrein-Beardsley, "Methodological Concerns about the Value-Added Assessment System," *Educational Researcher* 37, no. 2 (2008).
2. Discussions of the No Child Left Behind Act include Patrick McGuinn, *No Child Left Behind and the Transformation of Education Policy, 1965–2005* (Lawrence: University Press of Kansas, 2006); Frederick Hess and Michael Petrillli, *No Child Left Behind Primer* (New York: Peter Lang, 2007). For critical assessments, see Diane Ravitch, *The Birth and Death of the Great American School System* (New York: Basic Books, 2010), and Deborah Meier and George Wood, eds., *Many Children Left Behind* (Boston: Beacon, 2004); Mike Rose, "The Mismeasure of Teaching and Learning: How Contemporary School Reform Fails the Test," *Dissent* (Spring, 2011) http://www.dissentmagazine.org/article/the-mismeasure-of-teaching-and-learning-how-contemporary-school-reform-fails-the-test. Montgomery County Superintendent Joshua Starr recently called for a three-year moratorium on standardized testing. The nation "needs to 'stop the insanity' of evaluating teachers according to student test scores because it is based on 'bad science.'" Valerie Strauss, "MOCO Schools Chief Calls for Three Year Moratorium on Standardized Testing," *Washington Post*, December 10, 2012. http://www.washingtonpost.com/blogs/answer-sheet/wp/2012/12/10/moco-schools-chief-calls-for-three-year-moratorium-on-standardized-testing/. (Montgomery County's success in improving achievement and shrinking the achievement gap is discussed in chapter 9.)

Forty-five states, including New Jersey, have adopted the "Common Core" standards, an initiative sponsored by the National Governors Organization, which seeks to bring diverse state curricula into alignment with each other. Those standards have been promoted by the Obama Administration, but how well will be implemented is less than clear. Rick Hess at the American Enterprise Institute sees "great potential value in states choosing to embrace common, high-caliber reading and math standards, if these are implemented with conviction and attention to how they will interact with current reforms. That said, seems to me there's a huge chance that the whole exercise will go south, with many states implementing the Common Core half-heartedly, while screwing with existing reforms and standards. Such an outcome would ultimately do more harm than good. After all, the easiest course for states that have adopted Common Core standards but have second thoughts is to leave 'em be, and then simply not follow through." Rick Hess, "The Common Core Kool-Aid," *Education Week* (Nov. 30, 2012) blogs.edweek.org/edweek/…hess…/the_common_core_kool-aid.html

3. Howard Fleischman et al., *Highlights from PISA 2009* (Washington, DC: Department of Education, 2010), http://nces.ed.gov/pubs2011/2011004.pdf.

4. Valerie Strauss, "Joel Klein's Snow Job," *Washington Post*, January 11, 2011, http://voices.washingtonpost.com/answer-sheet/guest-bloggers/joel-kleins-snow-job.html. Chapter 9 assesses Klein's record in greater detail. See also Richard Rothstein, "Joel Klein's Misleading Autobiography," *American Prospect* (Oct. 2012), http://prospect.org/article/joel-kleins-misleading-autobiography.

5. On education and citizenship, see Meira Levinson, *No Citizen Left Behind* (Cambridge, MA: Harvard University Press, 2012).

6. David Kirp, "Is Michelle Rhee a 16th Century Throwback?" *Huffington Post*, March 11, 2011, www.huffingtonpost.com/david-kirp/is-michelle-rhee-a-16th-c_b_842858.html.

7. Flavio Cunha and James Heckman, "Investing in Our Young People," *NBER Working Paper # 16201* (2010), www.nber.org/papers/w16201; Eric Knudsen, James Heckman, Judy Cameron, and Jack Shonkoff, "Economic, Neurobiological, and Behavioral Perspectives on Building America's Future Workforce," *PNAS* 103, no. 27 (2006); David Kirp, "The Widest Achievement Gap," *National Affairs* 1, no. 5 (2010); Paul Tough, *How Children Succeed: Grit, Curiosity, and the Hidden Power of Character* (New York: Houghton Mifflin Harcourt, 2012).

8. The cheating scandals are discussed in chapter 9.

CHAPTER 8

1. See generally Deborah Yaffe, *Other People's Children* (New Brunswick, NJ: Rutgers University Press, 2007).

2. *Abbott v. Burke* (2012), http://caselaw.findlaw.com/nj-supreme-court/1568842.html; John Mooney, "Christie Sets Path with Picks for NJ Supreme Court," *NJ Spotlight*, January 24, 2012, www.njspotlight.com/stories/12/0124/0136/.

3. James Spillane and Amy Coldren, *Diagnosis and Design for School Improvement Using Distributed Practice to Lead and Manage Change* (New York: Teachers College Press, 2011) (managing instructional improvement); Frederick Hess, *Common Sense School Reform* (New York: Palgrave, 2006) (climate of high academic expectations); Raymond McNulty and Willard Daggett, "Best Practices of High Performing High Schools," *Leadership* 34, no. 4 (2005) (embrace change); Thelma Melendez de Santa Ana, "Bold Ideas for Secondary School Reform," *Principal Leadership* (2011) (lead change); Mary Ann Lachat and Steven Smith, "Practices That Support Data Use in Urban High Schools," *Journal of Education for Students Placed at Risk* 10, no. 3 (2005) (use data effectively); Mary Courtney and George Noblit, "The Principal as Caregiver," in A. Renee Prillaman, Deborah Eaker, and Doris Kendrick, eds., *The Tapestry of Caring: Education as Nurturance* (Norwood, NJ: Ablex, 1994) (nurture students).

4. See John Olson, "Research Upholds Value of Programs," *Interscholastic Athletic Administration* (1993); D. Feitz and M. Weiss. "The Impact of Girls Interscholastic Sport Participation in Academic Orientation," *Research Quarterly for Exercise and Sport* 55, no. 4 (1984).

5. On the relationship between perseverance and academic success see David Kirp, "Invisible Students: Bridging the Widest Achievement Gap," in Christopher Edley and Jorge Ruiz de Valasco, eds., *Changing Places: How Communities Will Improve the Health of Boys and Men of Color* (Berkeley and Los Angeles: University of California Press, 2011).

6. Chad Duhon, Anja Kurki, Ryan Williams, and Jiuping Chen, *Identifying Top-Performing High Schools for the "Best High Schools" Rankings* (Washington, DC: American Institutes of Research, 2012). This research is summarized in "Best High Schools" *US News & World Report* (2012) www.usnews.com/best-high-schools/features/bhs-homepage.

7. See, e.g., Tim Sass, *The Stability of Value-Added Measures of Teacher Quality and Implications for Teacher Compensation Policy* (Washington, DC: CALDER. National Center for Analysis of Longitudinal Data in Educational Research, 2008).

8. Winnie Hu, "Bullying Law Puts New Jersey Schools on Spot," *New York Times*, August 31, 2011, www.nytimes.com/2011/08/31/nyregion/bullying-law-puts-new-jersey-schools-on-spot.html?pagewanted=all; Adam Cohen, "Why New Jersey's Anti-Bullying Law Should Be a Model for Other States," *Time*, September 6, 2011, http://ideas.time.com/2011/09/06/why-new-jerseys-antibullying-law-should-be-a-model-for-other-states/.

9. Eric Cain, "High Teacher Turnover Rates Are a Big Problem for America's Public Schools," *Forbes*, March 8, 2011 www.forbes.com/sites/erikkain/2011/03/08/high-teacher-turnover-rates-are-a-big-problem-for-americas-public-schools/.

CHAPTER 9

1. Richard Elmore, *School Reform from the Inside Out* (Cambridge, MA: Harvard Education Press, 2004), 79.

2. Although Union City is a relatively small urban district, nationwide nearly half of all students are enrolled in districts the same size or smaller. http://nces.ed.gov/programs/digest/d10/tables/dt10_091.asp.

3. The account of Montgomery County's schools draws on a visit to the school district and interviews with key officials, among them former superintendent Jerry Weast and chief of staff Brian Edwards, as well as Stacey Childress, Denis Doyle, and David Thomas, *Leading for Equity: The Pursuit of Excellence in Montgomery County Public Schools* (Cambridge, MA: Harvard Education Press, 2009).

4. A modest amount of socioeconomic integration has been achieved through Montgomery County's inclusionary zoning program, which requires developers to include homes for low-income families in new developments. Heather Schwartz, "Housing Policy Is School Policy: Economic Integrative Housing Promotes Academic Success in Montgomery County, Maryland" (New York and Washington, DC: Century Foundation, 2010), http://tcf.org/publications/pdfs/housing-policy-is-school-policy-pdf/Schwartz.pdf.

5. See Cindy Rich, "Poverty in Montgomery County: Out from the Shadows," *Washingtonian*, May 16, 2011, www.washingtonian.com/articles/people/poverty-in-montgomery-county-out-from-the-shadows/.

6. Stacey Childress, Denis Doyle, and David Thomas, *Leading for Equity: The Pursuit of Excellence in Montgomery County Public Schools* (Cambridge, MA: Harvard Education Press, 2009), 107.

7. In 2012 Montgomery County switched to what it calls Curriculum 2.0. Its website explains that "[w]e are upgrading the existing MCPS curriculum for the elementary grades in a way that will better engage students and teachers, and provide more instructional focus to subjects such as the arts, health, information literacy, science, social studies and physical education. . . . Under the federal No Child Left Behind law, educators and parents have been rightly concerned that content areas outside the core, tested subjects of reading and mathematics have not received sufficient instruction time. Curriculum 2.0 addresses this concern head on. By teaching thinking and academic success skills across all subjects—reading, math, information literacy, health, the arts, science, social studies and physical education—our students will receive a more comprehensive, challenging and engaging learning experience in the early grades." www.montgomeryschoolsmd.org/curriculum/2.0/faq.aspx

8. The Texas Historical Association dryly notes that "the land used for the Aldine school and cemetery was donated by [one of the original families]. In 1900 the school had twelve students and one teacher. By 1971 the school had been abandoned, and all that remained of Aldine by 1988 was the cemetery." "Aldine, TX" (Denton, TX: Texas State Historical Association, n.d.), www.tshaonline.org/handbook/online/articles/hra90.

9. The account of the Aldine schools draws on Heather Zavadsky, *Bringing School Reform to Scale: Five Award-Winning Urban Districts* (Cambridge, MA: Harvard Education Press, 2009), as well as interviews with Zavadsky and Aldine Superintendent Wanda Bamberg.

10. A profile titled, fittingly, "Grow Your Own" notes that "Aldine has kept up its steady progress. The district has not lurched from one reform strategy to another. It has not hired on a succession of superintendent saviors. It has made progress without the knock-down, drag-out fights that the media can't resist. Instead, Aldine has stuck with strategies it formed over ten years ago and trusted its own veteran staff to lead the hard work of school improvement." www.learningfirst.org/visionaries/WandaBamberg.

11. See, e.g., Eric Hanushek, "The Impact of Differential Expenditures on School Performance," *Educational Researcher* 18, no. 4 (1989).

12. The account of the Sanger school district draws heavily on Jane David and Joan Talbert, *Turning around a High Poverty School District: Learning from Sanger Unified's Success* (2012 unpublished draft, on file with the author) as well as several conversations with and emails from David. An interim report appears at www.stanford.edu/group/suse-crc/cgi-bin/drupal/sites/default/files/Sanger-Report.pdf. See also Richard DuFour et al., *Raising the Bar and Closing the Gap: Whatever It Takes* (Bloomington, IN: Solution Tree Press, 2010).

13. "Diplomas Count," *Education Week*, June 7, 2012, http://thesangerherald.com/articles/2011/06/23/opinion/our_opinion/doc4e034cb9498e0604995789.txt.

14. Because California law prohibits bilingual classes, newcomers attend English as a Second Language classes, a decidedly second-best approach. See William Ryan, "The Unz Initiatives and the Abolition of Bilingual Education," *Boston College Law Review* 43, no. 2 (2002). For a discussion of how bilingual education is taught in Union City, see chapters 1, 2, and 6.

15. See Frederick Hess, *Spinning Wheels: The Politics of Urban School Reform* (Washington, DC: Brookings Institution, 1998).

16. The Aldine school board has embraced the reform efforts. As Superintendent Bamberg tells me: "When test scores were low in the mid 1990s, the board really led the charge for improvement together with the superintendent. They have been very supportive of all initiatives to bring about improvements. They monitor data carefully and we give them lots and lots of information."

    Aldine is a clubby world, one that most superintendents would envy. "We have not held the last two board elections because there were no opponents running against the sitting members," says Bamberg. "We have probably the most stable board in the area and probably the state. When board members decide to retire, they usually retire before their term is finished. Then the remaining board appoints someone to fill the position. When the election comes around, the group runs as a slate of incumbents. The district has been criticized for this but it has kept the work focused on students and not individual agendas."

17. Steven Brill, *Class Warfare: Inside the Fight to Fix America's Schools* (New York: Simon & Schuster, 2011).

18. Montgomery County's commitment to collaboration between the union and the school system led to the adoption of a remarkable strategy for evaluating, helping—and, when necessary, firing—bad teachers. Dismissals, even of certifiable incompetents, are nearly impossible in most places, and the fact that they remain on the school payroll gives critics of public education good reason to complain. But with the union's backing, Montgomery County does things differently. There, all teachers are appraised on a regular basis and those who are identified as subpar receive lots of coaching. A panel of teachers and principals reviews their progress, and those who don't improve lose their jobs. Michael Winerip, "Helping Teachers Help Themselves," *New York Times*, June 5, 2011, www.nytimes.com/2011/06/06/education/06oneducation.html?pagewanted=all

19. Jane David and Joan Talbert, "Turning around a High Poverty School District: Learning from Sanger Unified's Success" (2012 unpublished draft, on file with the author).

20. Ibid.

21. In Texas, teachers unions cannot engage in collective bargaining. Aldine has a local union, mainly composed of nonprofessionals, which sometimes represents teachers and employees in grievance hearings.

22. Stacey Lee, *Unraveling the "Model Minority" Stereotypes: Listening to Asian American Youth* (New York: Teachers College Press, 1996).

23. Recall the history of Orange, New Jersey, discussed in chapter 3, a natural (though unhappy) experiment that demonstrates that the "continuous improvement" approach to reform can work well in a black community. To recapitulate: Orange

recruited administrators from Union City and put in place the core tenets of Union City's approach. Elementary school students' test scores rose, and there were signs of improvement in the upper grades as the reforms took effect there. But at that point politics prevailed over policy. Board members who recruited these administrators lost an election to the old guard, which junked the reforms and fired the newcomers. Almost immediately the test scores plummeted.

24. Parents' engagement must be factored into the equation—the more parents are involved in the education of their children, the better the odds that they will do well—and the fact that Union City has been able to keep parents close helps to explain the glowing outcomes. See Don Davies, "Schools Reaching Out: Family, School, and Community Partnerships for Student Success," *Phi Delta Kappan* 72, no. 5 (1991). But in years past, Union City parents stayed away from the schools, feeling that their presence was unwanted, and altering that perception took a great deal of work. At each Union City school the district has community liaisons (like Maria Kanik at Washington School), longtime residents who know how to work with the social services bureaucracies to get families the help they're entitled to. Other successful districts have made the same calculation. In Montgomery County, the teachers have become so convinced of the value of this outreach that, in one budget-crunch year, they agreed to forgo a scheduled salary increase in order to keep the liaisons on the payroll.

25. Clay Risen, "The Lightning Rod," *Atlantic*, November 2008, www.theatlantic.com/magazine/archive/2008/11/the-lightning-rod/7058/.

26. The lead-by-intimidation educators fancy themselves as following the lead of business; in that, they're mistaken. See Adam Bryant, "How to Become a Bus Driver, Not a Bulldozer," *New York Times*, Oct. 6, 2012, www.nytimes.com/2012/10/07/business/ken-rees-of-think-finance-on-leading-a-growing-company.html.

27. "Getting Tough," *Time*, February 1, 1988, www.time.com/time/magazine/article/0,9171,966577,00.html.

28. Bill Turque, "Rhee Says Laid-Off Teachers in D.C. Abused Kids," *Washington Post*, January 21, 2010, www.washingtonpost.com/wp-dyn/content/article/2010/01/22/AR2010012204543.html?hpid=topnews. In fact, one of the 266 laid-off teachers had been accused of having sex with a student.

29. Amanda Ripley, "Rhee Tackles Classroom Challenge," *Time*, November 26, 2008, www.time.com/time/magazine/article/0,9171,1862444-2,00.html#ixzz0dv23UBsE.

30. Matthew Di Carlo, "Michelle Rhee's Empty Claims about Her D.C. Schools Record," *Washington Post*, January 31, 2012, www.washingtonpost.com/blogs/answer-sheet/post/michelle-rhees-empty-claims-about-her-dc-schools-record/2012/01/30/gIQAATFjdQ_blog.html.

31. Jack Gillum and Marisol Bello, "When Standardized Test Scores Soared in D.C., Were the Gains Real?" *USA Today*, March 28, 2010, www.usatoday.com/news/education/2011-03-28-1Aschooltesting28_CV_N.htm. A follow-up investigation, which dragged on for several years, was limited to a single school, where cheating was found to have occurred. Investigators said they restricted the scope of their inquiry because they believed news coverage of the scandal would limit future cheating; critics complained of a cover-up. Jay Mathews, "D.C. Schools Cheating Report Thin and Biased," *Washington Post*, August 11, 2012, www.washingtonpost.com/

blogs/class-struggle/post/dc-schools-cheating-report-thin-and-biased/ 2012/08/11/569d3f5c-e40d-11e1-a25e-15067bb31849_blog.html; Greg Toppo and Marisol Bello, "D.C. Investigates Just One School in Test-Cheating Scandal," *USA Today*, August 8, 2012, www.usatoday.com/news/education/story/2012-08-08/dc-schools-cheating/56888224/1.

32. Jack Gillum and Marisol Bello, "When Standardized Test Scores Soared in D.C., Were the Gains Real?" *USA Today*, March 28, 2010, www.usatoday.com/news/education/2011-03-28-1Aschooltesting28_CV_N.htm.

33. Jeneba Ghatt, "Atlanta's Cheating Ways," *Washington Times*, July 7, 2011, communities.washingtontimes.com/neighborhood/politics-raising-children/2011/jul/7/atlantas-cheating-ways-school-officials-test-score/. Suspicious test scores have been found in about 200 school districts, including such big city districts as Philadelphia and Denver. Heather Vogell, John Perry, Alan Judd, and M. B. Pell, "Cheating our Children: Suspicious School Test Scores across the Nation," *Atlanta Constitution*, March 25, 2012, www.ajc.com/news/cheating-our-children-suspicious-1397022.html.

34. When Mitt Romney unveiled his proposals to reform education in the spring of 2012, he stressed the paramount importance of expanding parental choice. Under his plan, all the federal funds that currently go to school districts with sizable numbers of poor children would be diverted to parents, who would be free to spend that money on public schools, charter schools, private schools, or home tutoring. Cautious politician that he is, Romney never used the word "voucher." He didn't need to, because his plan speaks for itself. Lanhee Chen, "A Chance for Every Child," May 23, 2012, www.mittromney.com/blogs/mitts-view/2012/05/chance-every-child-0.

35. *School Vouchers: Characteristics of Privately Funded Programs* (Washington, DC: Government Accounting Office, 2002), www.gao.gov/new.items/d02752.pdf.

36. Patrick Wolf, "The Comprehensive Longitudinal Evaluation of the Milwaukee Parental Choice Program: Summary of Final Reports," Fayetteville (AR): School Choice Demonstration Project, University of Arkansas (2012), www.uaedreform.org/SCDP/Milwaukee_Eval/Report_36.pdf. See also "Keeping Informed about School Vouchers" (Washington, DC: Center for Educational Policy, 2011), www.cep-dc.org/.

37. Stephanie Simon, "Louisiana's Bold Bid to Privatize Schools," *Reuters*, June 1, 2012, www.reuters.com/article/2012/06/01/us-education-vouchers-idUSL1E-8H10AG20120601. In November 2012, a Louisiana state court judge ruled that it violated the state constitution to fund vouchers with money legally dedicated to public schools.

38. Kevin Drum, "Louisiana Gives Us a Taste of Mitt Romney's Education Policy," *Mother Jones*, July 2, 2012, www.motherjones.com/kevin-drum/2012/07/louisiana-gives-us-taste-mitt-romneys-education-policy; Stephanie Simon, "Louisiana Sets Rules for Landmark School Voucher Program," *Chicago Tribune*, July 23, 2012, http://articles.chicagotribune.com/2012-07-23/news/sns-rt-us-usa-education-louisianabre86n00j-20120723_1_voucher-program-voucher-students-voucher-advocates.

39. [Editorial], "The Year of School Choice," *Wall Street Journal*, July 5, 2011, online.wsj. com/article/SB10001424052702304450604576420330972531442.html.

40. See Jeffrey Henig, *Spin Cycle: How Research Is Used in Policy Debates—the Case of Charter Schools* (New York: Russell Sage, 2009).

41. The best charter schools spend more money than the public schools—considerably more—while enrolling fewer special needs students and English Language Learners. Such differences make comparisons with public schools nearly impossible. See Bruce Baker, Ken Libby, and Kathryn Wiley, *Spending by the Major Charter Management Organizations: Comparing Charter School and Local Public District Financial Resources in New York, Ohio, and Texas* (Boulder, CO: National Education Policy Center, 2012), http://nepc.colorado.edu/publication/spending-major-charter.

42. See, e.g., Christina Clark Tuttle et al., "Student Characteristics and Achievement in 22 KIPP Middle Schools" (New York: Mathematica, 2010).

43. *Charter School Performance in Pennsylvania* (Stanford, CA: CREDO, Stanford University, 2011), http://credo.stanford.edu/reports/PA%20State%20Report_20110404_FINAL.pdf

44. www.broadprize.org. The three runners-up each receive $150,000 for scholarships. Heather Zavadsky, *Bringing School Reform to Scale: Five Award-Winning Urban Districts* (Cambridge, MA: Harvard Education Press, 2009) describes five of the prize-winning districts. Although depictions of the Broad Prize winners in Zavadsky's book and the foundation's website focus on the positive, none of these successes came easily. Were it otherwise, there would be many more such cities and no need for such a prize.

    Consider the situation in Boston. *A Decade of Urban School Reform*, a book-length account of Boston's triumphs and travails, mainly celebrates the accomplishments of its longtime superintendent, Tom Payzant. But it doesn't ignore the unfinished business even after his eleven-year run—"silos" within the central administration, as middle-level managers behave like empire builders, not cooperators; discomfiture on the part of teachers with an unfamiliar pedagogy that some believe demands too much of the students; and perennially simmering racial tension. Boston's public schools have become much better since the mid-1990s, when Payzant arrived, but much remains to be done. "The bottom line," writes Paul Reville, a principal during Payzant's tenure who later became Massachusetts Secretary of Education, "is that large numbers of students are leaving school unprepared for the challenges of the future." Paul Reville, ed., *A Decade of Urban School Reform: Persistence and Progress in the Boston Public Schools* (Cambridge, MA: Harvard Education Press, 2007)

45. See, e.g., Gordon MacInnes, *In Plain Sight: Simple, Difficult Lessons from New Jersey's Expensive Effort to Close the Achievement Gap* (New York: Century Foundation, 2009) (Union City).

46. Richard Elmore, *School Reform from the Inside Out* (Cambridge, MA: Harvard Education Press, 2004), 79 (italics in original). "Highly effective" California school districts—defined as districts that recorded higher achievement test scores than others with a comparable mix of students—"tended to rely more on a common culture of values to shape collective action than on bureaucratic rules and controls," one of these studies concludes. "The shared values typically focused on

improvement of student learning as the central goal, evidence of steady, sustained improvement, a positive approach to problem-solving in the face of unforeseen difficulties, a view of structures, processes, and data as instruments for improvement rather than as ends in themselves." In Texas, the leaders of successful districts "created a normative climate in which teachers and principals were collectively responsible for student learning and in which the improvement of instruction was the central task." A third study, this one looking at instruction in high-poverty classrooms, showed what type of leadership *doesn't* work. Initiatives backfired when school chiefs were "long on pressure and short on support." See Joseph Murphy and Phillip Hallinger, "Characteristics of Instructionally Effective School Districts," *Journal of Educational Research* 81, no. 2 (1988); Mary Ragland, Rose Asera, and Joseph Johnson, *Urgency, Responsibility, Efficacy: Preliminary Findings of a Study of High Performing Texas School Districts* (Austin: University of Texas, Charles A, Dana Center), www.utdanacenter.org/downloads/products/urgency. pdf. See generally James Spillane, *Standards Deviation: How Schools Misunderstand Education Policy* (Cambridge, MA: Harvard University Press, 2004); Michael Knapp, ed., *Teaching for Meaning in High Poverty Classrooms* (New York: Teachers College Press, 1995).

47. Joel Klein, "The Failure of American Schools," *Atlantic*, June 2011, www.theatlantic. com/magazine/archive/2011/06/the-failure-of-american-schools/8497/.

48. [unsigned], "Joel L. Klein," *New York Times*, May 8, 2012 topics.nytimes.com/top/ reference/timestopics/people/k/joel_i_klein/index.html; Sharon Otterman and Jennifer Medina, "New York Schools Chancellor Ends Eight Year Run," *New York Times*, November 9, 2010. www.nytimes.com/2010/11/10/nyregion/10klein. html?pagewanted=all.

49. Joel Klein, Condoleezza Rice et al., *U.S. Education Reform and National Security* (Washington, DC: Council on Foreign Relations, 2012), www.cfr.org/united-states/us-education-reform-national-security/p27618.

50. Sharon Otterman and Jennifer Medina, "New York Schools Chancellor Ends Eight Year Run," *New York Times*, November 9, 2010, www.nytimes.com/2010/11/10/ nyregion/10klein.html?pagewanted=all.

51. Aaron Pallas, "Joel Klein versus Those 'Status Quo Apologists,'" *Washington Post*, June 15, 2011, www.washingtonpost.com/blogs/answer-sheet/post/joel-klein-vs-those-status-quo-apologists/2011/06/15/AGkIeeWH_blog.html.

INDEX